GERMAN POLITICS
AND THE
SPIEGEL
AFFAIR

GERMAN POLITICS
AND THE
SPIEGEL
AFFAIR

A Case Study of the Bonn System

Ronald F. Bunn

LOUISIANA STATE UNIVERSITY PRESS / BATON ROUGE

For my mother

PREFACE

Anyone who employs the case study approach, as I have tried to do here, for inquiring into the functioning of a political system treads upon slippery methodological ground. Certain of these difficulties are acknowledged in the introductory chapter, but two underlying assumptions of my approach need to be made explicit here. First, I reject the "topical" interpretation which concludes that the *Spiegel* Affair was momentarily a sensational but essentially a trivial hiatus in the development since 1949 of the West German political system. Sensationalism there was—and, from the perspective of a political scientist, irrelevancy there was—in certain facets of the affair. But beneath its facade of sensationalism and partial political irrelevancy, the *Spiegel* Affair exposed problems and stylistic qualities which transcend topicality and suggest insights of broader significance for an understanding of the Bonn political system. Second, I have not wholly accepted a personality interpretation that stresses to the virtual exclusion of other considerations the clash of personalities who were directly involved in the *Spiegel* Affair. Without discounting the contributions which personality factors and individual leadership styles made to the shaping of the controversy, I am persuaded that these personalities were functioning within a framework of styles and procedures that are partially institutionalized and may persist for some time to come in the Bonn system.

Work on this book was interspersed over a period of four years, and I am indebted to several sources for the support that enabled me to initiate the study and eventually to complete it. The field research was begun in 1963 when, as a

Senior Fulbright Research Scholar attached formally to the University of Bonn, I spent the better part of a year in West Germany. Subsequent aid from the Louisiana State University Research Council permitted me to interrupt my regular teaching duties and to return to West Germany for additional research and interviewing.

During my visits in West Germany I discussed various aspects of this project with civil servants, journalists, academicians, political party staff members, and Bundestag deputies. Certain of them were directly involved in the *Spiegel* Affair and most of them, in any event, would prefer to remain anonymous as interviewees. I have not in every instance accepted either their interpretations or versions of what happened, but rarely did I find them unwilling to share with me their knowledge of the subject. Without their friendly and professional cooperation, this study would not have been possible. For assistance of another sort I am particularly indebted to Dr. Carl-Christoph Schweitzer, associated at the time with the office of the Federal President *(Bundespräsidialamt),* and Dr. Karl Lohmann, *Persönlicher Referent* of the president of the Bundestag, both of whom gave me more time than I had any right to expect in arranging contacts and appointments. I am also grateful to the directors and staff personnel of the following institutions for answering my questions, facilitating my research, and making available to me both published and unpublished materials: *Der Spiegel* Archives (Hamburg), EMNID Institute (Bielefeld), *Institut für Demoskopie* (Allensbach), the Bundestag Library (Bonn), and the Press Evaluation Section *(Presseauswertungabteilung)* of the Bundestag Library. None of these persons or institutions is responsible for errors of fact or interpretation. Thanks are due also to *Der Spiegel Verlag* (Hamburg) for permission to reproduce in English translation the Foertsch article, to the editors of the *Public Opinion Quarterly* for permission to use material that I first published in their journal, and to D. Van Nostrand Company, Inc., for permission to use certain of the material originally published in *Politics and Civil Liberties in Europe* (1967), edited by William G. Andrews and me.

To my wife Rita and our three daughters Robin, Kathy, and Beth, I am grateful for many things, but most especially for keeping the writing of this book in its proper perspective. Finally, it is a pleasure to dedicate the book to a person I have admired for many years.

RONALD F. BUNN

October, 1967
Houston, Texas

CONTENTS

I Prelude to a Crisis   3

II The *Spiegel* Action   37

III Framing the Issues: Initial Press
and Public Reactions   58

IV The Making of a Political Affair   92

V Political Bargaining, I   118

VI Political Bargaining, II   142

VII Epilogue   176

Appendix I, The Foertsch Article   185

Appendix I, The Thirty-four News-
papers Constituting the Sample   217

Index   223

INTRODUCTION

By the early 1960's supporters of the pluralistic, participatory political system could find in the Bonn system much to be pleased about. At various stages of its development, the system had demonstrated a relatively strong capacity for functional efficiency and policy effectiveness. Cabinet instability had been kept to a minimum. The aggregation of interests and inputs had been facilitated through the emergence of a bipolarizing tendency which was a dramatic departure from the fragmented and disintegrative party system of the Weimar period. An apparent stylistic shift away from ideology and dogmatism toward pragmatism and negotiation, as well as the discernible blurring of rigid class and social cleavages, seemed to confirm the conclusion that perhaps West Germany was at least on the threshold of achieving that difficult blending of pluralism and consensus within which the parliamentary system most easily operates. Given the limited set of options available to the successive Adenauer governments in the crucial policy areas of foreign affairs and reunification, the Bonn system appeared to be both relevant and decisive in its output function.

Without discounting the significance of these accomplishments, however, many observers viewed the West German political scene with either reservations or profound skepticism. Aside from the views of the extreme cynics that at the earliest possible moment the West Germans could be expected to revert to a system akin to that of the Nazi era, more reasoned assessments detected disturbing weaknesses in the Bonn system. The *Kanzlerdemokratie* of the Adenauer era reminded its critics of a paternalistic-authoritarian leadership style which they identified with an earlier and disastrous tendency in German politics. It was also suggested that too many West Germans, reacting against the bitter experiences of misguided loyalties during the 1930's, were in fact apathetic toward, if not alienated from, the Bonn system—that they were tolerant of and even grateful to the system for satisfying their immediate needs but that they could hardly be counted on for support if, in the future, it should encounter serious domestic or foreign policy difficulties. Others alluded to the "improvised" or "suspended" nature of the system. They felt that it was more a creature of externally imposed circumstances than of genuine popular endorsement, and in any event too unsettled in its basic configurations to permit serious speculation about its permanence or durability. And, the critics warned, in their apparent zeal for internal order and harmony, West Germans may have gone too far, replacing controversy and dissension with over-consensualism and conformity in which criticism of public authority was neither encouraged nor possible. Even that venerable instrument in the past of German opposition and dissent, the Social Democratic Party, was accused of having betrayed its followers in its drive to power by abandoning its function of providing meaningful alternatives to prevailing policies.

This is not the place for us to examine systematically these arguments or to evaluate their merits, but the questions they pose are relevant to this study.[1] Nor is it necessary to our task to insist that the *Spiegel* Affair was either the first or the most significant test of the viability of the West German parliamentary system, or to suggest that all of the facets of

[1] Extensive data have been collected in an effort to discover whether a popular attitudinal base exists in West Germany for a stable democratic political system. For a review of the findings, see Sidney Verba, "Germany: The Remaking of Political Culture," in Lucian Pye and Sidney Verba (eds.), *Political Culture and Political Development* (Princeton, 1965), 130–70.

the Bonn system were exposed during the processing and resolving of the crisis induced by the affair. But there can be no doubt that the affair was significant, that it eventually brought into play certain of the most articulate and active elements of the Bonn system, and that it ultimately posed for the West German public several key questions about the strengths and weaknesses of their political system. And it is because of these consequences of the *Spiegel* Affair that we propose here to examine it, with emphasis on the causes of the controversy and the responses of the political system to it.

A related purpose of this study is to test the methodological assumption that the analysis of a political affair is a useful technique for inquiring into the nature, problems, and stylistic qualities of a political system. What there is in the political system which when ignited by certain events erupts into a major political affair or crisis, and the manner in which its primary institutions and personalities respond provides material for a case study of the functioning of the system.

The meaning of the term "political affair" is largely conditioned by popular and journalistic usage, and no precise definition of the term can be derived from the various connotations commonly attached to it. Quite generally, however, references to political affairs as they have occurred over the past years in Western political communities suggest situations which are characterized by behavior, conduct, or action on the part of one or more persons endowed with political authority and which are of such a nature as to arouse a significant level of unfavorable reaction among the various strata of the political community, or at least among the more politically active and articulate groups within the community. Within this loosely drawn framework, moreover, it would seem that a political affair is typically a rather narrow-range event, induced by a fairly specific act or mode of conduct compressed within a relatively short span of time. The type of action, conduct, or behavior which induces what we conceive to be a political affair does not lend itself to a rigorous classificatory scheme. But if one examined the primary elements of certain of the more consequential political affairs, including the famous Dreyfus Affair in France, a strong case could be made for concluding that the act or conduct which most probably accounts for the political affair is one which conflicts with the presumed rules of the game. By the latter we mean the fundamental norms, whether embodied in positive legal codes or in traditional and conventional mores, which constitute the political culture by which a community determines what is acceptable and unacceptable in the political system.

Thus a political affair is not simply a situation characterized by public controversy over decisions and acts of public officials. It is something more than this. A political affair, as we understand the term, is a situation that touches upon the question of "morality," of allegiance to the political community, or of the congeniality of the methods and character of a public official with the prevailing political culture. Officials involved in political affairs are criticized most heavily not because of any technical incompetence or, as the popular jargon might put it, because of "honest errors of judgment," but rather because of questionable motives or apparent character defects.

The occurrence of a political affair also seems to require a certain level of sophistication of the political communications apparatus. Without sufficiently widespread knowledge of the act, conduct, or behavior—of the "violation" of the rules of the game—there can be no criticism of the intensity and scope which is one of the distinguishing features of a political affair. The important roles which the press, political parties, and other organized publics have played in political affairs of the past are suggestive of the setting within which political affairs might occur.

No observer of West German politics can ignore the ghost of Hitler lurking somewhere in the background of major political controversies that have erupted from time to time in postwar Germany. Sooner or later most of them are juxtaposed against the Nazi experience, with one or more groups in the controversy invoking the German past as its standard of comparison and asking whether Germany has "really" purged herself of values identified with national socialism. Even had there been no Third Reich, the *Spiegel* Affair would have raised significant questions about the state of health of the West German political system. But it seems equally clear that without the Nazi legacy many Germans, and foreign observers, would not have taken so passionate an interest in various facets of the affair nor would the protagonists in the controversy have framed their objections so intensely and harshly.

The immediate cause of the *Spiegel* Affair may be traced to the night of October 26, 1962. On that evening attorneys of the West German Federal Prosecutor's Office, assisted by Hamburg criminal police and officers of the Security Group of the Federal Criminal Office, converged on the Hamburg and Bonn offices of the news magazine *Der Spiegel*. The files and archives of the Hamburg central office were impounded. Three members of the editorial staff were taken into immediate custody. Rudolf Augstein, the publisher of *Der Spiegel*, could not be located that evening by the police, but upon learning of the warrant for his arrest he turned himself in to the authorities on the following day. Conrad Ahlers, an associate editor, was vacationing with his wife in Spain. In the early hours of October 27, he and his wife were awakened in their hotel room in Torremolinos by Spanish police, provisionally arrested, and placed in a jail for the rest of the night in nearby Malaga. In the weeks that followed additional arrests were made, including those of Colonel Adolf Wicht of the Federal Intelligency Agency *(Bundesnachrichtendienst)* and Colonel Alfred Martin of the Federal Defense Ministry. Altogether eleven suspects were confined for varying lengths of time as a "precautionary measure." The Hamburg offices of *Der Spiegel* were placed under police surveillance, and for some thirty days federal investigators searched its files and archival collections. On the morning following the raids and initial arrests the Federal Prosecutor's Office announced that the action had been prompted by a strong suspicion of publication by *Der Spiegel* of "state secrets" in such a way as to "endanger the security of the Federal Republic as well as the safety and freedom of the German people." Spokesmen for the federal prosecution explained that the suspicion arose primarily out of the feature article written by Ahlers for the October 10, 1962, issue. The charges specifically against Augstein and Ahlers were "betrayal of country, treasonable falsification of information, and bribery."[2]

Within a week after the October 26 raids and arrests, Federal Minister of Justice Wolfgang Stammberger, one of the five Free Democratic Party (FDP) members of the national coalition government headed by Konrad Adenauer, offered his resignation. Shortly thereafter the FDP leadership threatened to withdraw entirely from the cabinet, precipitating the first of two cabinet crises which developed during the affair. The three question periods (November 7 to 9, 1962) in the Bundestag concerning various aspects of the action against *Der Spiegel* were among the stormiest in Bonn's experience. On the last day of the questioning Franz Josef Strauss, federal defense minister and leader of the Bavarian Christian Social Union (CSU), admitted personal

---

[2] The charge of bribery was later dropped.

involvement in the action by having requested through the West German military attaché in Madrid the assistance of the Spanish police in arresting Ahlers. This admission by Strauss, coupled with other events, induced the second cabinet crisis as the FDP, which had agreed on November 5 to remain in the government, withdrew all five of its members from the cabinet. Strauss eventually resigned his ministerial post and had to abandon, at least temporarily, whatever aspirations he had to the federal chancellorship. Before the *Spiegel* Affair had run its course, Adenauer was compelled to fix a specific time for his retirement from the chancellorship.

These and other consequences of the *Spiegel* Affair developed against the backdrop of an extensive and acrimonious public debate concerning certain aspects of the investigation against *Der Spiegel*. Students objected by demonstrating in the major West German university communities. Academicians petitioned political leaders requesting either clarification or repudiation of the techniques employed in the investigation. An important segment of the West German press immediately criticized the action as heavy handed, if not illegal, and journalists' and publishers' associations protested against an alleged threat to the legitimate freedom of expression. Frustrated since 1949 by its failure to gain sufficient electoral support to form a national government and occasionally chided even by its supporters as an ineffectual opposition party in the Bundestag, the Social Democratic Party (SPD) was presented with a promising opportunity to prove its ability as an organized critic of the Adenauer government. A few observers were soon comparing the *Spiegel* Affair with the Ossietzky Affair[3] of the Weimar era or, more sweepingly, with the

[3] In violation of the terms of the Versailles Treaty, the Reichswehr contracted with the Junkers-Werke, a German aircraft factory in Dessau, to build in the Soviet Union aircraft for both the German and Russian armies. The contract was kept confidential and its financing was not con-

Dreyfus Affair. Within a few weeks of its inception approximately 90 percent of the West German adult population had become informed of one or more key aspects of the controversy.[4]

Various interpretations may be placed on the *Spiegel* Affair.[5] The suddenness of the raids, the nighttime inter-

tained in the budgets submitted to the Reichstag for approval. In addition, the Reichswehr had constructed in the Soviet Union chemical factories for the production of various gases. To maintain contact with these operations, German officers traveled to the Soviet Union under false passports. When the Junkers-Werke encountered financial difficulties with the Reichswehr, it relayed confidential memoranda to certain Reichstag deputies, seeking their support. One of the memoranda came to the attention of the British and was published in the December 3, 1926, issue of the *Manchester Guardian*. The Social Democratic Party had the report translated back into German and printed it in its party organ, *Vorwärts*. The SPD Reichstag delegation then moved a vote of no-confidence against the government of Chancellor Wilhelm Marx *(Zentrum)*. The motion passed by a vote of 249 to 171 on December 17, 1926. On April 12, 1929, *Die Weltbühne*, published in Berlin by Carl von Ossietzky, carried accounts written by Walter Kreiser that the Reichswehr was continuing the arrangements in the Soviet Union for the production of military aircaft, without the expenditures' submission to the Reichstag for approval, and, again, in violation of the Versailles Treaty. Charged with treasonable publication, Ossietzky was convicted in November, 1931, by the *Reichsgericht* in Leipzig and sentenced to eighteen months' imprisonment. Seven months after he began serving his term on May 10, 1932, he was granted amnesty. Shortly after Hitler came to power in 1933, Ossietzky was again arrested. In 1936 he received the Nobel Peace Prize. Ossietzky died on May 4, 1938, allegedly as a result of mistreatment in a Nazi concentration camp. See Kurt R. Grossman, *Ossietzky, Ein deutscher Patriot* (München, 1963) and *Das Parlament* (May 1, 1963), 10.

[4] See below, p. 163.

[5] In addition to the extensive newspaper commentary on the *Spiegel* Affair, useful analyses may be found in: Jürgen Seifert, "Die Spiegel Affäre," in Erich Kuby et al., *Franz Joseph Strauss, Ein Typus unserer Zeit* (München, 1963), 233–314; Theodor Eschenburg, *Die Affäre, Eine Analyse* (Hamburg, 1962); Otto Kirchheimer and Constantine Menges, "A Free Press in a Democratic State?" in Gwendolen M. Carter and Alan F. Westin (eds.), *Politics in Europe* (New York, Chicago, Burlingame, 1965), 87–138; and John Gimbel, "The 'Spiegel Affair' in Perspective," *Midwest Journal of Political Science*, IX (August, 1965) 282–97. A projected three-volume collection of commentaries and documents, under the general editorship of Jürgen Seifert, will in the future be an indispens-

rogations of certain of *Der Spiegel's* staff members, and the exceptional manner in which Ahlers was arrested in Spain were to the harshest critics uncomfortably reminiscent of the style of Nazi Germany. To those critics who resisted the temptation to draw analogies with the Nazi past, the action suggested at least overzealous law enforcement that seemed both disproportionate to what the circumstances required and insensitive to the role of the press in a constitutional system. Legal specialists pointed out the ambiguity of the law of treason in West Germany and the failure of the criminal code to distinguish adequately between the overt and perhaps unwitting publication of state secrets and the covert transmission of state secrets to unauthorized persons. The methods used against *Der Spiegel* raised doubts in some circles as to whether the national ministries and bureaucracy could be entrusted with the powers which the Adenauer government had been seeking through constitutional amendment in the event of a national emergency.[6] The complaint was also made that if the law did proscribe the publication of the type of information contained in the article written by Ahlers, perhaps the law, not *Der Spiegel,* was at fault. Finding nothing in the article that vitally jeopardized West Germany's security or

able source of information on the *Spiegel* Affair. The first two volumes, now in print but appearing after the completion of the present study, are titled: *Die Spiegel-Affäre: Die Staatsmacht und ihre Kontrolle* and *Die Spiegel-Affäre: Die Reaktion der Öffentlichenkeit* (Olton und Freiburg im Breisgau, 1966). David Schoenbaum's *The Spiegel Affair* (New York: Garden City, 1968) also appeared after the completion of the present study.

[6] Strongly encouraged by the German Trade Union Federation *(Deutscher Gewerkschaftsbund),* the Social Democratic Party has refused to support the government-sponsored emergency power proposals. Without SPD support, it has been impossible to secure in parliament the two-thirds vote necessary for amending the Basic Law to include the major provisions. Certain of the less controversial elements of the proposals did receive SPD support in the closing weeks of the 1965 Bundestag session. Until the full emergency power provisions are adopted, the three former occupying powers retain certain legal rights of emergency regulation in the German Federal Republic.

national interests, these critics charged the government, and particularly Strauss, with having failed to keep the public accurately informed of the military capabilities and limitations of the Bundeswehr and NATO, both of which had been treated in the incriminating article.

A few observers probed deeply into the psychic condition of the West German citizenry in attempting to account for what they perceived to be a significant public criticism of the authorities for the action against *Der Spiegel.* To these commentators the popular reaction was another illustration of a widespread alienation that persists in West German toward the Bonn system and which had found in the magazine both a symbol and a spokesman. Other observers, reasoning along different lines, concluded that the charge of treason no longer arouses the public response it might have produced in an earlier Germany. Charges of treason and crimes against the "Reich und Volk," so the argument went, had been used too often in the German past to mask violations of human decency to permit similar charges now to be accepted at face value. In short, it was asserted that the West German authorities may have misjudged the public mood if they assumed that the charge of treason would justify to the public, even during the Cuban missile crisis, the drastic measures initiated on the evening of October 26, 1962.[7] Finally, since the article which prompted the investigation dealt essentially with

[7] On October 22, 1962, the warrants for the arrest of Augstein and Ahlers were issued in confidence by the Federal High Court *(Bundesgerichtshof)* upon the request of the Federal Prosecutor's Office. On the same day President Kennedy announced in his radio and television speech the discovery of offensive missile sites in Cuba and the countermeasures which the United States government was taking. Therefore, the Cuban crisis, though abated, was still in progress when the October 26 raids were made on *Der Spiegel's* offices and the search and seizure warrants were executed. The Cuban crisis was later cited by certain public officials to justify the timing and the swiftness of the *Spiegel* action.

military policy, it gave additional impetus to the continuing controversy in West Germany as to whether the Bundeswehr should have a nuclear deterrent capability.

These diverse approaches to an interpretation of the *Spiegel* Affair converge at several points. But the particular framework within which the affair is examined will result in different emphases and concentrate on varying aspects of the affair. No attempt is made here to provide an exhaustive account of the *Spiegel* Affair in all of its complex relationships. A definitive history of the affair is not our purpose. It undoubtedly would include, but also range beyond, the aspects upon which the present study focuses. Moreover, only incidental attention is given to certain of the specialized legal questions raised by the controversy.[8] These technical-legal features of the affair are slighted not because they are trivial but because they are tangential to our central purpose of placing the affair within the broader context of the political system. Nor have we considered in depth either the implications of the *Spiegel* Affair for freedom of the press in West Germany or, more specifically, the important impetus provided by the affair for reforms in the West German penal code.[9] Instead, this study is designed primarily to examine the functioning of the West German political system as it sought to respond to and resolve the crisis produced by the affair. The *Spiegel* Affair resulted in certain demands being imposed upon the political system. What were these demands, why did they arise, how were they projected into the decision processes, and through what techniques and strategies were they negotiated?

[8] See Kirchheimer and Menges, "A Free Press in a Democratic State?" for a discussion of the primary legal and juridical problems raised by the *Spiegel* Affair.

[9] See Martin Löffler, *Der Verfassungsauftrag der Presse* (Karlsruhe, 1963), for an attempt to place the *Spiegel* Affair within the context of the "constitutional" function of press criticism.

The problems and limitations of generalizing about political systems through case studies have been elaborated elsewhere.[10] In a sense, no case is "typical," for in each situation the relevant issues, the alternatives available to the participants in the decision process in resolving the issues, and the relative degree of involvement of various participating groups and institutions may vary. Also the selection of a "crisis" rather than a "routine" or more regularly recurring policy decision as the focus of the case study may inject distorting variables into the study. These qualifications do not, we believe, invalidate the methodological soundness of the case study in general, or the "crisis" case study in particular, in seeking to contribute to an understanding of how a political system functions. They do suggest caution in extrapolating generalizations from a single case study. Properly conceived, a case study is a supplement to, not a substitute for, broadly framed inquiries into the functioning of political systems.

The intent of this study has determined that we forego a general description of the post-1949 political history of the German Federal Republic. By way of background, however, it is relevant to review in the following chapter certain events which occurred immediately prior to the *Spiegel* Affair and which partially conditioned the atmosphere surrounding the affair. Chapter Two delineates the most controversial aspects of the raids and arrests of October 26, 1962. For our purposes, the affair consisted of two phases: (1) the formative phase, during which the issues were initially framed and projected broadly into the political arena; and (2) the bargaining phase, during which the agents, particularly the party and governmental leaders, most directly involved in negotiating the issues sought either to moderate the controversy or to

[10] Cf. particularly Leon D. Epstein, *British Politics in the Suez Crisis* (Urbana, 1964), 1–6, and James B. Christoph, *Capital Punishment and British Politics* (London, 1962), 7–8.

translate the issues into demands upon the decision processes. The formative phase provides the focus of Chapters Three and Four; the bargaining phase is treated in Chapters Five and Six. What observations can be made about the Bonn parliamentary system in light of its response to the *Spiegel* Affair? In the concluding chapter we attempt to answer this question.

GERMAN POLITICS
AND THE
SPIEGEL
AFFAIR

Chapter I

PRELUDE TO A CRISIS

During 1946 the idea of creating in Germany a news magazine patterned after the American news weekly *Time* or the London *News Review* seems to have originated with Sergeant Harry Bohrer of the British Press Control Authority in Hanover. With the encouragement of his superior, Major John Chaloner, deputy chief of the Press Control Authority, Bohrer recruited a small staff of Germans, including twenty-two-year-old Rudolf Augstein. The first issue of the magazine, titled *Diese Woche*, appeared in November, 1946. In that issue the magazine offended the British authorities by reproducing a letter written by British publisher Victor Gollancz to the *News Chronicle* criticizing his government for encouraging a sumptuous Christmas celebration in Britain while the Germans were on near-starvation rations. As a result of the protest filed by the British military government with the Press Control Authority for its sponsoring a magazine that followed such an editorial policy, Bohrer and Chaloner dissolved the British connection with the magazine by allowing Augstein and two associates to assume ownership of the license. Augstein renamed his newly acquired magazine and under the title *Der Spiegel* the first issue appeared on January 4, 1947.[1]

From the outset the magazine adopted an aggressive style that placed it in a distinctive category in postwar German journalism. *Der Spiegel's* persistently critical treatment of policies and personalities of the successive Adenauer govern-

[1] See Löffler, *Der Verfassungsauftrag der Presse*, for the background and evolution of the magazine, particularly pages 23-27.

3

ments, its sensational exposés of prominent West German officials, coupled with disappointment in various circles with both the party system and the press community as instruments of criticism, eventually earned it the title "the loyal opposition" in the eyes of its followers. Within five years its original circulation of a few thousand grew to 118,000; by 1962 its weekly circulation exceeded a half million copies and its readership extended to five million persons.[2]

Under the guidance of publisher Augstein, Der Spiegel borrowed from Time a format which, while permitting primary attention to political news, was designed to appeal to the varied interests of a reasonably sophisticated reader.[3] In

[2] Circulation figures for Der Spiegel are taken from Löffler, ibid., 25. Other sources offer figures which vary slightly from those given by Löffler. For example, Paul Sackarndt, Der Spiegel—Entzaubert, Analyse eines Deutschen Nachrichtenmagazins (Essen, 1961), places the original circulation of Der Spiegel at about thirty thousand copies. (p. 12) By January 1, 1963, Der Spiegel is credited by Löffler, ibid., p. 25, with an average weekly circulation of 573,000 copies. Discrepancies in the circulation figures for the first year may be explained by the magazine's relying partially during its first year upon black-market paper in order to print more than the fifteen thousand copies allowed by its paper quota. The 1962 readership figure for Der Spiegel is taken from Erich Peter Neumann, Die Spiegel-Affäre in der öffentlichen Meinung (Address before the Institut für Publizistik of the University of Munich, offset print, n.p., June 19, 1963), 4. By July, 1963, circulation was reported by Augstein to be around 680,000 copies, with a readership representing some 11.5 percent of the West German population between fourteen and seventy years of age. Der Spiegel, July 17, 1963, p. 3. According to a survey conducted at the end of 1962 the educational structure of the magazine's readership, as compared with the average readership of West German periodicals, is as follows:

Terminal Level of Formal Education	Der Spiegel's Readership	Average Periodical Readership
Volkschule (to ages 14/15)	64%	80%
Mittlere Reife (to ages 16/17)	24%	16%
Abitur (ages 18 and above)	12%	4%

(Source: Neumann, p. 5.)

[3] See both Löffler, Der Verfassungsauftrag der Presse and Sackarndt, Der Spiegel.

an average issue slightly more than half its space is devoted to political news and public affairs; the remaining space is distributed among such diverse categories as sports, business, culture, science, and medicine. Issues periodically contain, in addition, special features, such as transcripts of interviews conducted by *Der Spiegel* reporters with prominent personalities, condensations of recent and controversial books (in several installments), or reports in depth on topics of particular interest to Germans. *Der Spiegel* stresses the personal flavor of the news, developing its reports around the personalities most directly involved in the subject being examined and interspersing its account with direct quotations. To give additional credence to its "inside dopester"-approach, the magazine takes pride in revealing intimate, and sometimes irrelevant, details about the personalities. Although lapsing into occasional tedium and longwindedness, the style of writing makes a valiant effort to emulate *Time's* use of the provocative phrase and suggestive aside.[4]

But *Der Spiegel* is not simply a German imitation of *Time*. Too much stress on the formalistic similarities of the two periodicals blurs the distinctiveness of *Der Spiegel* and the

[4] In a talk in 1953 before the *Industrie-Club*, Augstein said of the *Spiegel* approach: "Persons are colorful and more interesting than abstract events. Persons put life in a story. Nothing is more interesting for a person than another person. The character of personality influences history." Quoted in Sackarndt, *Der Spiegel*, 13. On the "personality" approach of *Der Spiegel*, a writer in a special issue of *Der Volkswirt* concludes: "To have produced the people who stand behind the economic and social happenings as the driving force is undoubtedly the service of *Der Spiegel*. The so-called serious press [in Germany] has consistently sought refuge in abstractions; in *Der Spiegel* people finally appear, their motivations, interests, weaknesses, and strengths." Cited in *Der Spiegel*, April 12, 1961, p. 98. The difficulty of adapting the German syntax to the *Time* literary style is reflected in Augstein's statement that "In *Der Spiegel* concise, colorful German is to be written, good German where possible, but there occasionally is the rub. . . . For terse and concise language inevitably leads in sentence structure to Anglicisms." Cited in Sackarndt, *Der Spiegel*, 12.

iconoclastic nature of its publisher and staff. The most important distinction arises from the missionary zeal with which it functions. Augstein and his associates have sought to fashion the magazine into a type of press organ which they feel has been lacking in Germany in the past: one that can reach a wide audience and, at the same time, assume the initiative in bringing to this audience the information and views which cannot be found in the daily press. Rejecting the taboos and stuffiness attributed to traditional German journalism, *Der Spiegel* does not simply condense and rewrite news accounts which have already been published or which are available through the wire services. It relies heavily on independent sources of information, has one of the largest dossier collections in Europe, and maintains probably the most resourceful staff of reporters in Germany. And success has bred success. It is to *Der Spiegel* that many Germans have come on their own initiative with grievances, complaints, and tips, some of which have led to the magazine's most sensational revelations.

Der Spiegel's jaundiced editorial eye has been cast in many directions over the years and has fixed as much on certain aspects of the "new" culture in West Germany as on those strands of the past which are construed as factors conditioning the rise to power of the national socialists. But in its avowed attempt to expose what it perceives to be the imperfections and hypocrisies of policies and personalities closely identified with the Bonn system, *Der Spiegel* has more than once been accused of a reportorial myopia that distorts the facts and culminates in irresponsible attacks. "Negativism is its *Weltanschauung*" is a complaint frequently made by its critics. In any event, this assumed function of protesting, of exposing, of acting as the keeper of the German conscience, as *Der Spiegel's* editors would define it, must be assigned considerable weight in any effort to understand the appeal which the magazine has to many of its readers.

One conclusion that can be drawn from the undoubted impact the magazine has made on the West German reading public is that, however far it may stray at times from acceptable standards of news gathering and reporting, *Der Spiegel* has struck a responsive chord among those West Germans who themselves have rejected certain traditions of the past but are not yet committed to satisfactory alternatives. In 1954 Karl Jaspers wrote: "In Western Germany, so far as the mass of the population is concerned, one cannot speak about a new democratic way of thinking. It is true that various Germans have expressed themselves on the basic ideas of democracy, on the constitutional state, on liberalism . . . [But] there is as yet no effective political thinking which derives from within and stands the test of every day life. Perhaps the inclination toward such thinking has even decreased in recent years."[5]

In 1955 Claus Jacobi, coeditor of *Der Spiegel*, observed: "West Germany today possesses no values for which the people would be prepared to sacrifice themselves, no symbols that inspire their reverence. For 12 years the Germans had a surplus of false ideals; today they have too few genuine ideas. No state consciousness had formed. In its place there is the German *Wirtschaftswunder* and the Old Man [Adenauer]."[6]

And in 1963, shortly after the occurrence of the *Spiegel* Affair, Anton Böhm, a prominent CDU (Christian Democratic Union) deputy in the Bundestag, still detected this widespread disorientation: "The historical break of National Socialism severed the contact of the Germans with

[5] "The Political Vacuum in Germany," *Foreign Affairs,* XXXII (July, 1954), 598.

[6] "Germany's Great Old Man," *Foreign Affairs,* XXXIII (January, 1955), 245.

their history. How deeply the cut went we did not correctly perceive in the years immediately after the catastrophe; only now are we beginning to understand it better. Demonic hate as a ruling maxim, the fundamental violation of justice and human dignity, the mockery of truth through the constitutionalization of lies, the unscrupulous misuse of the willingness to sacrifice and the belief in authority, before all however the atrocities and mass murders of Hitlerism created between the Germans and their history a barrier that sometimes seems insurmountable."[7]

These statements alone, of course, do not prove the existence of an ideological vacuum in West Germany out of which might grow an emotional attachment to periodicals such as *Der Spiegel*. But the available evidence is highly suggestive. In the comparative study by Gabriel Almond and Sidney Verba of the political cultures of West Germany, the United States, Britain, Italy, and Mexico, for example, one of the questions posed to the population samples asked: "Speaking generally, what are the things about this country that you are most proud of?" Only 7 percent of the West German sample cited "Governmental, political institutions," as contrasted with 85 percent in the United States, 46 percent in Britain, and 30 percent in Mexico. Italy, with a political developmental history that provides certain analogies with that of Germany, showed even a smaller percentage citing their governmental and political institutions as objects of pride. As a result of the attitudinal patterns derived from these and other polls, Almond and Verba concluded that in West Germany there "is a highly pragmatic—probably overpragmatic—orientation to the political system; as if the intense commitment to political movements that characterized Germany under Weimar

[7] "Krise des Staatsbewusstseins," *Die politische Meinung*, VIII (July-August, 1963), 50.

and the Nazi era is now being balanced by a detached, practical, and almost cynical attitude toward politics."[8] Equivocation, if not outright hostility, among the West Germans toward their political system, at least during the formative, or Adenauer, era, is also suggested by the results of various polls published in the 1957 *Jahrbuch der Öffentlichen Meinung.* In June, 1956, for example, the question was asked: "What do you really feel about our present constitution—I refer to our state's Basic Law? Do you find it, by and large, good or not good—or have you still no opinion?" Twenty-nine percent responded "Good," 6 percent said "Not good," and, most significantly, 65 percent were either "Undecided," or "Not familiar with the constitution."[9] Polls conducted in the early 1960's still indicated that at least 60 percent of the West German adults were "politically uninterested."[10]

Generalizing upon the basis of findings such as these is hazardous. In light of the German experiences during and after World War II and the novelty of the Bonn system at the time these polls were conducted, it is hardly surprising that considerable popular detachment existed with regard to the political system. Political apathy, the sense of improvisation induced by the continued division of Germany, a "healthy" skepticism borne out of bitter experience, and a preoccupation with materialistic goals—these explanations, rather than those that stress aggressive hostility toward the Bonn system, may be the appropriate conclusions to be inferred from the

[8] Gabriel A. Almond and Sidney Verba, *The Civic Culture: Political Attitudes and Democracy in Five Nations* (Boston and Toronto, 1965), 64, 313.

[9] Elizabeth Noelle and Erich Peter Neumann (eds.), *Jahrbuch der Öffentlichen Meinung 1957* (Allensbach am Bodensee, 1957), 165.

[10] Viggo Graf Blücher et al (eds.), *Der Prozess der Meinungsbildung* (Bielefeld, 1962), 13. West Germans born between 1940 and 1946 have a comparable or slightly lower level of "interest" in politics according to Walter Jaide, *Jugend im Blickpunkt* (Berlin-Spandau, 1963), 55–62.

findings. Yet, whether they longed subjectively for a political system that could attact their positive support and enthusiasm or were objectively concerned about the apparent gap between the popular strata and the Bonn system, a rather sizable community of dissidents had developed prior to the *Spiegel* Affair. While not always in agreement with *Der Spiegel's* editorial views or policy orientations, many of these probably found the magazine's iconoclasm to be an agreeable antidote to what they perceived to be the prevailing atmosphere.

It would be a mistake, however, to explain the magazine's following solely in terms of an ideological vacuum or lack of commitment to positive political values. Without condoning what they regard as *Der Spiegel's* occasional malicious and unprincipled methods, many reasonably "committed" and politically satisfied Germans have also given qualified support to the magazine for contributing to a more vigorous and informed political dialogue than may have existed in earlier periods of German history. Moreover, West Germany is not unique in experiencing the type of political deviancy to which *Der Spiegel* seems to have an appeal. With the decline of the old ideological cleavages, premised on economic, class, and religious tensions that have been partially obliterated or blurred in many modernized societies, observers have noted a new wave of dissent, particularly among the intellectuals and younger age groups, against the stifling conformity of an over-consensualized and over-pragmatized political culture.[11] In any event, by 1962 *Der Spiegel* had emerged as not only the most widely circulated weekly news magazine in West Germany but also as an effective organ of opposition to and criticism of the governing elites. It is not exclusively

[11] See, for example, the conjectures in Robert A. Dahl, "Epilogue," in Robert A. Dahl (ed.), *Political Oppositions in Western Democracies* (New Haven, 1966), 387–401.

the wisdom of hindsight to conclude that any attempt by these authorites, whatever their motives, to restrain the magazine in either its news gathering or reporting functions would invariably arouse considerable popular reaction.

Der Spiegel: "The Loyal Opposition"

Almost from its inception *Der Spiegel* asserted its role as an aggressive and enterprising critic of established authority. The first major sensation resulted from a report in its September 27, 1950, issue in which it charged that approximately one hundred Bundestag deputies had been paid one thousand to twenty thousand German marks each for voting to locate the provisional capital of the Federal Republic in Bonn. The allegedly bribed deputies came from most of the parties represented in the Bundestag, although they tended to cluster in the minor parties which had supplied the votes in 1949 that permitted Adenauer to be elected chancellor. In an elaboration upon the charge *Der Spiegel* revealed in its December 13, 1950, issue that Federal Finance Minister Fritz Schäffer might have been involved in the bribery by diverting funds from the CDU/CSU treasury to the smaller parties. Even before the second article appeared, a resolution was introduced in the Bundestag by the delegations of seven of the nine parties requesting the creation of a special committee of inquiry to investigate the bribery charges.[12] As a result of the evidence obtained in twenty-four open hearings, thirteen executive sessions, and from two thousand pages of testimony, the *"Spiegel Committee,"* as it had come to be called, submitted a detailed report to the Bundestag.[13] The committee traced the contentions by *Der Spiegel* to unfounded rumors arising from statements made by a Bundestag deputy

[12] *Verhandlungen des Deutschen Bundestages, 1. Wahlperiode 1949, Anlage—Band 6, Drucksache, 1950, No. 1397.*
[13] *Ibid., Anlage—Band 11, Drucksache, 1951, No. 2274.*

in private conversation. However, the report disclosed that both Schäffer and Bundestag deputy Franz Josef Strauss had either been involved in or informed of the diversion of CDU/CSU campaign funds to the Bavarian Party "in order for the Bavarian Party to pay its well-known debts." No evidence was discovered by the investigators that would sustain the charge that the money was intended to extract specific voting commitments from the Bavarian Party deputies; to the contrary, the committee concluded that the "specific charge that around 100 members were bribed is false."[14] Nevertheless, three deputies were accused by the committee of having testified falsely before it, and five Bundestag members eventually resigned their seats as a result of the committee's findings.

Der Spiegel's reputation as an enterprising muckraker was given additional impetus by its July 9, 1952, article titled "Be Careful Over the Phone." The article connected Konrad Adenauer and Herbert Blankenhorn in 1948 with a French secret service agent, Hans Konrad Schmeisser (alias René Levacher). According to *Der Spiegel*, Blankenhorn, executive secretary at the time of the British zone CDU organization, was authorized by Adenauer to give periodically to the French agent Schmeisser information that might be of interest to the French government. Among the reports allegedly turned over to Schmeisser was the "Speidel Plan," devised privately by former Wehrmacht general Hans Speidel for the defense of western Germany against a Soviet invasion. According to *Der Spiegel's* informants, Schmeisser was also given a list of Germans who, apparently in the opinion of Adenauer, could be relied upon under the "right" conditions to work for the permanent separation of the Rhineland from Germany. For these favors Blankenhorn reportedly received food and money, and both he and Adenauer were assured by

[14] *Ibid.*, p. 23.

the French government that they and their families would be safely taken to Spain in the event of a Russian invasion of Germany. *Der Spiegel* also disclosed that Blankenhorn had asked Schmeisser to make a contribution of 800,000 German marks to the CDU 1949 campaign fund. In 1953 Adenauer and Blankenhorn sued *Der Spiegel's* publisher and editors and its informants for libel; in the preliminary hearing of the suit, Augstein and Schmeisser (one of the informants) gave the complainants "satisfaction" by denying that they had intended to question the "loyalty" or "honor" of the complainants. The suit was then dropped.[15] The SPD (Socialist Democratic Party), however, pursued the charges in the Bundestag by directing a parliamentary question to the federal government requesting that Adenauer discharge "his obligation to the German people" by clearly and definitively confronting these accusations.[16] Adenauer responded in the Bundestag by denying the accuracy of the *Der Spiegel* report and alluded cryptically to the "unreliable" past of the informants.[17]

In the years that followed, *Der Spiegel* persisted in publishing news stories which, if sensationally presented, seemed basically well informed and served to spark the political interest of a relatively apathetic and economically preoccupied public.[18] By the late 1950's Franz Josef Strauss had

[15] The issues and events surrounding the Schmeisser Affair are summarized in the *Archiv der Gegenwart*, XXV, 5380-A, 5508-C.

[16] *Verhandlungen des Deutschen Bundestages, 2. Wahlperiode 1953, Stenographische Berichte, Band 27 (1955),* 6202.

[17] *Ibid.,* 6202–6204.

[18] Among the more notable exposés by *Der Spiegel* during this period are the following: In its August 17, 1955, issue *Der Spiegel* reported the antisemitic statements of Dr. Eberhard Taubert, vice-chairman at the time of the *Volksbund für Frieden und Freiheit.* The magazine revealed that these statements had been brought to the attention of the Federal Ministry for All-German Questions by the publisher of the *Allegmeine Wochenzeitung der Juden in Deutschland,* but the Ministry had replied that although it was aware of Taubert's antisemitic leanings it did not

emerged as *Der Spiegel's* prime target of criticism, prompted by both his policy views and his stylistic qualities.

Skeptical of Adenauer's policy of armed strength and military alliance with the West as a means of inducing the Soviet government to negotiate the German reunification problem, Augstein and his colleagues became increasingly alarmed by the apparent commitment of Strauss (who became defense minister in 1956) to the view that the Bundeswehr must share in atomic weaponry systems.[19] Equally important for an

feel free to expose him for fear of being accused of "communistic" sympathies. Shortly after *Der Spiegel* exposed Taubert's antisemitism, he resigned his position in the *Volksbund,* a private association of German expellees who seek the return of the areas east of the Oder-Neisse Line to a reunified Germany. Public school teacher Ludwig Zind in April, 1957, in a restaurant-tavern in Offenburg made antisemitic statements in the presence of a Jewish citizen of Offenburg, Kurt Lieser, and alluded to the "mistake" that the Nazis made of "not burning enough Jews." After lodging a complaint with the school authorities, Lieser finally received notice that a formal criminal action would be filed against Zind but that in the meantime no grounds existed for suspending Zind. The case seems to have been kept relatively quiet until *Der Spiegel* exposed in its December 18, 1957, issue the delay on the part of the public educational authorities in taking action. Zind was then promptly charged with violation of the Jewish Defamation Law; however, Zind fled to Italy and escaped rendition since the charge against him was construed as a "political crime." He was convicted in *absentia* and sentenced to a year's imprisonment. Zind was later reported to be residing in Egypt. In its June 11, 1958, and October 22, 1958, issues, *Der Spiegel* reported that Land Finance Minister Nowack of Rhineland-Palatinate had illegally profited from speculation in the trading of stocks in a partially publicly owned enterprise in his *Land.* Nowack was ex-officio chairman of the board of directors of the firm, three-fourths of its stock being owned by the *Land* government. The *Landtag* (*Land* parliament) finally created a parliamentary committee of inquiry to investigate the charges. It confirmed *Der Spiegel's* charges. Nowack resigned and was later convicted of illegal activities. In its July 9, 1958 issue *Der Spiegel* revealed that the state prosecutor in Bonn had evidence of widespread corrupt practices and influence-peddling in the federal government. One of the cases involved the personal aide of Chancellor Adenauer, Hans Kilb, who had been given two automobiles for his personal use by a Daimler-Benz dealer. After the exposé by *Der Spiegel,* the authorities took steps to curb the acceptance by civil servants of gifts from private groups.

[19] The evolution and justification of *Der Spiegel's* position on the rearming of West Germany and particularly on the equipping of the

understanding of the anti-Strauss tendency of the magazine was the growing conviction that Strauss did not possess personal qualities suitable for high public office in a democratic system.[20] In 1961, as Strauss's rise to political influence was climaxed with his being selected chairman of the Bavarian CSU—a position which, when coupled with his position as federal defense minister, made him a leading contender in the future for the chancellorship—*Der Spiegel* mobilized its journalistic resources to alert West Germany to the impending danger. Its cover story of April 5, 1961, the first in a series of reports on Strauss in succeeding weeks, underscored the magazine's concern. Alluding to the *"Endkampf"* in which the German Federal Republic would have to choose between Strauss and democracy, the magazine warned:

Three weeks ago Franz Josef Strauss, 45 years old, took the next to last step [by being selected CSU chairman] in the direction of the chancellorship. . . . The Federal Republic, its back to the wall, must now confront him head-on, and in so doing either accept him or shake him off. Without the agreement of the CSU, without the agreement of this permanent "pressure group" . . . it is no longer possible to select the head of the government, in view of the existing majority composition which controls the Bundestag.

Strauss brought suit to prevent *Der Spiegel's* repeating a number of references in the *"Endkampf"* article. A Nürnberg court, in granting the temporary restraining order, specifically forbade the repetition by the magazine of the statements

---

Bundeswehr with atomic weapons are reflected in the collection of essays first published in *Der Spiegel* and reprinted in Rudolf Augstein, *Spiegelungen* (München: List Verlag, 1964).

[20] *Der Spiegel* has not been alone in questioning Strauss's personal qualifications for leadership in a democratic system. The most systematically developed criticism of Strauss's political style is found in Erich Kuby et al., *Franz Josef Strauss, Ein Typus Unserer Zeit* (Wien, München. Basel: Verlag Kurt Desch, 1963).

that (1) Strauss did not conform to the ground rules of a "civilized" person; (2) he was an "opportunist"; (3) he refused to trust those who thought differently than he; (4) he was likely to use the Bundeswehr as an instrument for achieving personal political ambitions; (5) it was to be feared that he would circumvent such organs of constitutionalism as the parliament and the Constitutional Court *(Bundesverfassungsgericht)*; (6) he did not respect the principle of equality of all citizens before the law; and (7) he sought tactical atomic weapons for the Bundeswehr "for the purpose of bringing the Americans, against their will, into a war with the Soviet Union."[21]

Three weeks later *Der Spiegel* returned to its crusade against Strauss. In an article titled "The Way to the Top," the magazine revealed a deliberate campaign by Strauss, in his drive toward the chancellorship, to secure in the next government the post as foreign minister, "in line with the teachings of his old mentor, Josef Muller [of Bavaria], that the way to the top [of the governmental authority] is through foreign policy."[22] He was accused of having planted friends in the Foreign Section of the Federal Press Office who were insuring that his views on foreign policy were given prominent coverage in the official news *Bulletin* and also of having arranged for military attachés in German embassies to keep him informed of political—not merely military—developments abroad. The friendship of important personalities in the German diplomatic corps was being cultivated by Strauss and, the magazine added, he had already promised the position of State Secretary in the Foreign Ministry to Herbert Blankenhorn, at the time German ambassador to France.

[21] *Der Spiegel,* June 21, 1961, column by Rudolf Augstein titled "Lieber Spiegel-Leser."

[22] *Der Spiegel,* April 26, 1961, pp. 23–24.

The Fibag Affair

Der Spiegel's 1961 offensive against Strauss gathered momentum with the May 31 issue. In an article titled "Hans and Franz," the magazine accused Strauss of having recommended to the American authorities the "Fibag" firm *(Finanzbau-Aktiengesellschaft)* for the construction in West Germany of a $75 million military housing project, without properly examining the legal or technical competence of the firm and primarily upon the urging of a Bavarian political supporter and personal friend, Dr. Hans E. Kapfinger, publisher of the Passau *Neue Presse.* According to the article, Kapfinger had been promised by the founders of the "corporation"—the firm had not been legally incorporated—a one-fourth share ($30,000) of the original capital stock simply for his "connections" and "promotional" talents. *Der Spiegel* reproduced facsimiles of letters showing that Strauss had written a "To whom it may concern" endorsement of Fibag's efforts to secure the American military housing contract in West Germany. A second letter was sent by Strauss's office to United States Secretary of Defense Thomas Gates, certifying that the Fibag's plans had been examined in the West German Defense Ministry and urging Gates to refer the "feasible" plan to the United States "experts."[23] A carbon copy of the second

[23] The full text of the body of the letter reads:

According to information which has come to the attention of my ministry the American army is interested in the construction of a considerable number of apartments for the use of personnel of the U.S. Army in Germany. Although the Federal Defense Ministry is not directly involved, the proposals of the Architectural-bureau Lothar Schloss which were submitted by him have been examined and Herr Schloss was given a copy of the attached letter of endorsement. This is the same firm which participated in 1956 in the American barracks project in France. That project, for understandable reasons, was awarded to a French firm.

I am taking the liberty of mentioning that the plan presented by the Architectural-bureau Schloss has been examined here and found to be feasible. If you are interested in pursuing further the matter of

letter was forwarded to Kapfinger, with an accompanying note from Strauss saying that "I don't think we should press the Americans too hard, since past experience suggests that it would lead to false impressions and negative results." In short, the "Hans and Franz" article asked: By what authority had Strauss intervened with the United States government in behalf of the Fibag firm, which did not legally exist, in connection with a project which did not officially concern him and through what motivations had Strauss been led to write these letters of endorsement? Moreover, why had Dr. Kapfinger been kept informed by Strauss of the efforts by the German Defense Ministry to promote the Fibag project?

For the *Spiegel* charges to produce a major controversy they had to be injected more directly into the mainstream of the political system. This was accomplished by the SPD Bundestag delegation when it submitted on June 15, 1961, a parliamentary question concerning *Der Spiegel's* charges.[24] Approximately a month later Strauss's reply was published in the Bundestag proceedings. He denied any impropriety on his part in handling the Fibag matter. Specifically, he claimed that: (1) one of the participants in the Fibag consortium, Lothar Schloss of Munich, was known to his ministry as one who in the past had done satisfactory construction work for the local authorities in Munich; (2) although the American military housing plan was of no immediate concern to the Defense Ministry, it was anticipated that sometime in the future the housing facilities might be turned over to the Bundeswehr, and for this reason it was his responsibility to ascertain whether in design and location the facilities would eventually be useful for German military housing; (3) on

a housing project for the U.S. Army in Germany, I suggest that this be examined and passed on to your experts.

[24] *Verhandlungen des Deutschen Bundestages, 3. Wahlperiode 1957, Drucksache* 2847.

June 1, 1960, agencies in his ministry had therefore scrutinized Schloss's plans and specifications and were satisfied that they met also the eventual needs of the Bundeswehr and that the anticipated American financing would be sufficient to implement the construction of the facilities at prevailing costs; (4) except for those presented by Schloss, no plans were submitted to the Defense Ministry for this particular project; and (5) the Defense Minister or his associates did not know of Kapfinger's financial interest, if there was one, in the Fibag firm—the communications between Strauss and Kapfinger concerning the Fibag plan had resulted simply from Kapfinger's inquiring about it. "It is not possible," he said, "for the Defense Ministry, in light of the multitude of petitions and letters it receives, to go into them routinely and examine them specifically to see if there is [an improper] connection between the inquiring party and the project."[25]

The flurry of attacks by *Der Spiegel* against Strauss during the spring of 1961, culminating in the Fibag exposé, could only superficially be construed as an attempt by the magazine to harm Strauss's electoral prospects in the forthcoming (September 17, 1961) Bundestag election. Strauss's popularity in Bavaria and that of his party, the CSU, were too strongly grounded to permit *Der Spiegel's* staff to imagine that the charges would seriously dilute his base of political support. The optimal expectation was that the charges would momentarily decelerate Strauss's advance within the ranks of the Bonn cabinet and surround him with sufficient controversy to make him unacceptable for the "next step," the Foreign Office, in his alleged drive toward the chancellorship.

In the summer of 1961 the Fibag controversy occasionally entered the Bundestag election campaign, but both the FDP and the SPD hesitated to make the charges a central issue. The evidence was inadequately developed for either party to

[25] *Ibid., Drucksache 2967.*

become too heavily committed to *Der Spiegel's* version, and soundings of public opinion did not reveal any substantial electoral mileage to be gained from stressing the matter. Considerations of campaign strategy also warned against focusing on the Fibag matter. The FDP was particularly reluctant to alienate Strauss, not because it necessarily agreed with his political style or his policy views but because it needed Strauss in the months ahead. Seeking to pick up support in the elections from normally Christian Democratic and marginal voters who were disenchanted with Adenauer and wanted him removed from the chancellorship, the Free Democrats campaigned strongly in 1961 on the promise of removing Adenauer. This was to be effected by entering a coalition with the CDU/CSU, but only on the condition that the CDU/CSU propose someone (preferably Ludwig Erhard) other than Adenauer for the chancellorship. Although the Free Democrats were unable to secure this concession from the CDU/CSU when the time came to negotiate on forming the new cabinet, the FDP leadership assumed prior to the election that Strauss might be persuaded to help the FDP dislodge Adenauer by throwing his CSU bloc of votes in favor of Erhard.[26] To attack Strauss during the campaign might therefore jeopardize its strategy during the later coalition negotiations. The SPD was motivated by slightly different reasons. Many of its members, followers, and Bundestag deputies shared *Der Spiegel's* skepticism of Strauss's qualifications for public office, but the strategists of the Social Democratic campaign reasoned that the image of their party as a responsible and constructive alternative to the CDU/CSU re-

[26] Cf. Peter H. Merkl, "Equilibrium, Structure of Interests and Leadership: Adenauer's Survival as Chancellor," *American Political Science Review,* LVI (September, 1962), 640–42. Strauss finally sought, during the 1961 coalition negotiations, a compromise of a one-year transitional chancellorship for Adenauer, who would then step aside for Erhard. This strategy failed.

quired it to emphasize the positive merits of its own program and leaders rather than the negative traits of its opponents. Superimposed upon all of these considerations was the sudden shift in August, 1961, of West German public attention to the erection of the Berlin Wall, with its becoming a primary focus of interest in the final stages of the campaign.[27]

Although the Fibag controversy was thus eclipsed by other events in the summer of 1961, *Der Spiegel* renewed and elaborated the Fibag charges following the Bundestag election. In its October 25, 1961, issue the magazine expressed dissatisfaction with Strauss's reply to the earlier SPD parliamentary question and revealed that twelve days after the appearance of the "Hans and Franz" article a letter went out from the Defense Ministry instructing Lothar Schloss to return Strauss's letter of endorsement; on July 25, 1961, a second letter was sent to Schloss urgently repeating the request that the endorsement letter be returned and warning that unless Schloss complied the Ministry would "inform all appropriate U.S. authorities accordingly." Implicitly, the magazine reasoned, this new piece of information suggested that Strauss was trying to cover up his error and supported its original contention that the Defense Minister had acted improperly in the Fibag matter.

In its January 31, 1962, issue *Der Spiegel* reproduced facsimiles of sworn affidavits of two major Fibag partners, Lothar Schloss and Karl Willy Braun. The affidavits affirmed that Kapfinger had not only been brought into the deal solely because of his friendship with Strauss but that Kapfinger had said in the presence of Schloss and Braun that he planned to share his profits from the project with Strauss.[28] Although

[27] See John W. Keller, *Germany, the Wall and Berlin: Internal Politics During an International Crisis* (New York, 1964).

[28] "Kapfingers Erzählungen," *Der Spiegel* January 31, 1962, pp. 22–24. The affidavit executed by Braun stated that: "After the signing [of the agreement between Schloss, Braun, and Kapfinger] Herr Dr. Kapfinger in

specifically denying that it believed Strauss would have deliberately supported the Fibag project out of personal financial considerations, *Der Spiegel* called upon Strauss once again to explain his involvement in the Fibag case. The magazine complained that the apparent inability to get the truth from the minister had implications not merely for the personalities involved but for the Bonn system: "If in view of all this 'carelessness' [by Strauss] the answer of the Minister to the modest question of the SPD is to be accepted as a full explanation, then there is no longer in this country any effective checks on the majority party, there is no effective public opinion and no system of control over the conduct of the members of the Government from the side of the opposition in parliament. In short, the 'purification of the State' remains a farce."[29] In keeping with its assumed role as the "real opposition" in West Germany, *Der Spiegel* formulated in its January 31 article its own set of questions to which Strauss was asked to respond. Strauss responded on February 4 by filing a libel suit against the magazine.

Undeterred by Strauss's court action, *Der Spiegel* pressed on and developed in its February 21 issue a complete account of the evidence it had in the entire Fibag controversy. Taking into consideration the sworn affidavits submitted by Strauss to the local court in Nürnberg-Fürth justifying his libel suit, *Der Spiegel* reasserted its charge that the minister had acted both improperly and impulsively in the Fibag matter. Whether Strauss had violated his legal obligations

---

the presence of Herr Schloss and myself conveyed the impression of his being satisfied with the arrangements and declared that it would be a windfall . . . [since] he assumed no financial risk. He added that he regretted he would have to share with Herr Minister Franz Josef Strauss his share of the 25 per cent. Nevertheless, he stressed that without Minister Strauss this project would not be possible and consequently this reward could not be denied him." An affidavit executed by Schloss on May 18, 1961, affirmed the accuracy of Braun's statement.

[29] *Ibid.,* 24.

the magazine did not presume to judge; it did insist that binding political norms had been transgressed, either out of narrow partisan considerations or a defective sense of propriety.

Three questions had emerged from the Fibag controversy: (1) Did Strauss permit his ministry to endorse the Fibag proposal without an appropriate examination of the plans and specifications and of the technical and legal competence of the Fibag group to implement these plans and specifications? (2) Did Strauss's ministry have any official competence to concern itself with the Fibag project? (3) Had Strauss intervened in behalf of the Fibag group for inadmissible reasons? By February, 1962, it was clear that the SPD, as the party of the opposition in the Bundestag, could no longer ignore a responsibility to pursue these charges against a member of the federal government.

Available to the SPD was a fairly limited set of alternatives. It could investigate the charges against Strauss outside parliament by conducting its own study and publishing its findings. But without the legal powers to call witnesses and receive official records, a private SPD investigation could hardly produce the type of exhaustive study which would be regarded as credible by the West German public. Moreover, in the event that Strauss then challenged the published findings of the SPD by filing a libel suit, the decision would be shifted to the courts, which, while competent to adjudicate the technical, legal issues of the dispute, would hardly be in a position to establish the political or motivational aspects of the dispute. Whether Strauss had acted "legally" is one question; whether he had acted "improperly" is a broader question that implies an extralegal judgment. A second alternative available to the SPD was to resort again to parliamentary questioning. Having already submitted one set of questions without solving the controversy, the Social Democratic leadership was skeptical of a second use of this method. In any event, the sole reliance on parliamentary questions has severe limitations in arriving at a final, credible judgment. Unless there is a mechanism for determining the complete accuracy of the answers submitted by the minister and for providing the other side an opportunity to bring its own evidence into the discussion, the Bundestag is dependent ultimately on the minister's version.[30] In addition, even if Strauss's answers to parliamentary questions were challenged in the Bundestag, he would most likely have been sustained in his version by the majority coalition, bound by party discipline. The assumption that a majority vote would sustain Strauss's version is subject to one qualification: the FDP conceivably would refuse to join with its coalition partner, the CDU/CSU, in upholding Strauss. At that stage of the Fibag affair, however, there was no reason to anticipate that the FDP would choose to vote against Strauss. The third alternative, and the one chosen by the SPD, was to call for the creation in the Bundestag of a special committee of inquiry. A minority party in the Bundestag has no difficulty in instigating this method of exploring public controversies, provided it has or can obtain the support of one-fourth of the membership of the chamber.[31] But in composition, procedures, and decisions the twin effects of party discipline and proportionality operate in Bundestag committees of inquiry to produce invariably a vote favoring the interests of the majority part or coalition.[32] In view of the remote possibility of the FDP's deciding to vote

[30] If the written answer of a Minister to a *Kleine Anfrage* is not acceptable to a deputy in the Bundestag, he may raise the question again in the Question Hour. *Geschäftsordnung des Deutschen Bundestages, Bundesgesetzblatt* II, p. 389 (1952), as amended BGBL II, p. 1048 (1955) and BGBl. I, p. 1 (1961), Articles 110–11.

[31] *Ibid.,* Article 61 (1).

[32] *Ibid.,* Article 11 provides that memberships of all committees of the Bundestag will be determined according to the proportion of numerical strength of the parliamentary parties.

against Strauss in the committee, the SPD anticipated that the coalition majority on the committee would "exonerate" Strauss.

Nevertheless, the SPD *Fraktion* (group) petitioned on March 13, 1962, for the creation of a special parliamentary committee of inquiry for the Fibag affair.[33] In accordance with the principle of proportionality, the appointed seven-man committee consisted of three members each from the CDU/CSU and the SPD, and one member from the FDP.[34] The chairmanship was assigned to CDU deputy Mathias Hoogen, also chairman of the Bundestag standing committee on law.

Prior to the submission of its report on June 20, 1962, the committee of inquiry held seven public and five executive meetings, heard thirty witnesses, examined documents from various federal ministries and agencies, and received sworn affidavits and records from the courts in which suits were pending or had been tried in connection with the Fibag charges.[35] The committee found that Strauss had committed several "administrative errors" in the handling of the Fibag matter, but it did not feel that the evidence supported a conclusion that he was improperly "motivated" or that he had committed an actual "service violation."[36] The report also concluded that Strauss had had no knowledge of the alleged financial interest of Kapfinger in the Fibag matter and that he had answered truthfully the original parliamentary question submitted by the SPD.[37]

The June 20, 1962, report of the Fibag committee was debated eight days later in the Bundestag on an order of

[33] *Deutscher Bundestag, 4. Wahlperiode, Drucksache IV/247.*
[34] The full membership of the Fibag Committee: CDU/CSU deputies Benda, Hoogen, and Weber (Koblenz); SPD deputies Heinemann, Jahn, Reischl; and FDP deputy Dahlgrün.
[35] *Deutscher Bundestag, 4 Wahlperiode, Schriftlicher Bericht des 1. Untersuchungsausschusses gemäss Antrag der Fraktion der SPD, Drucksache IV/512,* p. 2.
[36] *Ibid.,* 1.
[37] *Ibid.,* 12–14.

business motion.[38] Gustav Heinemann, one of the SPD members of the committee, complained that, contrary to the precedent fixed by eight earlier parliamentary committees of inquiry, no written version of the committee report had been circulated among the minority party members prior to its being released to the public and that the witnesses before the committee had not been subjected to oaths during their oral testimony. Upon the urging of the SPD *Fraktion* that the committee's life be extended and that it be charged with adhering to more acceptable procedural standards in developing its report, the FDP *Fraktion* in a surprising move supported the SPD. Ewald Bucher, executive secretary of the FDP parliamentary delegation, introduced the motion satisfying the SPD position and added: ". . . we are concerned that he [Strauss] emerge from the twilight [of suspicion] . . . and that we in parliament emerge from the twilight [of suspicion that we failed to perform properly our investigatory function].[39] By the narrow margin of 226 to 224 the motion carried and the Fibag committee was instructed to resubmit its report after obtaining relevant additional evidence and after providing the minority the opportunity to express more fully its estimate of the findings. The vote on the recommittal motion was a straight party vote, with the FDP and SPD supporting it and the CDU/CSU opposing it.[40] In justifying the latter's opposition to the motion, Hoogen complained that "he had the impression that the truth was not desired, but rather the opposition wanted means with which to smear the Defense Minister Strauss."[41] That its coalition partner, the FDP, had aban-

---

[38] *Deutscher Bundestag. 4 Wahlperiode, Verhandlungen des Deutschen Bundestages, Stenographischer Berichte, 37 Sitzung,* (June 28, 1962), pp. 1581ff.

[39] *Ibid.,* 1582.

[40] CDU deputy Hans Richarts mistakenly voted in favor of the recommittal motion. FDP Ministers Starke, Mischnick, and Scheel did not vote.

[41] See footnote 47.

doned it was duly noted by the CDU/CSU *Fraktion* in a statement issued shortly after the vote: "The CDU/CSU cannot overlook the fact that the FDP *Fraktion* by its recent action has given credence to the politically inspired Fibag controversy. The CDU/CSU *Fraktion* expects the Committee of Inquiry to take up its work as soon as possible with the purpose of presenting to the House a final report. It is of the opinion that the reception of this report by the plenary session should not be delayed by the summer recess."[42]

Although the second Fibag committee report was indeed entered in the public record by August 30, 1962, the summer recess of the Bundestag delayed a debate on the report. October 25, 1962, was fixed by the "Council of Elders" *(Ältestenrat)*[43] as the date upon which it would be in order to move a consideration of the second report. With the CDU/CSU and FDP members voting in the majority, the committee's findings may be summarized as follows:

1. It was impossible to determine with precision whether Kapfinger in fact had alluded by name to Strauss when in a conversation on April 13, 1960, he mentioned to Schloss and Braun that he would have to share his anticipated profits from the American housing contract. The SPD joined the majority in voting that in the absence of firm evidence to the contrary Strauss could not be charged with having had a personal financial stake in the outcome of the Fibag deal.

2. The majority found that Strauss may have committed "indiscretions" or "errors" in handling certain phases of the Fibag proposals, but he did not violate an official "service obligation." The SPD minority found that Strauss had, in fact, committed a *Dienstpflichtverletzung* by personally promoting the interests of a

---

[42] *Archiv der Gegenwart,* XXXIII (1963), 9960/6.

[43] The Council of Elders, consisting of the Bundestag president, vice-presidents, and representatives from the parliamentary parties in proportion to their numerical strength in the chamber, recommends the agenda of the Bundestag. *Geschäftsordunung des Deutschen Bundestages, ibid.,* Articles 13 and 14.

private group and without official jurisdiction or competence in the matter.

3. The majority found that Stauss had answered the SPD *Kleine Anfrage* to the "best of his knowledge." The SPD minority found that Strauss had lied to the Bundestag, particularly by asserting that his ministry had known, prior to the Fibag proposal, of Schloss's background as a satisfactory contractor with the Munich *Finanzbauamt*. In fact, the SPD minority claimed Strauss's ministry had to phone the Munich office, after the Fibag proposal had been discussed, to confirm that Schloss had performed work for it in the past.[44]

The October 25, 1962, debate (one day prior to the *Spiegel* raids and arrests) on the second Fibag committee report resulted in the Bundestag's accepting the report, but not without heated exchanges between the SPD and the government parties. Rolf Dahlgrün, the FDP member of the Fibag committee who acted as rapporteur for the second report, recognized the problem presented by the principle of proportionality in constituting committees of inquiry when they had to investigate partisan controversies and conceded the virtual impossibility of securing an "impartial" decision because of party disciplined voting on the committees. In an extended speech, SPD deputy Gerhard Jahn summarized the background of the Fibag controversy and the findings of the committee, and then proceeded to admonish Franz Josef Strauss:

. . . the committee would not have been necessary in the first place if Herr Strauss had himself volunteered the necessary information. I would like to say something quite plainly to the Herr Minister: His word, his binding word, which he as a Minister offers, has a claim to be heard by us and to be accepted by us. We would listen and accept it. He certainly ought in the future to make use of this invitation. Some difficulty would have been

[44] 2. *Schriftlicher Bericht des 1. Untersuchungsausschusses gemäss Antrag der Fraktion SPD, Deutscher Bundestag, 4. Wahlperiode, Drucksache* IV/639.

spared us all and him. Of course, we are not so foolish to expect that those in responsible positions can not and do not make mistakes. When we know that he strives to avoid a repetition of such a mistake or similar mistake, when we know that he is aware of his mistake, then that is a clear position which considerably facilitates the relationship between him and us, between him and this House. This includes his preparedness occasionally to practice some self-criticism and to abstain from viewing these matters as personally objectionable. Without the Minister contributing his part, the whole thing is impossible.[45]

Jahn concluded his speech by warning the government, and Strauss, that "if questions such as these . . . arise in the future, we shall . . . regard it as our obligation to see to it that the necessary degree of clarity and certainty is achieved."[46] When the debate ended that day, the Bundestag accepted the final report and dissolved the Fibag committee of inquiry.[47]

The Foertsch Article

In the midst of both the Fibag exposé and numerous other 1962 skirmishes[48] between Strauss and *Der Spiegel,* the

---

[45] *Verhandlungen des Deutschen Bundestages, Stenographischer Bericht,* **43**. *Sitzung* (October 25, 1962), 1876–77.

[46] *Ibid.,* 1877.

[47] Erich Kuby, as critical of Strauss's personal qualifications for public office as is *Der Spiegel,* concludes in his account of the Fibag Affair that Strauss probably did not know of or expect any financial "reward" for his role in the Fibag project. Kuby suggests that Kapfinger may have manufactured the story about Strauss's share in the deal in order to convince Schloss and Braun that Kapfinger should receive his full 25 percent and not have to accept a lower share. Erich Kuby, *Im Fibag-Wahn* (Reinbek bei Hamburg: Rowohlt Taschenbuch Verlag, 1962), 91.

[48] *Der Spiegel* maintained a barrage of criticism against Strauss throughout 1962. In its September 26, 1962, issue an article titled "Onkel Aloys" cited information which suggested Strauss had used his influence to favor political supporters in Bavaria, including Dr. Aloys Brandenstein (a family friend of Strauss's wife), with contracts for munitions production. Strauss eventually sued *Der Spiegel* for libel in the "Onkel Aloys" Affair. The Barth Affair also occurred during 1962, partially through the efforts of *Der Spiegel* and SPD deputy Gerhard Jahn, indicating that Strauss

magazine undertook a second major inquiry concerning Strauss. This time it focused on his policy views. The cover of the October 10, 1962, issue carried a picture of General Friedrich Foertsch, inspector-general of the Bundeswehr.[49] This was the magazine's method of revealing the subject of the issue's feature story. In this case it was misleading, for the key figure in the feature article was not Foertsch but Defense Minister Strauss. Introduced with references to the recently conducted NATO Fall Exercise (Fallex 62), the article analyzed the problems confronting NATO in devising an effective strategy in the event of a war initiated in Europe by the Soviet Union. But more than that, the author critically examined Strauss's alleged determination to increase the atomic and nuclear fire power of the Bundeswehr at the expense of conventional power.

According to the article, more than eight thousand words long, Fallex 62 was the first NATO exercise based on the assumption that World War III would start with a major attack in Europe. The war began with the exploding of a Soviet atomic bomb of medium force over a West German airbase. Additional atomic and nuclear strikes were made against NATO airbases and missile installations in West Germany, England, Italy, and Turkey. But the Russians did not succeed with their initial attack in knocking out NATO's capacity to retaliate. Because of an assumed fourteen-day period of alert prior to the initial attack, a large number of NATO planes were either in the air or transferred to other

---

had improperly intervened in a military review of Strauss's demotion of Wing Commander Barth of the West German Air Force for carelessness in flying across the East German border. See Kirchheimer and Menges, *ibid*, 93–94.

[49] Dated October 10, 1962, the issue of *Der Spiegel* in which the article appeared was actually released to the public two days earlier and is a sequel to an article, *"Stärker als 1939?"*, which was published in the June 13, 1962, issue. A translation of the Foertsch article appears in Appendix I.

bases before the first strikes. Many of their missiles had been effectively camouflaged. Altogether about two-thirds of NATO's nuclear and atomic arsenal escaped the first raids. In spite of this, NATO's units did not halt the advance of the Soviet forces. Most of northern Germany, including Schleswig-Holstein, was occupied within a few days by the enemy. No effort was made to hold Hamburg by bloody street-to-street fighting reminiscent of World War II. Ten to fifteen million civilians in both the United Kingdom and West Germany were killed as a result of the combined ground and air attacks. "Even greater losses" were inflicted upon the United States by nuclear explosions. "Chaos was indescribable" in West Germany in the forward zones of fighting. Facilities for the care of the retreating civilian population were "completely inadequate." West Germany's nine divisions which represented its contribution to NATO's exercise were ill equipped, undermanned, and without sufficient numbers of noncommissioned officers. Weapons for the thousands of West German reservists were nonexistent. The Bundeswehr received from the NATO inspectors the lowest possible rating on the basis of their performance and degree of readiness: "conditionally prepared to defend" *(bedingt abwehrbereit)*.

Against the backdrop of this rather dramatic and grim presentation, *Der Spiegel* then proceeded to unfold its analysis of the dispute that allegedly existed in the West German Defense Ministry between those who have stressed the necessity of responding to an attack from the East in such a way as to avoid the escalation of the conflict into a nuclear war and those who see no alternative for the West but to assume that it must respond at the outset with an immediate nuclear retaliation.

The Foertsch article contends that Strauss's highly skeptical view of the feasibility of any kind of conventional war in Europe led him to embrace a "preemptive attack" strategy that calls for an immediate and massive nuclear attack on the Soviet Union, even before the Soviet Union resorts to tactical nuclear weapons in the combat areas. Air Force General Kammhuber, who at one time was the inspector of the West German Air Force, is presented as a prime supporter of the Strauss concept of preemptive attack and as having urged, with Strauss's endorsement, that the Bundeswehr be equipped with a weapons system that can strike as far east as the Ural Mountains. Strauss and Kammhuber began laying the foundations for their preemptive striking force through the Starfighter program. Fighter bombers would provide the initial delivery system for the atomic and nuclear bombs. Later the Starfighters would be phased out and replaced by medium-range missiles. The Strauss group premised its long-range planning on the basis of the preemptive strike concept, even though it is inconsistent, according to the Foertsch article, with the strategy accepted upon United States insistency by NATO. The latter assumed a selective series of responses, each progressively more destructive and exacting increasingly higher tolls from the aggressors than the previous stage. Only if this "selective strike" strategy failed would the stage of rapid escalation arrive for NATO forces.

The selective strike strategy, coupled with the "forward defense" plan which NATO conceded years ago during the negotiations with the first West German Defense Minister, Theodor Blank, required a substantial contribution in ground forces from West Germany. Thus under a revised NATO directive, Plan MC 96, effective the Foertsch article notes from 1964 to 1970, the West German Defense Ministry estimated that the Bundeswehr would have to be increased to 750,000 troops. To raise, train, equip, and maintain this large a force, armed at the same time with the medium-range missiles desired by Strauss, would cost 30 billion German marks, or 10 billion in excess of the amount the Adenauer government had decided it could annually afford for military defense.

In conclusion, the Foertsch article revealed that, short of meeting the goals contained in Plan MC 96, the West German Defense Ministry was considering three alternatives: (1) an armed force of 580,000 men, costing annually 20 billion German marks; (2) 580,000 men with the medium-range missiles desired by Strauss, costing annually 23 billion German marks; and (3) 500,000 men, including the missiles, at an annual cost of 20 billion German marks. Although the first of these alternatives is favored by one group of officers as being most consistent with NATO's strategy, Strauss and his supporters are portrayed as opting for the third alternative, the least compatible of the three with the views of NATO and the Kennedy administration for reducing the threat of a nuclear war in Europe.

Shortly after the appearance of the Foertsch article, when the attention of the world was directed to it by the sensational police action of October 26, 1962, observers differed in their initial estimates of both the significance and confidential nature of the information contained in the article. Although George Vine of the London *Daily Mail* concluded that the revelations "would have got Augstein in hot water anywhere in the world,"[50] and several foreign journalists expressed mild surprise at *Der Spiegel's* apparent access to the details of NATO's Plans MC 70 and 96,[51] the weight of the opinion seemed to support essentially the conclusion of the respected American military affairs journalist Hanson W. Baldwin: *"Der Spiegel's* criticisms of some phases of West German defense preparations are fairly severe. But to well-informed Americans the

[50] November 2, 1962.

[51] Cf. *Les Dernières Nouvelles* (Strassbourg), October 29, 1962; *Voix der Nord* (Lille), October 28, 1962; *La Libre Belgigue* (Brussels), October 29, 1962.

article appears to carry little information that was not generally known to the Russians or to other observers, except for the assertion that the West German Army had been placed in the lowest NATO category of readiness. . . . All these . . . and many other weaknesses have been publicly identified and commented upon in the past. Therefore, the extreme reaction of the West German Government to the publication of the article is somewhat mystifying to observers in this country."[52]

The West German Federal Prosecutor's case against *Der Spiegel* eventually raised, in fact, two sets of related questions: Did the article reveal information not hitherto available to the public and, if the answer to the first question is in the affirmative, did the article, because of the nature of the incriminating information, objectively jeopardize the national security and welfare of the Federal Republic? It soon became apparent that the three areas of information contained in the article most vulnerable to suspected treasonable publication concerned (1) the details about the Fallex 62 manuever, (2) the budgetary specifics of the alternatives available to the West German defense planners, and (3) the existence and configuration of the disagreement among West German military and defense planners aroused by Strauss's alleged commitment to the preemptive strike strategy. Although data falling within the first of these categories provided the focus of press

---

[52] New York *Times,* November 26, 1962. For substantially the same conclusion, see also the following commentaries: Edorado Rezzonico, "Der Spiegel e Strauss si battono da 2 anni," *Vita* (Rome), November 15, 1962; Vladimiro Mihely, "La Germania allo Specchio," *Il Lavoro Italiano* (Genoa) November 17, 1962; Marguerite Higgins, "Mirror, mirror, told it all," New York *Herald Tribune,* November 12, 1962; and Gerd Wilcke, "German weekly is accused anew," New York *Times,* November 30, 1962. Although not as detailed, and not mentioning specifically the low rating the Bundeswehr had received, a report on the inadequancy of civilian defense planning exposed during Fallex 62 had already appeared, prior to *Der Spiegel's* article, in the September 29–30, 1962, edition of the *Deutsche Zeitung mit Wirtschaftszeitung* (Köln).

speculation during the initial stage of the *Spiegel* Affair, it appears in retrospect that these revelations, however sensational, were not as decisive as the material within categories two and three in prompting the investigation. And it is most likely that Strauss and his associates reasoned, upon the basis of the information in these two categories, that informers did indeed exist within the Defense Ministry and by making contact with *Der Spiegel* were working to undermine his position both within the ministry and in the public arena.

The Foertsch article was available to the public on October 8, 1962, since the issue (dated October 10) in which it appeared was placed in circulation two days prior to its cover date, in accordance with standard procedures. On either October 8 or 9 (the exact date is still unknown) an official of the Federal Prosecutor's office in Karlsruhe expressed in a phone conversation with an official in the Defense Ministry in Bonn the suspicion that the Foertsch article contained state secrets.[53] In the course of the conversation a request was made of the Defense Ministry to examine the article for security leaks and to prepare a formal opinion specifying the items, if any, that seemed to be within the category of classified security information. On October 13, the Defense Ministry informally confirmed to the Federal Prosecutor's Office that "military secrets" were contained in the article; on October 19, the written opinion was formally transmitted to the federal attorneys. At the request of the Federal Prosecutor's Office, the examining judge of the Federal High Court, which has original jurisdiction in treason cases, issued on

---

[53] *Der "Spiegel"-Bericht, Darstellung der Vorgänge beim Ermittlungsverfahren gegen Verleger, Redakteure und Informanten des Nachrichtenmagazins "Der Spiegel"—Bericht der Bundesministerien des Auswärtigen, des Innern, der Verteidigung und der Justiz,* published in the *Bulletin des Presse und Informationsamtes der Bundesregierung,* No. 23 (February 5, 1963), 202. This official report issued by the federal government on the procedures employed in the Spiegel investigation is hereafter cited as *Der "Spiegel"-Bericht.*

October 23 warrants for the arrest of Ahlers and Augstein and search and seizure orders against the persons, residences, and offices of Ahlers and Augstein, and *Der Spiegel's* offices, archives, and premises. Significantly, the notation was added to the court orders that they could be implemented "at night-time." Three days later the orders were executed.

Chapter II

THE SPIEGEL ACTION

In the early evening of October 26, 1962, Erich Fischer, an advertising salesman in Düsseldorf for *Der Spiegel,* had just finished some last-minute grocery shopping for his wife when he was accosted by officials of the Security Group of the Federal Criminal Office. The car he was driving bore Hamburg identification letters on its license plates and was registered in the name of *Der Spiegel* publisher Rudolf Augstein. The officials asked Fischer for his identification papers. Having left them at home, he produced instead his driver's permit. Two additional Security Group officials then appeared. One of them showed Fischer a photograph, apparently of the person they were seeking. Unable to identify positively the person in the photograph, he was instructed to accompany the officials to the nearest police station. Shortly after arriving at the police station, Fischer asked that his wife be told of his whereabouts. When a police officer placed the call, Frau Fischer was requested to describe her husband in order to verify the identity of the man they had in custody. Two hours after his arrest, Fischer was advised that he was free to leave the police station. He had not been told why he was picked up. An hour after Fischer had been seized, a message was sent by the Security Group office in Bad Godesberg to the Federal Prosecutor's Office in Karlsruhe. The communique reported that the driver of the car in Düsseldorf with the Hamburg identification letters and registered in Augstein's name had been taken into custody, but, it continued, an error had been committed. Erich Fischer had been mistaken for Rudolf Augstein. Upon receipt of this information the Federal Prosecutor's Office ordered the immediate execution of the "measures." The order went out at approximately 8 P.M.[1]

Under West German law, the Federal Prosecutor's Office *(Bundesanwaltschaft)* is responsible for investigating suspected acts of treason and, if the investigation warrants, it then presents the charges with supporting evidence to the Federal High Court *(Bundesgerichtshof)* for possible adjudication.[2] The federal criminal police may be used to assist the federal attorneys in carrying out these investigations, but before any arrests or searches are made the "proper" notice must be given to the government of the *Land* (German state) in which the actions are contemplated.[3] The Federal Interior Ministry has supervisory control over the Federal Criminal Office, to which the federal police are assigned, and the responsibility for giving proper notice to *Land* governments.[4] According to official sources, the notification prior to the *Spiegel* actions was given at approximately 8:30 P.M., October 26, 1962.[5] State Secretary Josef Hölzl of the Federal Interior Ministry telephoned his counterpart, Ludwig Adenauer (a nephew of Konrad Adenauer), of the North Rhine-Westphalian *Land* Interior Ministry and told him that "police actions within North Rhine-Westphalia were imminent." Hölzl cautioned that particulars of the actions could not be divulged over the telephone, but that in the morning a full explanation would

---

[1] *Der "Spiegel"-Bericht,* 196–97.

[2] *Gerichtsverfassungsgesetz vom 12 September 1950 (Bundesgesetzblatt* 455; III 300–302), as amended by a law of 8 September 1961 (BGBL. I 1665) Article 134; and *Strafvollstreckungsordnung vom 15 Februar 1956 (Bundesanzeiger* No. 42), as amended on 15 December 1961 *(Bundesanzeiger* No. 248).

[3] *Gesetz über die Einrichtung eines Bundeskriminalpolizeiamtes (Bundeskriminalamtes) vom 8 März 1951* (BGBl. I, 165).

[4] *Ibid.*

[5] *Der "Spiegel"-Bericht,* 197.

be transmitted to the North Rhine-Westphalian Interior Ministry via the wires of the police communications system. While Hölzl was phoning Ludwig Adenauer, Ministerial Director Rudolf Toyka of the Federal Interior Ministry, who had been dispatched earlier to Hamburg, went to the residence of Hamburg Interior Minister (Senator) Helmut Schmidt (SPD) and informed him of the measures which were about to be taken within the jurisdiction of the *Land* of Hamburg. During their conversation Toyka requested on behalf of the Federal Prosecutor's Office the assistance of the Hamburg criminal police in carrying out the raid on the central offices of *Der Spiegel*. Senator Schmidt agreed to issue the necessary instructions and immediately phoned the director of the Hamburg police. The director, however, already knew of the impending action, having been directly informed at 8:40 P.M. by an official of the Federal Criminal Office.[6]

The Bonn Action

At the time of the action against the Bonn bureau, the staff included, among others, Hans Dieter Jaene, an associate editor of *Der Spiegel* and director of the Bonn bureau; Hans-Roderich Schneider, a reporter; and Hans Schmelz, a specialist in military and national security policy. At about 8:30 P.M. a representative of the Federal Prosecutor's Office, accompanied by officials of the Security Group of the Federal Criminal Police, went to the Bonn bureau, which they found locked. Other officials of the Security Group were dispatched to pick up Schneider and Jaene. Schneider was found at his apartment and was asked to come to the Bonn bureau. Apparently the bureau had already been under surveillance, for the officials instructed Schneider to bring with him the papers which he had been seen taking with him when he left his office earlier that evening. The "papers" turned out to be

[6]*Ibid.*

newspapers.[7] When told that a search was to be made of the Bonn bureau, Schneider protested that the bureau's director Jaene was the appropriate person to contact. Officials who had already been sent to pick up Jaene found him at about 9 P.M. at his home. Jaene was simply advised that an attorney of the Federal Prosecutor's Office wished to speak to him at the Bonn bureau. At 9:45 P.M. Jaene arrived at his office, where he learned that a search had been authorized by an examining judge of the Federal High Court (*Bundesgerichtshof*). The search began at 10 P.M. and "extended over several hours."[8] Jaene was provisionally taken into custody.

In a legal brief which was later prepared by *Der Spiegel's* defense counsel a number of details have been provided about the Bonn phase of the action.[9] Upon arriving at the Bonn bureau Jaene was shown the search and seizure order issued by the Federal High Court. The attorney of the Federal Prosecutor's Office asked Jaene to assist in expediting the search. Jaene declared that, since he did not know specifically what the prosecutors were after, he was in no position to help. He was then told the search was directed toward information pertaining to the preparation of the Foertsch article. He contended that there was not in his bureau any material relating to this particular article. Nevertheless, the search was begun. At Jaene's request a list was prepared by the investigators of the materials which they decided to impound. Jaene refused to accept the list as originally worded; a second and more detailed enumeration of the seized material was then prepared and given to him. The office was not sealed, and certain of the impounded documents were

[7] *Verfassungsbeschwerde der Spiegel-Verlag Rudolf Augstein & Co., KG, Hamburg—1 BvR 586/62—Schriftsatz der Beschwerdeführerin vom 1 Mai 1963*, p. 33. This legal brief, and supporting documents, prepared by *Der Spiegel's* legal counsel is hereafter cited as *Verfassungsbeschwerde.*

[8] *Der "Spiegel"-Bericht*, 202.

[9] *Verfassungsbeschwerde*, 33–34.

left overnight in the Bonn bureau. Shortly after he was taken to the Security Group office in nearby Bad Godesberg, Jaene was advised by an attorney of the Federal Prosecutor's Office that he was being held temporarily under suspicion of "betrayal of country" because of possible complicity in the preparation of the Foertsch article. Jaene affirmed by sworn affidavit that he had had nothing to do with the article, but he was requested to remain there overnight for further questioning. Apparently there was some discussion between Jaene and a federal attorney about the legal grounds upon which he could be detained, but eventually Jaene voluntarily acquiesced in the request that he remain in the Security Group office that night. In the company of federal investigators he was allowed to pick up some overnight toilet articles at his home. On the following day, at about 11 A.M., Jaene returned with officials of the Security Group to the Bonn bureau for additional searching. When Jaene asked about the legal authority for the second search, he was told that it was technically a continuation of the one which had been initiated the previous evening. A more thorough search was made and additional documents and files were removed by the investigators. Later that day Jaene was released from police custody and told by a court official that he was no longer under suspicion of having committed or conspired to commit treason.

Hans Schmelz was en route to Budapest when the October 26 raid was launched against *Der Spiegel's* Hamburg and Bonn offices. Accompanied by *Der Spiegel* reporter Ferdinand Simoneit, Schmelz was carrying out an assignment to conduct an interview with Hungarian Deputy Premier Gyula Kallai. On October 27 an order for Schmelz's arrest was issued because of his suspected participation in the preparation of the Foertsch article. While he was still absent from West Germany on October 28, but in the presence of his wife, his apartment was searched. According to *Der Spiegel's* version, officials of the Security Group seized a "large number of writings," particularly those which "in any way concerned military matters," including materials about the Weimar Reichswehr and the Röhm putsch of 1934. A private telephone directory belonging to Frau Schmelz and Schmelz's bank records were also seized.[10] From Vienna on Tuesday evening, October 30, Schmelz telephoned the Security Group offices in Bad Godesberg to get official confirmation that he was the subject of an arrest order. He promptly returned to West Germany and shortly before midnight of October 31 placed himself in custody of the Security Group officials in Bad Godesberg. He reportedly was offered, but declined, political asylum by the Hungarian government.

The Hamburg Action

Originally situated in Hannover, the central office of *Der Spiegel* had been moved in 1951 to the Pressehaus in downtown Hamburg. At the time of the raids, the Pressehaus contained not only the central office and archives of *Der Spiegel* but also the editorial offices of the daily newspaper *Hamburger Echo,* the weekly newspaper *Die Zeit,* and the weekly magazine *Der Stern. Der Spiegel* leased about one hundred rooms in the building, with additional facilities located in the nearby Miramar-Haus. Its Hamburg staff at this time numbered more than two hundred persons.[11]

Shortly before the raid on the Hamburg offices, a task force was organized by the Security Group of the Federal Criminal Office to assist the Federal Prosecutor's Office. Before proceeding to the Pressehaus, the members of the group were briefed on their duties and plan of operation. During the briefing session, according to the official account, particular emphasis was placed on the highly confidential nature of their

[10] *Ibid.,* 35.
[11] *Der Spiegel,* November 7, 1962, p. 55.

mission, the rules of procedure which they must observe in carrying out the action, and the necessity of acting in an "absolutely correct" manner from the legal point of view.[12] The plan of operation, devised by the Federal Prosecutor's Office, stipulated that:

. . . for the purpose of later examination, everything in the offices of the accused Augstein should be secured in such a way as to prevent any possible obstruction of the investigation. First State Attorney Buback particularly stressed that the task force should immediately remove all persons who happened to be present in the offices to be searched and then place the offices under lock and seal.

The offices of *Spiegel* in the Pressehaus and those also in the new building (Miramar-Haus) would have to be searched in the presence of officers of the publishing company. In doing this, care would have to be taken that none of them in leaving the offices took with him any materials or documents which might have a bearing on the case. After this had been accomplished, the doors of the offices would have to be locked and sealed.[13]

In the document later prepared by legal counsel for *Der Spiegel,* the following observation is made concerning the task force's plan of operation:

Apparently the Federal Prosecutor's Office had planned simply to lock and seal the offices without an immediate searching of them. Failing to have anticipated that considerable activity would be going on [in *Spiegel's* offices] at the time of the raid, they concluded that merely a few officers of the Security Group could do the locking and sealing without any difficulty. In this matter, as in the case of the whereabouts of Augstein, Ahlers, and Jacobi, the Federal Prosecutor's Office was poorly informed. On the sixth and seventh floors of the Pressehaus work was in progress on issue Number 44/1962. Engaged in this work were the Chief Editor, the Germany II Department, the Economic Department, the Sports Department, the Picture Department, the Archives, and all facilities of the "Chief of Service," who has the final

---

[12] *Der "Spiegel"-Bericht,* 202.
[13] *Ibid.,* 202.

responsibility for the editing of each issue. Altogether there were about 60 persons working that evening in the offices.[14]

The task force converged on the Pressehaus at 9 P.M. *Der Spiegel* coeditor Johannes K. Engel, who had just left the Pressehaus and was walking toward his car, was immediately taken into custody. On the fifth floor the task force encountered a porter and asked to be directed to the office of publisher Augstein. It was discovered that Augstein had already left for the day. Locating coeditor Claus Jacobi in his office, the officials announced that he was to be placed under provisional arrest. Jacobi was shown the search order issued against the business and editorial offices of *Der Spiegel* and was advised to instruct all employees to evacuate immediately. Jacobi demurred on the ground that he was not authorized to make such a decision. Two members of the task force were then assigned to keep Jacobi under surveillance in his office.

Commissioner Schütz, the Security Group official in charge of the task force, instructed two of his men to locate the other entrances to the Pressehaus which were not yet guarded, while he and the remaining officers under his command attempted to get the employees to evacuate. Through radio communications, three members of the "flying squad" of the Hamburg criminal police were asked to assist in clearing the premises. By this time, many of the employees had assembled in one of the main corridors. In the words of the official account, "excited groups gathered together and, using unfortunate expressions, claimed that they were not going to leave the premises. . . . The task force leader urged them to use prudence and reason." When the protestations of the employees continued and grew "threatening," Commissioner Schütz warned them that by their conduct they could incur

[14] *Verfassungsbeschwerde,* 37.

criminal liability for obstructing the law. "In this manner a type of sit-down strike occurred."[15]

At this point Commissioner Schütz's problem was compounded by the hesitancy of the three "flying squad" Hamburg policemen to cooperate in clearing the premises of all employees. Schütz had informed the gathered employees that, if they continued to refuse to leave voluntarily, he would have them forcibly ejected. He called upon the three men to help him carry out this threat. The leader of the "flying squad" questioned whether his instructions authorized this type of official assistance. A brief conference was held between the Security Group officials and the "flying squad." Schütz "most emphatically" repeated his request for assistance from the three policemen and argued that it was essential to have the premises cleared of all employees in order to prevent the danger of evidence being stolen or destroyed.[16] The leader of the "flying squad" policemen finally agreed to permit his group to render this type of help. By this time Director Dr. Land of the Hamburg Criminal Police had arrived with twenty Hamburg criminal police officers, who were immediately posted throughout the *Spiegel* complex of offices. A houseplan of the Pressehaus was obtained from one of the housemasters and a systematic effort was begun to clear all offices of employees and to place the offices under lock and seal. By midnight of October 26, most of the *Spiegel* offices in the Pressehaus and those on the second floor of the Miramar-Haus had been cleared of employees and sealed. Keys to these offices were placed in envelopes and deposited with a representative of the Security Group who was stationed in the porter's room.

Der Spiegel and other organs of the West German press were quick to seize upon several episodes which occurred

---

[15] *Der "Spiegel"-Bericht,* 202.
[16] *Ibid.,* 202–203.

during the evening of October 26, as evidence of ineptness on the part of the authorities. One of these episodes was the mistaken arrest of Erich Fischer. A second such episode concerned Leo Brawand, an associate editor of *Spiegel.* Brawand's office in the Pressehaus was on the seventh floor, removed from the center of activity surrounding the initial phase of the Hamburg raid. Although the details have been variously reported, it appears that during the inspection of the offices, the investigators and policemen overlooked Brawand. According to the account in one of West Germany's most reliable newspapers, two officials of the Security Group entered his office, walked around, saw no one in the office, and concluded that the room was vacant.[17] Actually, Brawand was in a large closet adjoining the office. When he heard the officials enter his office, he remained in the closet. A few minutes after they departed, he emerged from the closet, phoned his wife over a direct line from his office to his home, and instructed her to alert the attorney Dr. Josef Augstein, brother of Rudolf Augstein, that some kind of police investigation was under way against *Spiegel.* Then he pressed a button on the intercom system connecting him with the office of Claus Jacobi, who was being held in his office by two Security Group officials. "Not unlike the scenario of an American gangster film" continues the newspaper account, Brawand, speaking in English in case the intercom system was being monitored, simply said to Jacobi: "I was in the closet. Josef is on the way." With scissors and a letter opener, he cut through the seal of the door of his office and left the building undetected. It was from Brawand's wife that Josef Augstein first received reliable confirmation of the rumor, already in circulation, that the police action was in progress.

A third incident is described by *Der Spiegel:*

[17] *Süddeutsche Zeitung* (Munich, October 29, 1962), p. 3.

A short time after Johannes K. Engel had been taken into custody, the Hamburg police were still looking for a vehicle with the identification numbers HH-SY 100 on its license plates and in which they believed they would find: a man by the name of Rudolf Augstein, one by the name of Johannes Engel and one by the name of Claus Jacobi. Whom the well informed police could have actually had in mind in seeking Rudolf Augstein was quickly figured out by a few *Bild* [*Bildzeitung,* West Germany's widely circulated tabloid] reporters, who had overheard the police radio. But why the police suspected that the *Spiegel* publisher and the two *Spiegel* co-editors were in this car was, at least for the moment, known only to the police: The vehicle belongs to Werner Dolata, a resident of Hamburg-Billstedt, Kleingartenverein Horner Brook, Colony Goldkoppel, Lot 175.

In the neighborhood of the garage where a few of the *Spiegel* people keep their cars each day, Dolata, by profession a foreman, was attending on Friday evening a conference which ended around 10 P.M. Dolata's car was parked near the Pressehaus. Without a topcoat and being very hungry he ran with a colleague to his car. This apparently aroused the suspicion of the police nearby that they must be *Spiegel* editors who were running away.

When Dolata drove up in front of his house, a car without any identification numbers revealing it to be a police car pulled up directly behind his car and two criminal police officers climbed out. They asked Dolata to leave his car doors unlocked and his briefcase inside the car: they said another policeman would arrive shortly to take the car and briefcase into protective custody. Dolata was requested to come with them. Since he refused, however, they accompanied him inside his home to talk with him. It was then established that the foreman had no connection whatever with *Spiegel.* The disappointed policemen issued Dolata a ticket carrying a fine of five Marks—because of driving too fast.[18]

A fourth incident, again described by *Der Spiegel,* resulted from the efforts by a detachment of Security Group officials to locate Claus Jacobi, who apparently unknown to them had already been arrested around 9 P.M. as he was leaving the Pressehaus.

[18] *Der Spiegel,* November 7, 1962, p. 61.

Shortly after 9 P.M. two gentlemen knocked on the door of *Spiegel* reporter Ernst Hess' apartment on Hochalle in Hamburg and asked to speak with Co-editor Jacobi. [Jacobi had formerly lived at this address.] About to take a bath, Hess shiveringly replied through a crack in the door that Jacobi, or his whereabouts, could probably be discovered by contacting the Hamburg offices of *Spiegel.*

Since the intruders were unpleasant to the half-naked Hess— one of them in the style of a salesman had placed his foot in the doorcrack—he ordered them away and by phone contacted the police: this was sufficient to persuade the investigators to beat a quiet retreat.

After half an hour of waiting the police still had not appeared, but thirty-five minutes after the call had been placed they showed up, apologizing for the delay: that evening there had been an unusually large number of traffic accidents to investigate. But they also suggested: in such cases in the future it would be advisable to call the neighbors for help. After the police officers heard Hess' story, they recommended that editor Jacobi be immediately alerted by telephone that men impersonating criminal investigators were looking for him. The police officers witnessed the repeated attempts [by Hess] to get a connection through to *Spiegel's* offices. But a telephone connection with *Spiegel,* at this time, was not to be had. At the central telephone exchange [of *Spiegel's* Hamburg Offices] sat criminal police investigators, and they were undoubtedly authentic.[19]

Commissioner Schütz and his task force experienced additional complications in attempting to carry out their plan of operation. About 9:45 P.M. Jacobi requested that a small staff of employees be allowed to continue the final phase of work on the next issue of the magazine; otherwise its scheduled appearance would be jeopardized. Schütz assured Jacobi that it was not their intention to prevent the publication of future issues of *Der Spiegel.* He tentatively agreed to an arrangement by which a small staff of ten employees, headed by Chief of Service Johannes Matthiesen, would remain in

[19] *Ibid.,* 58.

the Pressehaus until the proofs of the next issue were ready for the press. State Attorney Buback, representing the Federal Prosecutor's Office in the operation, tentatively approved this decision. Final approval came from his superiors in the Federal Prosecutor's Office at 2.45 A.M. on October 27, but one condition was attached: Buback was instructed to secure the proofs of the next issue. Later accused of precensorship, the authorities reasoned that:

Since the proofs could have a bearing on the case, it had to be determined whether they contained information related to the Foertsch article and which might be regarded as evidence for purposes of the investigation. For this reason it was necessary that the proofs be laid before the investigators. The leader of the Task force, in the company of two other officials, sought out Chief of Service Mathiessen and asked him to make the proofs available. During the discussion it was explained to him that if he did not give his express approval, the Criminal Police were not authorized to look through these materials. Mathiessen then stated that he agreed to their looking at the proofs. But to the further question as to whether he had the authority to give such permission, he remarked that, of course, one would have to expect possible objections by the publishing company and, accordingly, he could only agree to the procedure by simultaneously lodging a protest.

The officials asserted that this protest could be construed as a denial of permission; in light of this they would simply have the proofs placed, in his presence, in an envelope which would be turned over to the examining judge of the Federal High Court for an authoritative decision. Mathiessen suggested that this procedure bordered on pre-censorship. The leader of the Task force countered that it was rather a measure taken in order to discover evidence relating to the Foertsch article. In any event, he added, the final decision would rest with the appropriate judge.

Mathiessen was asked to make sure that all the proofs were there. After about 45 minutes he affirmed that the proofs were complete. They were then, in his presence, placed into a large envelope and sealed. The seal was initialed by Mathiessen and members of the Task force. A courier sent by the First State

Attorney Buback transmitted them, in turn, to the examining judge of the Federal High Court. None of the members of the Security Group looked through the proofs. Later when Mathiessen asked when the decision of the judge could be expected, he was told by the leader [of the Task force] that printing of the proofs could continue as planned and that the new issue could be distributed.[20]

The final work on the next issue of *Der Spiegel* was completed about 5 A.M., on the twenty-seventh. The premises were evacuated by the remaining employees and placed under lock and seal. In Hamburg the total office space which was sealed exceeded thirty thousand square feet. On October 31, 92 percent of this space was still under police control. By November 12 some 25 percent of this space was still sealed off by the authorities.[21]

The search for evidence among the archives, reputedly containing one of the most extensive dossier collections in West Germany and consisting of several million separate items, seemed at times to have been a task much beyond the capacity of the relatively small staff of investigators assigned to it by the Federal Prosecutor's Office. A system was quickly devised by which empoyees of *Der Spiegel* were allowed to go into certain of the areas under police control in order to make temporary use of materials for forthcoming issues, although this arrangement was far from satisfactory in the view of *Der Spiegel's* editors. Under this system, some 56 specific and written requests, involving some 325 separate items or documents, were approved by the Federal Prosecutor's Office while the searching of the offices and archives was still in progress.[22] Each of the temporarily released items was scrutinized by a representative of the Federal Prosecutor's Office before it was turned over to *Der Spiegel's* staff and had to be

promptly returned after the staff was finished with it. At
8:45 P.M. of November 25, 1962, thirty days after the initiation of the action against *Der Spiegel,* the publishing company finally had free access to all of the space originally
sealed by the authorities.

Number 44 of *Der Spiegel,* dated October 31, 1962, appeared as scheduled. Virtually completed by the time the
October 26 raids occurred, except for editing and proofreading, it contained no reference to the affair. With Number 44 distributed, *Der Spiegel's* staff went to work, no doubt
rather zestfully, on the story of the *Spiegel* action. Number
45, dated November 7, 1962, featured Rudolf Augstein on
the cover and a *Titel* story titled "They Came by Night." Approximately two-thirds of its contents dealt with the raids and
initial arrests. In spite of a greatly increased press run, the
issue was quickly sold out. Whatever the ultimate consequences of the action for *Der Spiegel* and its publishers, one
result was immediately evident: *Der Spiegel's* weekly circulation made a dramatic jump.

The Arrests

Much of the criticism against the October 26 action centered around certain of the procedures and the timing of the
searches of the Hamburg and Bonn offices. But of equal
interest to many of the critics and observers of the action were
the scope and circumstances of the arrests which were made
during the first few weeks after the raids. In the initial stages
of the search and seizure actions, beginning on October 26
and extending through the remaining days of that month, the
roundup of persons was confined to those directly concerned
with the publishing and editing of the magazine: Rudolf
Augstein; coeditors Jacobi and Engel; Conrad Ahlers, author
of the Foertsch article and one of several associate editors of

the magazine; the Bonn bureau Director Jaene; and Schmelz of the Bonn bureau.

The seemingly elusive Rudolf Augstein was neither at home nor at his office in the Pressehaus when the investigators launched their raids. The West German press gave extensive treatment to almost all conceivable aspects of the investigation, but in a rather curious oversight failed to account for Augstein's activities immediately prior to and during the Hamburg raid. It is known that he had been in the Pressehaus earlier that day. Speculation later suggested that he had been warned in advance that a raid was imminent and fled the Pressehaus shortly before the raid to put his personal affairs in order before his anticipated arrest. However, in spite of assertions to the contrary, it is doubtful that Augstein and his associates had been alerted that an inquiry was under way in the Federal Prosecutor's Office concerning the Foertsch article; certainly there is no evidence to confirm the suggestion that they were aware of the specific plan to raid the Hamburg and Bonn offices.[23] At noon, Saturday, October 27, Augstein, having learned of the warrant for his arrest, turned himself in to the authorities in Hamburg.

According to information supplied by *Der Spiegel's* legal counsel, Rudolf Augstein's home was searched in the presence of both his wife and John Jahr, a Hamburg publisher and former business associate of Augstein. The search began about 9:30 P.M., October 27, and lasted some two and one-half hours. A "large number of private papers were taken, including letters written during the war by Augstein and a

[23] Shortly after the October 26 raids and arrests, government spokesmen asserted that Colonel Wicht of the Federal Intelligence Agency alerted Augstein eight days before the raids occurred, that an investigation of the Foertsch article had been undertaken by the Federal Prosecutor's Office and the Federal Defense Ministry. In March, 1965, the Federal Prosecutor's Office admitted as erroneous the charge against Wicht.

notebook containing his school themes."[24] Augstein was kept in police confinement until February 7, 1963.

Coeditor Johannes K. Engel, as already mentioned, was seized by members of the Security Group as he was leaving the Pressehaus just as the raid was beginning on the evening of October 26. He was kept under confinement for twenty-four hours, then released on October 27 with the stipulation that he keep himself readily available for questioning.

The other coeditor, Claus Jacobi, who was placed under arrest on the evening of October 26, accompanied members of the Security Group to his home in Kuckels (Holstein), just outside Hamburg. According to *Der Spiegel*:

Around midnight Anneliese Jacobi was awakened by the noise of a passing car. Through the bedroom window she saw several men coming through the garden with a flashlight. Reassured by a familiar whistle signal from her husband, she came to the door. Her husband was accompanied by three criminal investigators. . . . With a glance at the men with her husband Anneliese Jacobi: "Do you really want me to open the door?" Claus Jacobi: "Don't look so upset, these men can't help it."

The search began upstairs, in the bedroom, guestroom and children's room of the Jacobi house. Frau Jacobi asked her husband: "What is that all about?" Immediately an investigator warned Jacobi: "I must point out to you that nothing is to be said about this."

They raised the mattresses and looked under the beds. They opened the writing desk of Anneliese Jacobi and assembled part of her private mail, they shook books, carefully pulled underwear out of the dresser and just as carefully put it back, even glanced at the toys of the Jacobi children. The children, who were asleep, were transferred by their parents to another room, so that all beds, including the children's, could be searched.

Basement, garage, and the pony stall, even the pony's straw became the object of a police search—nothing was omitted. The search lasted about two hours. By two o'clock (A.M., October 27), a pile of papers had been collected and seemed to be

[24] *Verfassungsbeschwerde,* 36.

of interest to the investigators—personal letters, old manuscripts, memoranda—and each item was listed on a receipt.

The next time Anneliese Jacobi heard her husband's voice was on Sunday morning. He called from a jail in Hamburg and told her he was under arrest.[25]

But of all the arrests arising out of the action against *Der Spiegel,* that of Conrad Ahlers was to arouse the greatest criticism. The circumstances surrounding his seizure and the procedures employed in bringing him within the jurisdiction of the West German authorities played a decisive role in converting the events of October 26-27 into a political crisis. An associate editor of *Spiegel* and author of the Foertsch article, Ahlers served from 1952 to 1954 as press officer in the "Blank Office," created in 1952 by the Adenauer government to conduct studies and negotiations anticipating the rearming of West Germany. When the Blank Office was superseded in 1955 by the newly formed Federal Defense Ministry, Theodor Blank became West Germany's first defense minister, a post he held until October, 1956, when Franz Josef Strauss assumed the position. After leaving his job as press officer in the Blank Office, Ahlers returned to newspaper work. For a while he was associated with the *Frankfurter Rundschau,* one of West Germany's largest dailies generally sympathetic with the views of the Social Democratic Party. From the *Frankfurter Rundschau* he went to *Der Spiegel.* His earlier service in the Blank Office and his professional interest in and writing on national defense matters made him one of West Germany's better informed journalists with extensive contacts in the agencies responsible for security and military policies.

Ahlers began working on the Foertsch article in the late summer of 1962. As is customary in the case of a forthcoming feature story, *Spiegel* gave advance notice of the

[25] *Der Spiegel,* November 7, 1962, p. 59.

Foertsch article in its September 19, 1962, issue.[26] The article was thus originally scheduled to appear in the next issue, that of September 26, 1962. The Fallex 62 maneuvers did not take place until September 21, 1962. The publication of the Foertsch article was postponed until the October 10 issue to permit a partial revision of the article in light of the results of Fallex 62.

On October 26, 1962, about 10 P.M., two officials of the Security Group went to Ahlers' Hamburg apartment in order to take him into custody and search his apartment. At the apartment they found Frau Ahlers' aunt, Fraulein Wildhagen, who was caring for the Ahlers children while their parents were on vacation in Spain. Fraulein Wildhagen explained to the men that Ahlers and his wife had been in Spain since October 20 and were due to return to Hamburg on November 8, 1962. She also informed the officials that earlier that day, October 26, Frau Ahlers had phoned from Torremolinos, near Malaga, Spain, that she and her husband probably would go to Tangiers on the twenty-seventh in order to visit briefly with a former school friend, Frau Dr. Vitanien. Frau Ahlers added, during the phone conversation, that in about three days they would again be in Torremolinos and would spend the rest of their vacation there before returning to Hamburg. The Security Group officials were able to confirm part of this information by discovering in the house search a notation on an airlines flight plan indicating that Ahlers and his wife planned to leave Spain by plane on November 6 and arrive in Hamburg on November 8, 1962.[27]

Whatever the explanation for the failure of the authorities to have known of Ahlers' departure on October 20 for Spain, this lack of accurate intelligence and planning on the part of the investigators resulted, during the night of October 26, in

[26] *Der Spiegel,* September 19, 1962, p. 105.
[27] *Der "Spiegel"-Bericht,* 197.

a series of hasty improvisations which had profound consequences for Franz Josef Strauss. The procedures and personalities involved in effecting the arrest of Ahlers while he was on Spanish soil constitute a complex story and are more appropriately treated in a later chapter. It is sufficient for our immediate purpose to note that the Spanish authorities were contacted during the night of October 26 and were requested to take Ahlers into custody, although the extradition agreement between West Germany and Spain did not authorize rendition of persons accused of political crimes, including treason. At approximately 3 A.M., October 27, Ahlers and his wife were awakened in their hotel room in Torremolinos by Spanish police and requested to accompany them to police headquarters in nearby Malaga. Ahlers was kept in confinement until he and his wife were returned to West Germany on a nonstop Lufthansa flight from Madrid to Frankfurt, arriving at the Frankfurt airport on Sunday, October 28. Ahlers was immediately arrested by West German investigators. His wife was permitted to proceed to their home on the outskirts of Hamburg. After his arrest in Frankfurt, Ahlers was kept in jail until December 22, 1962.

In the weeks following the October 26 raids additional arrests were made. Hans Detlev Becker, publication director of *Der Spiegel,* was appointed temporary editor-in-chief shortly after the arrests of coeditors Jacobi and Engel. On November 2, 1962, he was taken into provisional custody, along with Colonel Adolf Wicht, a Bundeswehr official on duty with the Federal Intelligence Agency. On November 29, 1962, Colonel Alfred Martin of the Federal Defense Ministry and Paul Conrad, a West German lobbyist in Bonn and Honorary Consul for the Republic of Tunisia, were seized. Dr. Josef Augstein, brother of *Der Spiegel's* publisher, was arrested on December 4. By the end of December these four individuals had been released from confinement.[28] Statements from the Federal Prosecutor's Office indicated that the strongest suspicions of treason centered on Rudolf Augstein, Conrad Ahlers, and Colonel Martin. Eventually the Federal Prosecutor's Office turned over to the Federal High Court whatever evidence the Office had in support of the accusations, particularly against Rudolf Augstein, Ahlers, and Martin. The judges of the Federal High Court would have to decide whether the evidence warranted a trial.

On the morning following the October 26 raids and initial arrests a spokesman in Karlsruhe for the Federal Prosecutor's Office issued a cryptic statement that the actions and arrests stemmed from "strong suspicion" of "betrayal of country, treasonable falsification, and bribery" on the part of *Der Spiegel's* publisher and certain of its staff through the publication, particularly in the Foertsch article, of "state secrets in such a manner as to endanger the welfare of the German people and the security of the Federal Republic."[29] The West German public would have to wait a bit longer before receiving an official elaboration of these charges and learning the basis of the accusations.

---

[28] Colonel Wicht was provisionally arrested for advising Ahlers and Becker, prior to publication, whether state secrets were contained in the Foertsch article. Eleven items of information contained in the draft of the article were checked by Wicht. He cleared ten of them; the one remaining item was "revised," according to Ahlers, before the article was published. Colonel Martin was discovered by the federal attorneys through material seized in *Der Spiegel's* offices as the informant who had passed information from the Defense Ministry to *Der Spiegel.* Martin, apparently disturbed by Strauss's views on strategic questions, first contacted in the spring of 1962 Paul Conrad, who, in turn, placed Martin in touch with his lawyer, Dr. Josef Augstein, brother of *Der Spiegel's* publisher. It was thus Josef Augstein who brought together Colonel Martin and *Der Spiegel.*

[29] *"Strafverfahren gegen das Nachrichtenmagazin 'Der Spiegel,' " Bulletin des Presse—und Informationamtes der Bundesregierung,* Bonn, No. 203 (October 31, 1962), 1716.

Chapter III

FRAMING THE ISSUES:
Initial Press
and Public Reactions

As was indicated earlier, two stages, functionally distinct but overlapping in time sequence, characterized the *Spiegel* Affair. The formative stage lasted approximately two weeks, extending perhaps to November 9, 1962, when the Bundestag ended its three days of debate on the affair. It was during this stage that the organized "publics" in West Germany framed their responses, projected them into the political arena, and shaped the tone and configurations of the controversy during its later stage. The primary group actors in the formative stage were elements of the press, the intellectual and academic communities, and the party system. The bargaining stage began shortly after Wolfgang Stammberger offered on November 1 to resign as Minister of Justice; it subsided on November 6 when the FDP agreed to remain in the coalition government and then erupted again in mid-November, when the FDP renounced its earlier commitment and withdrew from the cabinet. This stage of the affair was formally closed on December 7 with the announcement of the formation of a new coalition cabinet.

Immediate Public Reactions

Among the first to enter the fray against the authorities for the October 26 police action against *Der Spiegel* were elements of the intellectual and student communities. Beginning with a small sit-in staged by some 150 students in downtown Frankfurt on the afternoon of October 30 and given impetus by a huge student demonstration involving some 2,500 students the following evening at the University of Hamburg, student protest demonstrations and sit-ins eventually occurred, in the ensuing weeks, in virtually all major West German university towns and cities. By the middle of November at least fifteen such demonstrations had been reported by the press, each involving from a few hundred to a few thousand university and technical college students. In the instances in which they were organized or sponsored, the leadership was most frequently identified with student groups sympathetic with the views of the SPD or the FDP (e.g. the *Sozialdemokratischer Hochschulbund,* the *Sozialistischer Deutscher Studentenbund,* and the *Liberaler Studentenbund*). On a few occasions counterdemonstrations occurred, and here the initiative most frequently came from the Christian Democratic-oriented student groups, such as the *Ring Christlich-Demokratischer.* Slogans appearing on the placards carried by the student demonstrators told essentially, and sometimes in ironic form, the nature of their initial reactions: "*Der Spiegel* is dead—freedom is dead"; "Long live German-Spanish friendship"; "Head in the sand, dear Fatherland"; "On to the total state"; "Germany indivisible—freedom indivisible?" "Carl von Ossietzky, 1929—Augstein, 1962?" "Augstein out [of jail]—Strauss in"; "My God, what is to become of Germany?" "Censorship is not permitted—Basic Law, Article 5"; "It concerns not *Der Spiegel*—it concerns press freedom"; "Basic rights for the Government's opponents"; and "Remember *Die Weltbühne*—Are we back to that?" In addition to demonstrations, the students protestors also used petitions as a means of expressing their concern. At the close of a student demonstration in Mannheim on November 3, for example, signatures were secured on a roll of blank newspaper for a letter of sympathy to *Der*

Spiegel. Three days later 102 Protestant seminary students at *Kirchliche Hochschule* near Bielefeld urged in an open letter to Federal President Heinrich Lübke that he use the prestige of his office to secure a prompt clarification of the procedures used in the *Spiegel* action. As the controversy extended into November, with no apparent solution in sight, the more formal apparata of student opinion, including the student government organizations *(Allgemeine Studentenausschüsse)*, were mobilized to try to secure from the authorities a fixing of responsibility for the improprieties surrounding the investigation.[1]

The first recorded expression of concern from the academicians is contained in an open letter, dated October 31, and signed by twenty nine medical and natural science professors and instructors at the University of Cologne:

We the undersigned—professors and instructors at the University of Cologne—have with serious concern learned of the necessity of an action against the news magazine *Der Spiegel.*

We disassociate ourselves from the possibly illegal methods of a journalistic news organ, but at the same time we wish to go on record strongly for the observance of press freedom as a foundation stone of the democratic order. In the interest of the security of our country on the one side and the constitutionally guaranteed basic right on the other side we seek by way of this letter to the Federal Justice Minister an expeditious clarification of the accusations which have been raised.

Since we are of the opinion that the political responsibility of the individual is a decisive component of the democratic order, we ask all like-minded citizens to submit similar letters to the Federal Justice Minister, so that by this action the concerned interest of the German public may be revealed.[2]

A few days later similar expressions of concern, also in the form of open letters to Minister Stammberger, were released by members of the faculty at Göttingen University and by

[1] See below, pp. 155–57.
[2] *Kölner Stadt-Anzeiger,* November 1, 1962.

teaching staff members of the public health clinic in Köln-Merheim.[3] However, in contrast to the relatively early involvement of the student protestors, the first serious wave of openly expressed concern by the teaching community did not appear until the middle of November, and at a point when it seemed that the Bonn system was incapable of satisfactorily explaining the controversial aspects of the investigation. In short, when the *Spiegel* Affair progressed to the second stage, when a crisis of confidence in the political system itself became the issue for certain observers, the concern of the teaching and academic professions became most apparent.[4]

The initial reaction of certain other elements of the intellectual community, including prestigious writers, artists, and publicists, was swift and unequivocal. Thus on the morning after the police action a telegram was sent to *Der Spiegel* pledging that "we are solidly with you and ask that you let us know what we can do to help." Among the eight signers were Günter Grass, Uwe Johnson, Alfred Andersch, Hans Werner Richter, and Hans Magnus Enzensberger. The following day a "manifesto," signed by forty-nine of West Germany's best-known writers, artists, and publicists condemned the action, renounced a public policy that kept "so-called" military secrets out of the public domain, and demanded Strauss's resignation:

> The German journalist Rudolf Augstein, publisher of *Der Spiegel,* has been arrested in connection with an alleged betrayal of so-called military secrets and under the charge of having revealed them to the public. An act of state arbitrariness against *Der Spiegel* accompanied this arrest. The undersigned express their respect for Herr Rudolf Augstein and are solidly with him. In an age which has made war impracticable as an instrument of policy, they hold the reporting to the public about so-called

[3] *Die Welt,* (Hamburg), November 1, 1962; *Kölner Stadt-Anzeiger* Cologne), November 3, 1962.

[4] See below, pp. 155–57.

military secrets a moral obligation, which they would on all occasions undertake to fulfill. The undersigned regret that the politics of the Defense Minister of the Federal Republic forces them to so sharp a conflict with the views of the authorities of the state. They call now finally for the resignation of this politically, societally, and personally discredited minister.[5]

In spite of later efforts on the part of a few signers of the above manifesto to qualify its reference to the moral obligation to make public military secrets and the ripple of criticism in a few newspapers against the oversensitivity of the signers to still unfounded rumors, most of the signers refused to retreat from the essential thrust of their statement.[6]

The Evolution of Press Attitudes
October 27–31, 1962

The timing of the raids prevented the West German newspapers from giving extensive coverage to the events in their October 27 editions.[7] The first press reports were therefore brief notices of what had apparently transpired the preceding evening, with no attempt at editorializing. At this point, and even in the days that followed, the press was handicapped by

[5] *Die Welt,* October 31, 1962. Thirty-six of the signers were members of "Gruppe 47," a conference of prominent West German writers and intellectuals who began meeting annually in 1947 to discuss and criticize their works. The additional thirteen signers included painters, sculptors, cabaret artists, and actors.

[6] One of the signers, actor Cürd Jurgens, promptly denied that he endorsed the implication that private citizens had the obligation to reveal "state secrets." Another signer, literary critic and journalist Rudolf Walter Leonhardt, hastened to explain that the manifesto's reference to so-called military secrets was intended to stress the fear that the concept "military secrets" is easily exploited by the authorities to keep the public uninformed about the "dangers of military and political situations." *Der Tagesspiegel* (West Berlin), November 1, 1962.

[7] Where the comments and views of the newspapers are identified in the body of the text by the name and issue of the newspaper, no additional references are given in footnotes. All of the press material cited in this chapter is contained in the "Spiegel"-Affäre files of the Press Evaluation Section of the Bundestag Library (Bonn).

the dearth of reliable information. Rumors were widespread and the information derived hastily from Hamburg police who participated in the raids was not wholly accurate.[8]

Few West German newspapers publish Sunday editions, but those that do attempted to piece together whatever information was available for front page stories. The Sunday press accounts referred particularly to the statement issued the preceding morning by the Federal Prosecutor's Office in Karlsruhe:

On the basis of published material which dealt with important questions of national defense in such a way as to endanger the position of the Federal Republic as well as the security and freedom of the German people, the offices in Hamburg and Bonn of the news magazine *Der Spiegel* have been searched on Friday, October 26, 1962, under the authority of an order issued by the Examining Judge of the *Bundesgerichtshof.*

Several associates of *Der Spiegel* have been provisionally taken into custody on account of suspicion of treason, treasonable falsification, and active bribery and will in the next few days be taken before the court for preliminary hearings. Against the publisher Rudolf Augstein there has been issued by the court an arrest order, which has been executed. The extensive investigation also concerns officers, civil servants, and employees of the Bundeswehr, who may also be suspected of having betrayed state secrets to *Der Spiegel* for monetary considerations. . . .[9]

[8] For example, the *Freie Presse* (Bielefeld) reported in its October 27, 1962, issue that "all bureaus of the news magazine in the Federal Republic have been searched and its documents have been seized." Actually the police raids and the investigations were confined to the Hamburg and Bonn offices of *Der Spiegel.* Also, the *Hamburger Abendblatt* on October 27 quoted the director of the Hamburg Criminal Police as having said that the West German Foreign Office was in charge of the investigation. In no sense was this allegation accurate. Indeed, one of the many complaints arising out of the incident was that the authorities had not taken the Foreign Office into confidence in attempting to secure in Spain the arrest of Ahlers.

[9] Cf. the October 28, 1962, issues of *Welt am Sonntag,* 12; *Der Tagesspiegel* (West Berlin), 1–2; and *Bild-Zeitung* (Hamburg), 1.

Offered without elaboration by a spokesman for the Federal
Prosecutor's Office, this statement was the first official indication of the nature of the charges against Augstein and his
colleagues. It made no reference to the continuing search and
impounding of materials in the Hamburg office of *Der Spiegel.*
Also on Saturday, following the issuance of the above statement, *Der Spiegel's* managing director Detlev Becker commented in a press conference on the events of the previous
evening. The Sunday editions stressed Becker's denial that
Der Spiegel had bribed anyone for information used in the
Foertsch article. Emphasis was given also to Becker's explanation that Conrad Ahlers, in preparing the Foertsch
article, first submitted to the "authorities" a set of questions
containing what Ahlers believed to be the material most susceptible to the interpretation of being state secrets. Becker
added that in all of these areas, except one, the "authorities"
advised Ahlers that no state secrets were involved. The material dealing with the one area in which Ahlers was told
state secrets were contained was "revised" before the Foertsch
article was published.[10]

For the most part the Sunday editions contained no editorials speculating about the political implications of the raids
and arrests. Not so, however, in the case of the East German
press, which quickly perceived the propagandistic value of
the actions against *Der Spiegel. Neues Deutschland,* the widely circulated organ of the East German Communist Party
(SED), speculated in its Sunday edition of the twenty-eighth
that:

> The complex of events [of recent days] will be found revealing,
> even in West Gremany. Information is still lacking about the par-
> ticulars of the action. But merely a superficial examination of it
> suggests the massive scale of the prevailing suppression of all ex-
> pressions of discontent by the subtle apparatus of the clerico-

[10] *Ibid.*

militaristic dictatorship in the federal regime. Where freedom of the press begins and ends is decided in the Bonn system by the generals and their fine War Minister [Franz Josef Strauss]. Where the constitution begins and ends is not a matter for the people to decide, but is under the jurisdiction of the militarists and ultras.

The East Berlin newspaper *National Zeitung* drew similar conclusions, noted the apparent collusion of "Fascist" Spain and West Germany in the arrest of Conrad Ahlers, and added: "In its analysis of the maneuvers the magazine revealed that the Federal Republic will be completely destroyed in the event of war. Because of this revelation the Adenauer government decides that there has been a betrayal of state secrets and of country."

But the East German newspapers were not the only foreign newspapers that immediately questioned the motives of the investigators. Over the weekend the liberal Stockholm *Dagens Nyheter*, a daily with one of the largest circulations in Sweden, was not editorially willing to discount the possibility that the action represented "a type of juridical blood vendetta." The Swiss *National Zeitung* carried in its October 29 issue a dispatch from its Bonn correspondent concluding that it "would be alarming for democracy in the Federal Republic if an extensive and irrefutable basis for the Friday night action is not quickly given by the Federal Prosecutor's Office." The respected *Neue Zürcher Zeitung* also noted on the twenty-ninth the speculation about the political motivations of the *Spiegel* action, but it cautioned that the speculation "did not as yet have a firm basis." The London *Times* refrained in its October 30 issue from judging the merits of the case against *Der Spiegel*, but it warmly praised the magazine as "one of the few West German publications ready to turn its criticism on any party or person when it judged something was amiss." However, it was the harsh indictment in the October 27 issue of prestigious *Le Monde* that caught the editorial eye of the West German press. Tentatively concluding that Strauss was probably responsible for the action against *Der Spiegel, Le Monde* reasoned that he had timed his "revenge" so that it would follow his "acquittal" by the Bundestag of the misconduct with which he had been charged in the Fibag Affair. A number of the major West German newspapers interpreted *Le Monde's* accusation as a significant clue to the seriousness with which foreign observers might view the *Spiegel* action and how damaging the episode might be for West Germany's image abroad.[11]

On Monday, October 29, the events concerning the *Spiegel* action rivaled the Cuban missile crisis for front-page space in all of West Germany's leading newspapers. Editorial comment was now appearing also in all parts of the Federal Republic. In its lead editorial on October 29, the *Frankfurther Allgemeine Zeitung,* often a supporter of the government, termed the action against *Der Spiegel* "the most decisive action of the postwar period against an organ of the press." The editorial writer expressed surprise that the authorities saw fit to carry out the action at night and allowed three days to elapse after the arrest and search warrants had been issued by the examining judge of the Federal High Court. He questioned the legal grounds for the seizure in Spain of Ahlers and his wife and warned that the political repercussions from this unparalleled action would jeopardize the prospects of the Bundestag's approving the proposed constitutional amendments granting emergency powers to the national government. In a front-page analysis, Alfred Rapp of the *Frankfurter Allgemeine Zeitung* wrote that the key question posed by the events of the past weekend was whether the action represented a serious invasion of the legitimate freedom of the press.

[11] Cf. the October 29, 1962, issues of the following: *Kieler Nachrichten, Frankfurter Allgemeine Zeitung, Westdeutsche Allgemeine, Münchner Merkur,* and *Stuttgarter Zeitung.*

He added:

When the maneuvers are now given publicity, when it is printed that in spite of atomic and nuclear weapons a Soviet advance can not be halted, that the *Bundeswehr* is not only undermanned but also ill-equipped and the like, one may only reply that the Soviets already knew these things without having to read *Der Spiegel*. Can there not be instances in which the press must feel itself obligated to write about the defects in the country's defense system? The rubber-stamp marked "state secret" will all too often be used—and not just in the military agencies.

In a final note of caution, however, Rapp concluded that before the public answers these questions it must await additional information. Hans Henrich of the *Hamburger Echo* editorialized that: "One may think what he will about *Der Spiegel*. But at the same time the '*Nacht und Nebel*' action has shown to even those reluctant to admit it that laws are needed not only to prevent precensorship but also to protect newspapers, periodicals, radio, and the like against wholesale seizures of their sources of information. Until there are such laws, one can only recommend to publishers and editors to store their information in safe places."

The *Weser Kurier* (Bremen) also complained in its editorial of October 29 of the extensive scope of the search and examination of *Der Spiegel's* materials. It reasoned that the investigation had gone far beyond the limits of any proper inquiry into the evidence relevant to the charges and that one could only conclude that the public authorities were attempting to intimidate the magazine by compiling an elaborate file on its sources of information. Similar charges were contained in the first editorial reactions of the *Hannoversche Presse*. More feared than any "revenge action" by Franz Josef Strauss, according to this paper, was the possibility that the public authorities had set a dangerous precedent for future violations of the legitimate freedom of the press.

The *Süddeutsche Zeitung* (Munich), in an editorial in its October 29 edition, suggested that two questions had been raised by the events of Friday evening: Had the law, in fact, been violated by *Der Spiegel's* publisher and editors as a result of material appearing in the Foertsch article, and had the methods used by the investigators conformed to legal and reasonable standards? The first of these questions, according to the editorial, would have to be decided by the appropriate court. But the second question was one on which the press was obligated to speak. In the opinion of the *Süddeutsche Zeitung* editorial writer, neither the staging of the action at night nor the extensiveness of the searches could be justified unless the Federal Prosecutor's Office had strong reason to believe that *Der Spiegel* was about to reveal, in forthcoming issues, additional information which was also suspected of containing state secrets. The authorities had not yet shown that such a suspicion existed. The writer continued that even under this condition the investigation and searches ought to be limited to the prevention of the immediate publication of the specific data. Under no circumstances, it concluded, could the authorities justify their apparent efforts to precensor an entire issue of *Der Spiegel*. Similar questions were raised in editorials of October 29 in such diverse newspapers as the *Münchner Merkur*, the *Rhein Zeitung* (Koblentz), the *Saarbrücker Allgemeine Zeitung*, the *Westdeutsche Allgemeine* (Essen), and *Der Mittag* (Düsseldorf).

Die Freiheit (Mainz), identified with the views of the Social Democratic Party, admitted in its October 29 editorial that it is not easy to fix the boundaries between freedom of the press and the interests of national security, but added that Franz Josef Strauss had a strong personal motive for silencing *Der Spiegel*. The belief that Strauss may have somehow taken a personal hand in the action against *Der*

Spiegel was reflected also in the October 29 issue of the *Kölner Stadt-Anzeiger,* in which Hans Gerlach, writing under the heading "Strauss' Revenge?" refused to discount the possible connection between the action against the magazine and the recent Fibag Affair. Supporting this suspicion, he suggested, was the weakness of the contention of the Federal Prosecutor's Office that the material in the Foertsch article jeopardized the national security of West Germany. In a not altogether appropriate analogy, he pointed to the continuous revelations and speculations in American newspapers about the military alternatives open to the United States in the Cuban missile crisis, which was still in progress.

Aside from the concern about the implications of the *Spiegel* action for the freedom of the press, criticism was voiced by several editorial writers on October 29 as they viewed the events against the backdrop of recent German history. Writing in the *Abendzeitung* (Munich), Jochen Willke objected that: "When a phone call to the office of *Der Spiegel* is greeted by 'The Security Group is in charge here!' a painful sensation arises that such words belong to a time past which has rightly been called the darkest days of our country." In reference to a statement released by Josef Hermann Dufhues, executive secretary of the CDU, that the investigation was aimed solely against *Der Spiegel* and not against the press in general, Willke countered: "It is more correct to say: It is a matter involving not merely *Der Spiegel* or the German press. It involves German democracy." But it was in the pages of the October 29 edition of the *Frankfurter Rundschau* that the parallel between the methods used in the *Spiegel* action and those associated with the Nazi era was most sharply drawn:

Fifteen years had passed after World War I when the year 1933 entered the books of history. Today seventeen years have passed since World War II and we record the year 1962. We know history never repeats itself in precise patterns; and no false analogies should be drawn. But we are sure that there is among us today in this country a serious concern as to how long the Germans can keep the freedoms which were given to them. . . . It is more than a coincident, it is a symbol, that the decisive act of this drama, the seizure of reporter Conrad Ahlers, was carried out at the request of Germany by the police of fascist Spain.

If now the doorbell rings in the early hours of the morning, we cannot console ourselves with the peaceful thought that it is nothing more than the milkman or the delivery boy with the breakfast rolls; if someone knocks on the door at midnight we no longer know whether, at worst, it is only a telegram or a drunk who, staggering home, has come to the wrong door. We must now consider the possibility of its being the political police who under cover of darkness are looking for traitors. If we hear children whimpring because late at night they are disturbed by someone searching their beds for material to be used in prosecuting their parents; if we hear that someone's writings and drafts of articles have been confiscated and taken to the censor; if we hear that the offices of *Der Spiegel* in Hamburg and Bonn have been suddenly invaded by armed police commandos and that colleagues in adjoining offices cannot be reached by phone—if we hear all this we cannot be certain any longer that these are simply reports coming out of Moscow, Prague, Leipzig, or from Berlin of 1944. Yet we are urged to keep calm. All this is happening, we are assured, in the name of freedom. . . . The allegedly incriminating article could not under any circumstances justify these events. It may be that purely formal grounds exist for suspecting treason. That is yet to be decided by the courts. However that may be, there is hardly a schoolchild who can really be persuaded that because of this article the Federal Republic has been placed in danger.

Not all of the major West German newspapers in their October 29 editorials were critical of the action. Among these newspapers the position most widely taken was that of withholding any adverse criticism until more information could be obtained of the basis of the accusations. In the meantime, it was argued, the public authorities were entitled to a presumption that they must have acted only under the most serious and careful consideration of the merits of the case. The *Kasseler Post,* which throughout the ensuing *Spiegel* Affair refused to join the ranks of the critics of the government, editorialized on October 29 that there was not a shred of evidence that Strauss had inspired or influenced the action against *Der Spiegel,* that only a gross exaggeration could lead to the assertion that the entire press community was under attack from the public authorities, and that the future would show whether those who now leap to *Der Spiegel's* defense were really serving the cause of democracy or merely their selfish partisan aims. The *Ruhr-Nachrichten* (Dortmund), a supporter of the views of the CDU, warned also against premature judgments in the matter but conceded that equally vigorous action should be expected by the authorities against public officials who may have leaked the information to *Der Spiegel.*

With the appearance of the October 30 editions, the tempo of West German press reaction to the *Spiegel* action quickened. The editorial in the *Süddeutsche Zeitung* suggested that with the continuation of the search by public authorities of *Der Spiegel's* files and archives a new element had entered the controversy. This harassment, the editorial emphasized, would be disastrous for a less financially secure publication and added, "Under the pretext of investigating a particular case the whole operation of the magazine is being hindered." The editorial writer warned that this procedure should be taken into account in the debate as to whether the federal government needed additional authority in times of national emergency. Implicity, the specter of the abuse of the emergency clause of Article 48 of the Weimar Constitution was being raised—a theme already raised in the October 29 newspapers and which found expression in other commentaries during the next few weeks.[12]

[12] Article 48 of the Weimar Constitution permitted the president, with

Erhard Becker, in the October 30 issue of the *Mannheimer Morgen,* called the action against *Der Spiegel* unparalleled in German history, with the exception of the extraordinary cases arising under conditions of war, revolution, or the Third Reich. "To inform and enlighten the public about defense matters is a duty of the free press," he wrote. Where the legitimate boundary lies between this obligation and that of respecting the requirements of national security, he admitted, was difficult to say. But the launching of the raids immediately after the Fibag debate in the Bundestag and three days after the court orders were issued put in doubt the alleged motives of the action.

In an unusual display of impatience with the public authorities, the *Frankfurter Allgemeine Zeitung* of October 30 carried a front-page analysis by one of its leading staff members, Bruno DeChamps. He bitterly denounced the statement by CDU Executive Secretary Dufhues that the matter involved merely *Der Spiegel,* not the entire press. DeChamps complained that in this case there could be no singling out of *Der Spiegel* from the press, since the methods used by the public authorities against any organ of the press indirectly affect all members of the press community. DeChamps posed several questions which, he insisted, the government could not ignore: (1) Did the Federal Prosecutor's Office take "politi-

---

the counter-signature of the chancellor or the appropriate minister, to issue emergency decrees. Although the chancellor was to remain responsible during the emergency period to the Reichstag, which could rescind the decrees, the intended safeguards against the abuse of Article 48 were circumvented through the willingness of President Hindenburg to dissolve the Reichstag, thus rendering it physically incapable of supervising the exercise of emergency powers. An excessively legalistic or formalistic interpretation can easily err on the side of regarding Article 48 and its use as a basic cause of the collapse of the system. A more adequate view of the provision, and its use, is that the heavy reliance upon it during the final months of the Weimar Republic was symptomatic of the impossibility of discovering within the Reichstag a cohesive coalition upon which a government could be formed.

cally-inspired" advice from Defense Minister Strauss in timing the action? (2) Why were the raids and arrests carried out under cover of darkness rather than at some "civilized" hour? (3) Why have the West Germans had to wait so long for the appointment of a Federal Public Prosecutor, and did the existing vacancy in this post have anything to do with the methods used?[13] (4) What really happened during the occupation of the Hamburg offices? DeChamps commented: "It would appear that this phase of the action was either so clumsily or ineptly handled as to disqualify the leaders of this operation from further service in the government." (5) On what authority was Ahlers arrested in Spain and required to return to Germany since neither the extradition agreement with Spain nor the statute of the International Police could legally be invoked in securing his seizure?[14] DeChamps concluded:

The excesses which agitate in this matter and produce distrust, finally, are due partially to a plain stupidity, to a clumsiness and coarseness, which a young and still not stable democracy as ours ought not to have to bear. One might have expected that all parties without exception [would have protested the handling of

[13] Prior to the *Spiegel* Affair, Justice Minister Stammberger had recommended Wolfgang Fränkel for the directorship of the Federal Prosecutor's Office *(Generalbundesanwalt)*. Immediately after the appointment on March 21, 1962, of Fränkel, however, the East German government exposed Fränkel's compromising role as a jurist in the Nazi era, amply verified by its revealing Nazi documents concerning court decisions in which Fränkel had participated. Fränkel was subsequently stripped of the *Generalbundesanwalt* position, thus leaving it vacant at the time of the *Spiegel* investigation. Publicly acknowledging his responsibility for having failed to inquire more carefully into Fränkel's background, Stammberger offered to resign as Justice Minister. Adenauer chose not to accept the resignation, but a number of CDU/CSU leaders, including Franz Josef Strauss, made no secret of their exasperation with Stammberger for his embarrassing the Adenauer government in the Fränkel case. The major aspects of this case are reported in *Archiv der Gegenwart*. XXXII (1962), 9979, 9988-E, and 10007-D.

[14] For an examination of the jurisdiction of Interpol in connection with the *Spiegel* Affair, see Emil Kirschbaum, "Interpol—Aufgaben und Begrezung," *National Zeitung* (Basel), November 10, 1962.

the action] . . . when instead it is said that this is no affair of the press, but one involving only *Der Spiegel,* it is implied that in the case of *Der Spiegel* one should not take too seriously a few violations of the free order and should overlook them. If one agrees with that premise, then something is rotten. We would be happy if someone could prove to us that it is not so, that the remark of Dufhues was simply misunderstood. But we cannot let it pass. For what stinks here concerns not only *Der Spiegel,* not only the press, but it concerns the whole democratic system in our country, which, without a free press, without universal press freedom, cannot survive.

Die Welt's lead editorial of October 30 refused to pass judgment on the legal merits of the charges against Augstein and *Der Spiegel.* It did, however, question the methods that were employed and were still being employed against the magazine. The seemingly interminable search of *Der Spiegel's* archives, the effort by police on the night of October 26 to read the proofs of the forthcoming issue, the extraordinarily slow process being used by the authorities to terminate its restrictions on the future operation of the magazine "violate certainly the spirit, and perhaps the letter, of the Bonn Basic Law."

The editorial writer for the *Westdeutsche Allgemeine* on October 30, apparently in a mood of exasperation, concluded that the alleged effort to censor the next issue of *Der Spiegel* was intolerable. If reports about the precensorship were correct, the investigation "has exceeded the permissible bounds of an inquiry of admittedly a very serious matter." The *Allgemeine Zeitung* (Mainz) complained that the investigation was too one-sided; why had no arrests occurred on the government side, of the "informants"? Kurt Gehrmann, in the editorial for the *Neue Rhein Zeitung* (Cologne) of October 30, complained that "We still do not know on which passages in the three weeks old article the charge of treason is based, even though this is the most sensational action against journalists in recent press history." This, indeed, Gehrmann concluded, was an "unusual case." Why did the authorities have to wait almost three weeks after the appearance of the article before launching the action? Why did not the Defense Ministry recognize immediately after the appearance of the Foertsch article on October 8, 1962, that *Der Spiegel* had betrayed state secrets? Alluding to a rumor that the investigation had been prompted by a private citizen's complaint, Gehrmann asked why the Federal Prosecutor's Office first needed prodding from a private citizen if so flagrant a case of treason was involved?[15] And "since when," he concluded, "is precensorship permitted in the Federal Republic?"

A central theme among the October 30 editorials of the relatively few major West German newspapers which refused to criticize the government's handling of the *Spiegel* investigation was that of warning the reader against premature conclusions. Werner von Lojewski, writing in the *Bonner Rundschau*, reaffirmed the position taken by his paper since the raids that the gravity of the charges against the magazine outweighed any of the criticisms that had been made of the procedures used by the authorities. He added, however, that the federal government was in danger of making a public martyr of Augstein by its hesitancy in fully informing the public of the basis of its actions. The *Deutsche Tagespost* (Würzburg) in its October 30 issue complained that the SPD was attempting to exploit the *Spiegel* investigation for partisan advantage, accused the SPD Bundestag delegation of being "legislative appendages" of *Der Spiegel,* and concluded that "hardly a bomb is dropped in the pages of *Der Spiegel* but

[15] Gehrmann is here alluding to the rumor that a citizen's complaint by Freiherr Friedrich August von der Heydte prompted the Federal Prosecutor's Office to initiate its investigation, culminating in the raids of October 26, 1962. See pp. 77–78 and footnote immediately below.

what the SPD echoes it in the Bundestag." Yet the *Deutsche Tagespost* editorial admitted that *Der Spiegel* had occasionally in the past played a positive role in West German politics, particularly in uncovering Nazi war criminals who had returned to responsible positions.

Until October 31, 1962, the primary thrust of the press criticism of the *Spiegel* investigation was in the direction of expressing concern for freedom of the press. Few major newspapers until this date took seriously the charge that Franz Josef Strauss had inspired the investigation or played a decisive role in its implementation. On October 31, however, a growing uneasiness was apparent among many West German newspapers about the circumstances surrounding the apprehension in Spain of Conrad Ahlers. Out of this uneasiness emerged a decided shift toward the view that the government—and particularly Franz Josef Strauss—was withholding information to which the public was entitled. As it became increasingly clear that not all the relevant information about Ahlers' arrest had been made known, a significant segment of the press community found it plausible that perhaps the government was either trying to hide something or did not itself know who or which agency had secured Ahlers' arrest in Spain. Whatever the reason for this dearth of official information on the Ahlers' episode, the press was no longer willing to ignore or belittle the possibility that Strauss had indeed assumed a key role in the investigation. Who had requested the Spanish police to take Ahlers into "provisional custody" and upon which legal grounds had this request been founded? Explanations from the Federal Prosecutor's Office, the Foreign Office, and the Federal Criminal Office seemed to absolve all of them from the responsibility of having initiated his arrest on foreign soil. But if none of these agencies had acted, which other agency or official had made the request and through which channels? *Die Welt* reflected the sentiments of many West German newspapers on October 31 when it declared:

It is of utmost importance to know how the Federal Prose-cutor's Office could effect in Spain the arrest of a German citizen, without apparently a formal request from the federal government. Interpol—so the government has declared—was not implicated in the arrest. The International Police may be brought in only in criminal, not in political, cases. The same restriction applies in the extradition agreement, renewed after the war, between Spain and Germany and which dates back to 1878. Therefore, how was it possible? Through the assistance of the Secret Service? Through the Falange, through the *Abendländische Akademie* [a nationalist-conservative organization]? We are being grotesque, but only because the incident is grotesque. . . . [It will remain grotesque] until the Federal Prosecutor gives a satisfactory ex-planation.

In examining in their October 31 editorials the possibility mentioned four days earlier by *Le Monde* that Strauss had improperly influenced the actions against *Der Spiegel,* and particularly the arrest of Conrad Ahlers, a number of major newspapers noted a couple of rumors that seemed to be interrelated. It had been widely reported in the press that the private party who had filed complaints against *Der Spiegel* for allegedly publishing state secrets was Freiherr Friedrich August von der Heydte, a professor of public law and political science at the University of Würzburg, a paratroop officer during World War II, and identified with certain "rightist" groups, such as the *Abendländische Akademie,* which are bitterly anti-Communistic and opposed to the abandonment of German claims to the territories east of the Oder-Neisse line. In connecting von der Heydte with the investigation, the *Westfälische Rundschau* queried why he had so recently been promoted to the rank of Brigadier-General, a rank never be-fore attained by a reserve officer. Was there a link between von der Heydte's promotion and his filing of the complaints against *Der Spiegel?*[16] The writer in the *Westfälische Rund-schau* laconically concluded that whoever "maintains that there is a connection will surely be sued." Second, new significance was being attached on October 31 to the rumor that Strauss had privately hinted two days before the October 26 raids that something was about to happen to *Der Spiegel.* The revelation was supposed to have occurred during the reception on the evening of October 24 at the Schloss Brühl (located between Cologne and Bonn), the scene of the annual reception given by the Federal President for Bundestag deputies. It had been reported that during this evening Strauss, in a somewhat inebriated condition, had become highly agitated in a discussion with a few prominent SPD Bundestag deputies and had stated, among other things, that *Der Spiegel* would soon be experiencing "difficulties." The story, in circulation for several days, was now being given attention in even the more cautious newspapers. Did Strauss in fact have prior knowledge of the October 26 raids? Had

[16] In reference to an earlier article in *Der Spiegel* dealing with the role of the Bundeswehr in NATO, Professor Heydte wrote in the July 6, 1962, issue of the *Deutsche Tagespost*: "What has here been revealed under the pretext of seemingly objective reporting in the form of truths, half-truths, and lies about the internal affairs of the Bundeswehr is more than a mere indiscretion in the conveyor belt. It borders, to the contrary, on deliberate treason at a time where there is involved the very existence of the state and the freedom of all of us." After *Der Spiegel* received a court order restraining Heydte from repeating this accusation, Heydte on October 1, 1962, lodged a "citizen's complaint" against *Der Spiegel's* publishing "state secrets." In his petition to the Federal Prosecutor's Office he cited six issues in which state secrets may have been revealed by *Der Spiegel.* In the *Deutsche Tagespost* Heydte later justified this course of action by reasoning that since in view of the restraining order against him there "remained to us no effective means other than that of complaining to the Federal Prosecutor of our suspicion." *Deutsche Tages-post, Sonderdruck, Zusammenfassung aus Nr. 130–38 vom 30 Oktober bis 17 November 1962,* p. 3. In a second complaint which he filed on October 11, 1962, with the Federal Prosecutor's Office, Heydte cited the Foertsch article as another example of treasonable publication by *Der Spiegel.* The Federal Prosecutor's Office later denied that its investigation against *Der Spiegel* was prompted by Heydte's complaints.

he been personally involved in their implementation? By a process of elimination, could not one conclude that he was the official who had secured the cooperation of the Spanish police in arresting Ahlers and having him returned to Germany? It was clear that Strauss could not continue to maintain silence as to his role in the events of October 26. Equally clear was the embarrassing situation into which these rumors were placing the CDU/CSU and the federal government.

Reactions of Press Associations

During the initial phase of the *Spiegel* Affair various associations of the West German press community began to voice their criticisms of the *Spiegel* action. A sampling of these group reactions is also significantly indicative of the role which the press community played in formulating the issues and stimulating the controversy which colored the atmosphere of the later stage of the Affair. As early as October 28, 1962, the board of directors of the Professional Association of Hamburg Journalists protested the methods employed in the October 26 raids, ". . . for there will be created among the population the impression that through these surprising actions . . . the state power can by force create a real hindrance for the legitimate periodical press every time there is the slightest suspicion of the nature involved in these actions."[17]

On the same day the directors of the Federal Press Conference *(Bundespressekonferenz)* wired both Federal Minister of Interior Hermann Höcherl and Federal Minister of Justice Wolfgang Stammberger for prompt clarification of the basis of the charges against *Der Spiegel* and an explanation of the methods employed in carrying out the investigation.[18] The Bonn Correspondents' Association wired Höcherl and Stammberger for a public statement defining the legal grounds for

[17] *Hamburger Echo,* October 29, 1962.
[18] *Ibid.*

the police action against the Bonn bureau of the magazine.[19] Speaking on October 28 as chairman of the Bavarian Journalists' Association, Ernst Müller-Meiningen, Jr., stated: "The move against *Der Spiegel* might prove itself to be a move against the entire German press. Not because the press is in any way to be identified with the accusation, which is a pending legal matter, but because here there appears dramatically what dangerous methods might do to endanger the constitutionality and freedom of the press."[20]

On Monday, October 29, the directors of the German Journalists' Association *(Deutscher Journalistenverband)* issued a public statement which underscored "emphatically" its agreement with the views of its Hamburg affiliate (cited above), charged that the methods used against *Der Spiegel* were "ill-advised," and "especially condemned the police control of the production of the next issue of *Der Spiegel.*" The statement concluded: "This is an obvious violation of the constitutional guarantee against pre-censorship."[21] The directors of the *Presseverband Berlin* publicly endorsed the foregoing statement.[22] The president of the Association of German Periodical Publishers *(Verband deutscher Zeitschriftenverleger)* wired Stammberger: "Request in the 'Spiegel Action' the avoidance of all measures which appear unnecessary for securing the evidence and which might jeopardize the freedom of the press. Continued sealing of publishing and editing rooms, thereby hindering further work, disturbing to the publishing profession."[23] Similarly, John Jahr, Hamburg publisher and former part owner of *Der Spiegel,* wired Stammberger that he wished, in "agreement with a large number of West German publishers," to protest the hindrances

---

[19] *The Times* (London), October 29, 1962.
[20] *Abendzeitung* (Munich), October 29, 1962.
[21] *Die Welt,* October 30, 1962.
[22] *Telegraf* (West Berlin), October 30, 1962.
[23] *Die Welt,* October 30, 1962.

imposed by the police and investigators on *Der Spiegel*. Jahr added in his telegram that some publications could be financially ruined by these procedures.[24]

On October 30 the climax of the initial press reaction to the *Spiegel* action was reached when the most respected organized spokesman for the international press community, the International Press Institute, released from its Zurich headquarters the following statement:

> The International Press Institute has learned with concern of the methods and scope of the police action taken against the Hamburg newsmagazine *Der Spiegel*.
>
> Without wishing to prejudge in any way the allegations now made against this magazine, which will no doubt be determined by due process of law, the Institute is under the impression that the unusual methods employed by the police on this occasion have interfered with the production of the magazine to an extent which goes far beyond anything called for by the incriminating article, which was published three weeks ago. It would appear that the democratic principle of freedom of the press has been disregarded in the determination to investigate an alleged criminal action by individual journalists.
>
> Unless safeguards exists against damaging well-established publications as a result of this type of police action, an atmosphere of insecurity is likely to be created for all journalistic activities.[25]

A Content Analysis

To conclude our treatment of the initial responses of the West German press community to the *Spiegel* action, a systematic analysis is necessary to indicate quantitatively the scope and nature of the editorial reactions. For this purpose a sample has been constructed, consisting of thirty-four daily newspapers (See Appendix II).

Variations in format, news content, editorial policy, and

[24] *Frankfurter Rundschau,* October 30, 1962.
[25] *IPI Report, Monthly Bulletin of the International Press Institute,* November, 1962, p. 12.

readership among the West German newspapers warn against neat generalizations. However, at the risk of oversimplification, we can distinguish four categories within which most of the daily newspapers might be classified: (1) "boulevard sheets," or tabloids, dependent on street sales for their circulation, heavily employing pictures and color, and generally inclined to "sensationalize" the news; (2) *Heimatzeitungen,* or "hometown" newspapers, which have limited circulations (rarely exceeding 10,000) and are essentially preoccupied with the reporting of local events in the smaller towns and communities; (3) *Generalanzeiger,* or "advertisers," which usually attempt a limited coverage of national and international news and occasionally editorialize on public issues, although their primary function is that of providing a medium for local advertisers and the reporting of regional news; and (4) a relatively small number of newspapers, frequently described as the "serious" press, which is neither as sensational as the tabloid press nor as locally oriented in news coverage as the *Generalanzeiger* and *Heimatzeitungen.*[26] Although certain of the tabloids, particularly the *Bild-Zeitung* with a circulation that regularly exceeds three million copies, reach large numbers of readers, these newspapers are too preoccupied with appealing to and stimulating the reading appetites of the mass reading public for any intensive and sustained contribution to an informed discussion of political issues. The *Heimatzeitungen* include a wide variety of the small-town and village newspapers. Some of them are independently owned, operated, and written, but many of them now depend on major newspapers *(Hauptausgaben)* for whatever reports they carry on national and international news

[26] This four-part classification system is a revised version of one offered by W. Phillips Davison, "The Mass Media in West German Political Life," in Hans Speier and W. Phillips Davison (eds.), *West German Leadership and Foreign Policy,* (Evanston, Illinois, and White Plains, New York, 1957), 244–46.

and for features, such as fictional serials and literary supplements. Their editorials on matters that transcend local importance are customarily reproductions of editorials carried in the *Hauptausgaben*. The distinction between a *Heimatzeitung* and a *Generalanzeiger* is frequently marginal, as the latter also contain in many instances "canned" editorials of the major newspapers with which they are affiliated. Moreover, both the *Heimatzeitung* and the *Generalanzeiger* are heavily dependent on the wire services for national and international news coverage. Within the fourth catgory are included those newspapers which are generally regarded as "prestigious." Although none of them can claim a circulation figure that even approaches that of the *Bild-Zeitung,* several of them have circulations in excess of 150,000 copies.

Each of the thirty-four daily newspapers comprising our sample falls within either the third or fourth categories, or tends to combine aspects of both groupings. All of these newspapers are regularly clipped by the Press Evaluation Section *(Presseauswertungabteilung)* of the Bundestag Library in Bonn for its own evaluation purposes. It must be stressed that the sample is numerically a small minority of the daily newspapers published in West Germany and cannot be accepted as definitive and representative of the entire West German press.[27] However it is sufficiently representative of

[27] Davison, *ibid.,* estimated that of the approximately sixteen million copies of newspapers in daily circulation in West Germany in 1955, the tabloids accounted for about three million, the *Generalanzeiger* between three and four million, and the *Heimatzeitungen* about five million. In the reporting period immediately prior to the *Spiegel* Affair, the authoritative *Die deutsche Presse 1961* (Institut für Publizitik of the Free University of Berlin, Berlin: 1961) places the total number of newspapers published in the Federal Republic (including West Berlin) at 1,636, with a combined circulation of twenty and a half million copies. A 1963 survey fixes the number of *daily* West German newspapers at 1,418, with only 185 of these actually maintaining news gathering staffs. Walter J. Schütz, "Wettbewerbsbedingungen und Konzentrationstendenzen der deutschen Tageszeitungen, Ergebnisse pressestatistischer Strukturuntersuchungen," in

the most widely circulated and prestigious daily newspapers
in West Germany (including West Berlin) to serve as a
meaningful index of the editorial responses of an important
segment of the press community.[28]

In Table I the newspapers constituting our sample have
been distributed among three categories: critical, sympathetic,
and unclassifiable. In the first of these categories we have
placed the twenty-one newspapers which in editorials and
reportorial commentaries between October 27 and October
31, 1962, seemed so preoccupied with either alleged procedural or substantive defects in the October 26 action against
Der Spiegel as to convey the preponderant impression of an
essentially hostile or critical attitude toward the public authorities for their undertaking against the magazine and its staff.[29]
In the second category are the six newspapers in our sample
which, in their editorials and reportorial commentaries during

Publizistik, Festschrift für Edgar Stern-Rubarth (Bremen, 1963), 363–79.
Using Schütz's findings, one observer concluded that "whoever wanted to
know in 1964 what the general press actually had to say about political
matters, he had at his disposal and for his orientation 185 papers." Man-
fred Kötterheinrich, "Die Konzentration in der deutschen Presse," in
Harry Pross (ed.), *Deutsche Presse seit 1945* (Bern, München, Wien,
1965), 78.

[28] For an attempt to evaluate the prestige and political importance of
the West German newspapers, see Günther Gillessen, "Die Tageszeitung,"
in Pross, *ibid.*, 119–34; Davison, *ibid.*, 244–51; and Karl D. Deutsch and
Lewis J. Edinger, *Germany Rejoins the Powers* (Stanford, 1959), 111–23.

[29] In determining the editorial positions of the newspapers, both editorials in the formal sense and commentaries by editorial staff writers
have been taken into account. Use of the latter is justified in certain cases
because of the tendency of many German newspapers not to distinguish
clearly between editorials and interpretative news reports. Weekly newspapers and other periodicals have been excluded from the analysis, primarily because their editorial reactions to the *Spiegel* raids appeared after
the period under consideration. This omission is not to deny the role
which they may have played in formulating and reflecting public responses to the events of October 26, 1962. The two most prominent
weekly newspapers in West Germany—*Die Zeit* and *Christ und Welt*
(Stuttgart)—both took essentially what we have termed here a critical
attitude toward the investigation.

this period, present an impression of supporting the public authorities in their action against *Der Spiegel* in spite of whatever indiscretions or miscalculations may have marred the procedures. Under "unclassifiable" we have included the seven newspapers within our sample whose editorial and reportorial responses were of such a nature as to prevent our placing them within either of the two other categories.[30] Each of the categories is broadly drawn and within each of them further refinements could be made.[31] In Table II we have classified the newspapers within each of these three categories in terms of their political orientation. Finally, in Table III, we have profiled the critical newspapers in terms of the asserted reasons for their basic hostility to the *Spiegel* action. Nine specific reasons for criticizing the action were found to be most frequently cited by these newspapers. Indicated by percentages is the extent to which these twenty-one newspapers, as a whole, relied upon each of these complaints in justifying their condemnation of the public authorities.

Table I shows that during the first five days following the October 26 raids a clear majority (61.8 percent) of the sample took an essentially hostile or negative view of the proceedings against *Der Spiegel*. Slightly less than 18 percent of the sample endorsed the actions against the magazine. Among the critical segment of our sample were the three best known and most prestigious West German dailies: the *Frankfurter Allgemeine Zeitung, Die Welt,* and the *Süddeutsche Zeitung.*

Only in a qualified sense does the classification in Table II

---

[30] A few newspapers in the unclassifiable category simply took no editorial position during the initial stage of the affair. Most of the unclassifiable newspapers presented however a type of "balanced" editorial position which could not be classified as either sympathetic or critical.

[31] A refinement particularly could be attempted in discovering the *intensity* of attitude toward the *Spiegel* action. Certain newspapers in our sample were obviously more critical or more sympathetic than others in the same category.

Table I

Classification of Newspapers by Editorial Response to the
Spiegel Action Between October 27 and 31, 1962

Classification	Newspapers*						Percent
Critical	2,	3,	4,	7,	9,	10,	61.8
	11,	12,	14,	17,	18,		
	20,	22,	25,	26,	28,		
	29,	30,	31,	32,	33,		
Sympathetic	1,	5,	6,	13,	15,	34,	17.6
Unclassifiable	8,	16,	19,	21,	23,		20.6
	24,	27,					

* Newspapers as numbered in Appendix II.

demonstrate a correlation between editorial response and political orientation of the newspaper. There appears to be a tentative confirmation of the generalization that the "leftist"-oriented papers, as contrasted with the "rightist"-oriented papers, were more likely to be hostile to the actions against *Der Spiegel*. Thus the three pro-SPD newspapers in our sample were all classifiable as critical; the one nationalist newspaper in our sample was classifiable as sympathetic. Yet between these poles in the "left-right" spectrum, the correlation is less defined. Although a third of the pro-CDU/CSU newspapers were sympathetic with the actions against *Der Spiegel,* more than half (55.6 percent) of this group refrained from developing a clearly classifiable position on the action. Also, the two pro-business newspapers, which cannot by any reasonable definition be regarded as "leftist," took critical positions. Significantly, the majority of the critical newspapers in our sample are independent in their political orientation and include a number of prominent newspapers, such as the *Frankfurter Allgemeine Zeitung,* that had

Table II
Distribution of Table I Categories, by Political Orientation

Political Orientation	Critical Newspapers*	Sympathetic Newspapers*	Unclassifiable Newspapers*	Total Number	Percent of Total Sample
Pro-CDU/CSU	22	1, 6, 15	8, 19, 21, 23, 27,	9	26.5
Pro-SPD	9, 11, 31			3	8.8
Pro-business	10, 12			2	5.8
Nationalist		13		1	2.9
Independent	2, 3, 4, 14, 17, 18, 20, 25, 26, 28, 29, 30, 32, 33	7, 5, 34	16, 24	19	55.9

* As numbered in Appendix II.

generally been supporters of the policies of the Adenauer governments.

What specifically did the critical segment of the sample object to? The nine elements of the action which aroused the most criticism are reproduced in Table III. Taken as a whole, these nine elements suggest that the critical editorial writers were motivated by two primary concerns: (1) procedures were being followed in the *Spiegel* action that might set future precedents jeopardizing the appropriate rights and functions of a free press, and (2) "acceptable" norms for the investigation of suspected violations of law appeared to have been sacrificed in favor of a discriminatory and "politically inspired" investigation of a magazine that had long been a persistent and enterprising critic of the policies and personalities, especially Strauss, of the successive Adenauer governments.

The rights of a free press were clearly uppermost in the thoughts of many editorial writers in the first few days following the *Spiegel* raids. The staging of the raids and the interrogation of suspects in the dead of night suggested a type of insensitivity on the part of the public authorities to the importance of the press in a participatory political system, an insensitivity which certain newspapers argued had broader implications involving the parallel between the timing of the raids and the "midnight" arrests of the Nazi era. The complaint of precensorship, specifically forbidden in Article 5 of the Basic Law, stemmed from reports of the investigator's seizing for examination the master proofs of the forthcoming issue of *Der Spiegel*. The impounding and searching of the archival material in the Hamburg central office seemed to challenge the presumed privileged source of information of a free press. The interruptions of future publication schedules caused by the temporary police occupation of the Hamburg offices and the provisional police monitoring of the internal and external communications systems of the Hamburg offices were interpreted as a type of economic harassment, intention-al or not, that would be financially disastrous for many press media.

But the critical segment of the sample also responded out of an apparent fear that "political" or "personal" considera-tions conditioned both the substance and the procedure of the investigation. This tendency was apparent by October 31, as the government seemed unable to supply the information needed to allay these fears. The complaint that was voiced

TABLE III

Primary Criticisms of the *Spiegel* Action by the
Twenty-One "Critical" Newspapers Between
October 27 and 31, 1962

Percentage of Newspapers Which Cited This Factor

Criticism	
The lapse of two weeks between the publication of the Foertsch article and the *Spiegel* action	52
The alleged attempt by the investigators on the night of October 26 to precensor the forthcoming issue of *Der Spiegel*	39
Prolonged and extensive searching and examining of materials and archival data in the Hamburg office of *Der Spiegel*	39
Confusion and questionable legality surrounding the procedures used in securing the arrest in Spain of Conrad Ahlers	35
Failure of the investigators to effect immediate arrests also against possible collaborators of *Der Spiegel* in positions of public re-sponsibility	35
The ambiguity of legal distinctions between freedom of the press and publication of "state secrets"	26
Staging of the Bonn and Hamburg raids and arrests at night	26
Possibility that Franz Josef Strauss improperly influenced the *Spiegel* investigations	26
Temporary monitoring by public authorities, immediately after the October 26 raids, of telephone and intercom system of *Der Spiegel's* Hamburg offices	22

by the greatest percentage of the critical newspapers—that too much time had elapsed between the appearance of the article and the October 26 action—implied the possibility that the investigation may have been partially intended as a retaliation for the magazine's role in the Fibag Affair. Why, the press complained, had there been a delay both in securing the search and seizure warrants (fifteen days from the time the Foertsch article was published) and in executing the warrants (a delay of three days from the time they were issued). Were the raids timed to coincide with the "acquittal" of Strauss by the Bundestag (on October 25) for his role in the Fibag incident? The seizure in Spain of Ahlers suggested collusion on the part of the Spanish and West German authorities that had little regard for the niceties of legal or international practices, particularly when viewed in the context of the extradition agreement between West Germany and Spain, which precluded the rendition of persons accused of political crimes and treason. And, aside from the strictly legal question in the Ahlers incident, here was additional basis for suspecting that officials in Bonn had intervened in such a manner as to call into question the essential motivation of the *Spiegel* investigation. Both the West German Foreign Office and the Federal Prosecutor's Office denied responsibility for the intervention of the Spanish police in securing Ahlers. By October 31, when it was known that the West German military attaché in Madrid had requested Spanish assistance in locating Ahlers, the critical newspapers were no longer willing to discount the possibility of Strauss's personal involvement in the Ahlers incident.

Aggravating the critical mood of the newspapers were two additional circumstances. The failure of the federal attorneys to bring charges promptly against those within the federal government who may have leaked "military secrets" to *Der Spiegel* strengthened the belief, as time went on, that the investigation was primarily designed to intimidate *Der Spiegel*. Moreover, the confused and contradictory account the press was receiving from the authorities about the various aspects of the investigation compounded the suspicious nature of the whole affair. At best, the official news releases and the statements reflected a poorly coordinated and hastily conceived investigation that bordered on gross incompetence. An even harsher interpretation concluded that the contradictions and omissions in the official news releases hinted at a deliberate attempt to avoid answers to some embarrassing questions.[32] Toward the end of the formative stage, the conviction was growing within the editorial community that one person, Franz Josef Strauss, could solve the riddle posed by these questions and ambiguities.

---

[32] Seifert, *ibid.*, 272–81, examines rather systematically the contradictions and confusion that characterized the official news releases during the first three weeks of the *Spiegel* Affair.

Chapter IV

THE MAKING OF A POLITICAL AFFAIR

The initial public and press reactions to the *Spiegel* action did not alone produce a political affair. The primary effect of these reactions was that of framing tentatively the issues and focusing the attention of both the broad reading public and the political elites on certain questions arising out of the nighttime raids and arrests. Whatever the merits of the initial criticisms and expressions of concern, a prompt, candid, and full explanation of the procedures used in the investigation might have contained the controversy and diverted it from the course which it eventually took. This type of response, however, was not immediately forthcoming from the public authorities, and by early November the primary participants in the national political system found themselves on the threshold of a rapidly escalating political crisis.

Both the SPD and the FDP played key roles in converting the *Spiegel* controversy into a major political affair. Although both parties invoked, to a limited extent, ideological and constitutional principles in ultimately justifying their responses, tactical considerations figured prominently in the calculations determining their responses. Tactically, the FDP found itself in a particularly complex situation; its position therefore was neither as predictable nor as consistent as that of the SPD.

The Party in Opposition: The SPD

After the occupation authorities had permitted the formation of political parties on a local and zonal level, remnants of the pre-1933 SPD leadership took up the task of reconstructing their organization and renewing contacts with their traditional sources of primary support: the industrial workers and certain strata of the public employees, salaried employees, and intellectuals. However, the revived SPD failed in 1949 to secure a majority of seats in the Bundestag. Striking a bargain with the non-Socialist parties, Konrad Adenauer, who was elected chancellor by a margin of one vote, formed a coalition government consisting of his own party (CDU/CSU), the FDP, and the German Party (DP).

Until his death in 1952 Kurt Schumacher plotted a vigorous and frequently uncompromising course of opposition for the SPD *Fraktion* in the Bundestag. The respected, but colorless, Erich Ollenhauer succeeded in 1952 to the parliamentary leadership of the SPD and under his guidance emerged the beginnings of a shift in both tactics and policies of the party in the hope of attracting a broader and more diversified electoral support. But before the shift took its full course, the party frequently found itself in support of policies which seemed to many West Germans wholly unrealistic and ill suited to postwar developments. It was not until late in the 1950's, climaxed by the adoption in 1959 of the Godesberg Program, that the SPD, striving toward a *Volkspartei* image, became reconciled to West German rearmament, military alliance with the West, and the social market economy policies of the successive Adenauer governments.[1]

[1] However, the SPD's endorsement in 1959 of these policies must be viewed in context of the qualifications also stipulated in the Godesberg Program. See Vorstand der Sozialdemokratische Partei Deutschlands, *Grundsatz Programm der SPD* (Köln, 1959), especially at p. 12 on armaments, p. 14 on private initiative and market competition, and p. 24 on regional alliances. As early as 1952 the traditional SPD emphasis on

In attempting in recent years to broaden its electoral base the SPD has been partially a victim of its heritage and traditions. In spite of its abandonment of rigid Marxist formulae for interpreting contemporary problems, the belief persists for many West German voters of an older generation that the SPD is the old party simply flying under new colors. To devout West German Catholics, particularly women, it is still the party of anti-clericalism and agnosticism. For many conservative farmers, self-employed artisans, and landowners (all members of the politically important *Mittelstand*), it remains the party of socialism and industrial proletarianism. And to the more traditionalist-inclined segment of the West German electorate, the SPD is tainted by an ideological heritage "alien" to the German culture. Whether any of these images is correct is beside the point; historically there is just enough basis for so viewing the party that whatever the SPD now claims to be its program and however the SPD leadership conducts itself, it will continue to have the problem of competing with the aggregative and pragmatically-oriented CDU/CSU for the support at the national level of the marginal voters and middle-class electorate.

Nevertheless, although between 1949 and 1962 the SPD had failed to realize its goal of forming a national government in post-World War II West Germany, it steadily improved its popular vote and its proportion of seats in the Bundestag. In the most recent election (1961) prior to the *Spiegel* Affair, the SPD for the first time in the postwar period broke through the "35 percent barrier" by polling slightly more than 36

---

economic planning and state controls was weakened in favor of combining economic planning with private ownership; in 1954 the SPD's *Aktionsprogramm* coined the phrase "As much competition as possible, as much planning as necessary." The phrase is repeated in the Godesberg Program. For the 1952 and 1954 policy statements of the SPD, see Ossip K. Flechtheim (ed.), *Dokumente zur parteipolitischen Entwicklung in Deutschland seit 1945* (Berlin, 1963), Vol. III, 64–86 and 93–105.

percent of the popular vote and securing 190 of the 499 seats with voting rights in the Bundestag.

If the *Spiegel* Affair had erupted just prior to a Bundestag election, the electoral mileage to be gained by the party from exploiting the government's embarrassment as a result of the controversy might have been maximized. However, from the SPD perspective the *Spiegel* Affair was not entirely timed to its advantage. As a result of the difficult coalition negotiations in 1961 between the FDP and the CDU/CSU, Adenauer had vaguely agreed to resign the chancellorship prior to the next regular Bundestag election. But the anticipated interim transferral of leadership was expected to occur within the internal processes of the CDU/CSU and without the need for an intervening Bundestag election. The next Bundestag election required by the four-year limitation fixed in the Basic Law would not occur before 1965. However, two important *Land* parliamentary elections were in the offing shortly after the outbreak of the *Spiegel* Affair. The *Landtag* election in Hesse was scheduled for November 10, 1962; the Bavarian *Landtag* election was to occur on November 25, 1962. Riding a crest of rising electoral support since 1961 in all *Landtag* elections,[2] the SPD leaders could not ignore the implications of the *Spiegel* controversy for these two elections. And, whether the initial response of the SPD is viewed in terms of partisan motives or principled indignation at apparent violations of democratic and constitutional norms, there was never any doubt that the SPD leadership, as spokesmen for the opposition in the Bundestag, understood that they would have to engage themselves and their parliamentary *Fraktion* in the *Spiegel* Affair.

If the SPD leaders initially reacted more slowly than certain of their followers would have liked, it was partly due

[2] Lowell W. Culver. "Land Elections in West German Politics," *Western Political Quarterly,* (XIX) (June, 1966), 304–36.

to the complexity of formulating a policy. Aside from the procedural problem that arises when a major political party must activate quickly its decision processes to formulate a position on a major and unexpected crisis, a number of other factors cautioned against too hasty a response. First, the significant press hostility to the *Spiegel* action did not necessarily reflect a correspondingly high degree of public hostility toward the action. Systematic opinion polls had not yet been taken and could not be expected for several weeks, nor could the various student demonstrations and protests from other groups be accepted as firm evidence of an overwhelming popular repudiation of the *Spiegel* action. Second, the objective facts about the action were still surrounded with ambiguity. The SPD leadership could not be certain, in spite of extensive newspaper coverage, just what had happened that might properly be exposed to criticism. The party had devoted too much attention to cultivating an image of "responsibility" and "moderation" to embrace uncritically the charges being levied against the government and Strauss by the newspapers. It was especially important, or so the SPD leadership reasoned, that the party not rush headlong into a defense of *Der Spiegel* at the risk of appearing to condone treasonable publication of state secrets. The Social Democrats, in short, did not wish to adopt a course of action that might later be turned against them and give credence to the long-standing accusation by the rightists that the Socialists were insensitive to German national interests. Finally, the well-established *Legalitätsprinzip,* the principle that criminal investigations are nonpolitical and nondiscretionary responsibilities of juridical authorities (examining judges and state attorneys), implied considerable immunity for the investigators from attacks or criticisms by political parties.[3] This principle suggested

[3] Although well established, the legality principle in German law is also ambiguous. It presumably means that, except for a few designated

to the SPD leaders that in formulating their response they (1) clearly distinguish between the "political" and "nonpolitical" agencies involved in the *Spiegel* action and (2) withhold any criticism of the "nonpolitical" agencies and officials until—and only then—the latter were definitely shown to have violated their trust.

The first reactions to the *Spiegel* action were expressed not by the party leadership collectively but, individually, by SPD Bundestag deputies. On Saturday, October 27, Fritz Sänger, a leading SPD spokesman in the Bundestag for the press, lodged a protest by phone with the Federal Prosecutor's Office that the criminal police and investigators were illegally restricting the freedom of the press by interfering in Hamburg with the efforts of private citizens to contact the *Spiegel* offices.[4] On the same day, Herbert Wehner, the controversial deputy chairman of the SPD Bundestag *Fraktion* and former (1927–42) member of the German Communist Party, issued a statement in which he complained of the methods being used in the action and chided the authorities by suggesting that if, as alleged, *Der Spiegel* was guilty of so grave a crime as treason, one might have expected the investigators to move with equal vigor against the informants within the government.[5] The protests from Sänger and Wehner were immediately taken up by a third SPD Bundestag deputy, Ulrich Lohmar, who had served since 1954 as the chief editor of

---

instances, all offenses require prosecution by the public attorneys. *Strafprozessordnung vom 12 September 1950, Bundesgesetzblatt 455* (and subsequent amendments), Paragraph 152, Section 2. Does this also mean, however, that the public attorneys have no obligation to consult with or permit themselves to be advised by the Minister of Justice in cases of obvious political importance? Paragraph 147 of the *Gerichtsverfassungsgesetz* stipulates that the Minister of Justice has "the right of supervision (Aufsicht) and direction (Leitung) . . . concerning the Federal Prosecutor's Office and the Federal Attorneys." *Gerichtsverfassungsgesetz vom 20 September 1950, 1949–50 Bundesgesetzblatt, 528.*

[4] *Welt am Sonntag* (Hamburg), October 28, 1962.
[5] *Deutsche Zeitung* (Cologne), October 29, 1962.

his party's journal, *Die Neue Gesellschaft*.[6] Lohmar called for a prompt meeting of the Bundestag standing committee on cultural and informational policy, of which he was deputy chairman. Lohmar's suggestion was rejected by the Christian Democratic committee chairman, Berthold Martin, on the ground that under the Bundestag rules of procedure such a special meeting could not be called without the initiative of the presiding officer of the Bundestag.[7]

The first official response of the SPD indicated its difficulty in determining specifically upon what its attack should focus. Four points were stressed in the party statement. (1) The case obviously had implications for freedom of the press and it was not simply, as CDU executive secretary Dufhues argued, a matter concerning one organ of the press; (2) All the available evidence pointed to a failure by the authorities to have given proper advance notice to the appropriate *Land* agencies of the use of federal police within the jurisdiction of the *Länder;* (3) The extensive search of *Der Spiegel's* archives appeared to be taking the form of an illegal search and seizure of material irrelevant to the specific cause of the accusation; and (4) The arrest in Spain of Ahlers required clarification. The SPD statement commented: "One might ask whether there exists an old camaraderie between the commando offices of Franco Spain and those of the Federal Republic."[8]

The developing dispute between the Hamburg and North Rhine-Westphalia *Land* governments, on the one hand, and the federal government, on the other hand, as to whether the

---

[6] *Ibid.*

[7] The Standing Orders of the Bundestag provide that "The [standing] committees may only deal with matters assigned to them, except insofar as these Standing Orders or a resolution of the Bundestag makes other provisions for particular committees." *Geschäftsordnung des Deutschen Bundestages, Bundesgesetzblatt 1952* II, p. 389, as amended BGBl. II, p. 1048 (1955) and BGBl. I, p. 1 (1961).

[8] *SPD Pressedienst,* October 29, 1962, P/XVII/219.

former had been properly notified in advance of the use of federal criminal police within their jurisdictions was seized upon by the SPD *Land* organizations. On October 29, for example, the SPD delegation in the North Rhine-Westphalia *Landtag* moved that the *Land* Interior Minister (Weyer, FDP) report within two days to the *Landtag* Committee for Internal Administration on the background of the police raids conducted on October 26 against the Bonn office of *Der Spiegel*.[9] The issue concerned the presumption expressed in the federal statute creating the Federal Criminal Office that, as a rule, criminal investigations arising under either *Land* or federal law were under the jurisdiction of *Land* authorities. The federal criminal police could be employed in criminal investigations within a *Land* only if the competent *Land* authorities (the *Land* Interior Ministers) so request or if the Federal Interior Minister, for "overriding considerations," orders them into the *Land*. If the Federal Interior Minister on his own initiative directs the federal police to undertake an investigation in a *Land*, he is obligated to inform "without delay" the *Land* Interior Ministers.[10] In the case of Hamburg, the appropriate authority, Interior Minister (Senator) Helmut Schmidt, was informed about thirty minutes in advance of the police raids on the Hamburg offices of *Der Spiegel*. In North Rhine-Westphalia the *Land* Interior Minister was not personally contacted prior to the Bonn raid. There the State Secretary, subordinate of the Minister, of the Interior Ministry was contacted a few minutes before the Bonn action was started. The procedure used by the Federal Interior Ministry vis-à-vis the North Rhine-Westphalia Interior Ministry looked particularly suspicious and politically inspired, since the State Secretary, Ludwig Adenauer (a nephew of the chan-

---

[9] *Die Welt*, October 30, 1962.

[10] *Gesetz über die Einrichtung eines Bundeskriminalpolizeiamtes (Bundeskriminalamtes), Bundesgesetzblatt I (1951)*. 165, paragraph 3.

cellor), was a member of the CDU while his uninformed superior, Weyer, was a member of the FDP.

The difficulties confronting the SPD at the national level in devising the most effective strategy for exploring the many questions about the *Spiegel* Affair were apparent by October 29. On that day, after a meeting of the SPD Presidium, it was announced that the party would request an immediate parliamentary investigation with a focus on the legality of the methods used in the actions against *Der Spiegel*.[11] Certain problems, however, were connected with the use of this technique and several of them had been revealed during the Fibag Affair. A parliamentary inquiry is slow; more than that, it is controlled by the majority coalition. If the FDP and the CDU/CSU remained united, as they had during the production of both the first and second reports of the Fibag Committee, the chances of getting an exhaustive inquiry into the *Spiegel* Affair were remote. At this point there was no reason to expect that the FDP would act differently than it had during the Fibag investigation. Another problem was presented, however, by the use of a parliamentary inquiry. Hints were now being circulated in Bonn that *Der Spiegel's* informants included members of the SPD Bundestag *Fraktion*.[12] Whatever the validity of these rumors—and at this point the SPD leadership had not checked out the accuracy of them—the

[11] Instead of calling for the formation of a special committee of inquiry, the SPD Presidium proposed that the Standing Committee on Law conduct the investigation. *SPD Pressemitteilungen und Informationen,* October 29, 1962, No. 292/62.

[12] SPD deputy Gerhard Jahn, executive secretary of the SPD Bundestag *Fraktion,* was one of the deputies rumored to have turned over classified information to *Der Spiegel.* In a radio interview on November 1, 1962, Jahn replied: "To the charges which have been raised against me I declare: I have betrayed no state secrets. I therefore have no reason to restrict in any way or to abandon my obligations which I have undertaken for the next few days in my constituency and in the Hesse *Landtag* campaign." *BPA Abt. Nachrichten, Rundfunkaufnahme, Deutsche Gruppe West, Hessischer RF II/1.11.62/1915/vt.*

party wished to avoid giving the government the opportunity of diverting attention from its own embarrassment by focusing on the possible involvement of SPD deputies in the preparation of the Foertsch article. In any event, the SPD Presidium's decision on October 29 to ask for a parliamentary inquiry, using either a special committee or an appropriate standing committee, was soon reversed. Instead, the SPD Bundestag *Fraktion,* upon the urging of *Fraktion* chairman Fritz Erler, decided first to use the technique of the Question Hour and to hold in abeyance the inquiry committee technique. This decision was announced on November 4.[13] Karl Mommer, executive secretary of the SPD Bundestag delegation, added that eighteen questions were to be immediately placed before the chamber.

Challenge and Response: The FDP

Forged out of an alignment among various "liberal" *Land* parties which were created during the period 1945–48 within the Western occupied zones, the Free Democrats have prided themselves on their refusal to insist upon doctrinal conformity, and the relatively diffuse decision authority within the FDP is reflective of the lack of a cohesive body of dogma to which the party's leadership elites are committed.

If the FDP has a generally accepted body of principles, it tends to cluster around two related, but not always compatible, traditions of libertarianism and economic neoliberalism. As advocates of libertarianism the Free Democrats have stressed such goals or values as individual responsibility, freedom of expression, religious toleration, anti-clericalism, separation of church and state (particularly in the public school system), and national unity in preference to the excessive particularistic tendencies best represented by the Bavarian

[13] *BPA Abt. Nachrichten, Rundfunkaufnahme, Deutsche Gruppe West, Deutschlandfunk /5.11.62/1900/vt. Anhang VIII (Fernsehen).*

Catholics. But it is the party's economic neoliberalism which has shaped many of its most persistent and distinguishing policy goals over the past few years and which has accurately identified the party as somewhat to the right of the CDU/CSU on the political spectrum. From its neoliberal economic perspective, for example, the FDP has derived, or at least rationalized, its emphasis on the free market system, anti-cartelism, "sound" (counterinflationary) fiscal and monetary policies, the profit incentives, a tax system which encourages private capital formation and investment, restraint in the expansion of the social welfare system, private property rights, and the maintenance of managerial prerogatives against the demands of organized labor for the right of codetermination *(Mitbestimmung)* in the making of decisions within the private and public sectors of the economy.[14]

The libertarian strain in the party's orientation was personified by the late Theodor Heuss, the first national chairman of the FDP. With his election in 1949 as the president of the Federal Republic and his removal from partisan political activity, there passed from the leadership ranks of the FDP a personality who, through the combination of intellect, experience, and prestige, might have provided the party a unifying national leadership around the humanistic goals of German liberalism. Following the elevation of Heuss to the federal presidency, the FDP was led nationally by a succession of personalities, such as Franz Blücher, Thomas Dehler, Reinhold Meier, and, more recently, Erich Mende—all of whom have had a difficult task of attempting to reconcile the party's libertarian views with its conservative economic persuasism.

If the libertarianism of the FDP found its strongest support

[14] Cf. Gerard Braunthal, "The Free Democratic Party in West German Politics," *Western Political Quarterly,* XIII (June, 1960), 332–48. See Flechtheim, *Dokumente,* III, for the official pronouncements of the FDP on policy questions.

in Protestant south Germany, especially in Baden-Württemberg, and in the city-state of Hamburg, the economic conservatism of the party has appealed most strongly to the business, professional, and middle-class groups clustered in North Rhine-Westphalia and Hesse. And it has been to the business community of these areas that the FDP has looked for the important financial contributions upon which the party is dependent if it is to wage a vigorous national campaign for seats in the Bundestag.

Central to an understanding of the behavior of various groups within the FDP during the Adenauer era was their impatience with the Adenauer policy of "inflexibility" toward the East both in trade relations and in seeking a basis for negotiating with the Soviet Union a reunification of the two Germanies. This tendency within the FDP groups is sometimes interpreted as a revival of irresponsible nationalism. This charge against the FDP is exaggerated and oversimplifies a complex problem which any political party in West Germany cannot neglect. Indeed, a persistent theme of nineteenth-century German liberalism, manifesting itself in the abortive attempts during 1848–49 to have incorporated into the German political system a greater recognition of popular accountability and individual rights, has been that of national unity—it being assumed that only in a unified state could the liberal goals be securely anchored. Moreover, within the more recent context of the postwar division of Germany, no party in the Federal Republic can ignore the natural, if passive, longings of the West Germans for a reunified state. However, what has been disturbing to many observers, both foreign and domestic, has been the periodic succumbing of the FDP to the temptation of framing its nationalistic program in terms reminiscent of the more intemperate and adventuresome demands of "rightist" groups of the Weimar era. Thus, in its attempt to enlarge its electoral support, the FDP has been particularly responsive to the interests of certain rightist elements who occasionally seem inclined to place such stress on the restoration of German unity as to discount the democratic and liberal values crucial to the give and take of the parliamentary system. And as a practical matter, the Free Democrats must try to attract voters away from minor rightist parties, which are particularly reluctant to abandon Germany's claims to territories east of the Oder-Neisse line. In their more strident form, these nationalistic overtones of the FDP's program found their strongest geographical support in Lower Saxony.

In 1949 the CDU/CSU and the SPD together received 60 percent of the total vote cast in the Bundestag election; by 1957 their combined share of the electorate had grown to 82 percent. Because of this bipolarization tendency and confronted as the FDP has been with internal divisions, speculation persists that the days of the FDP as a party of representation in the Bundestag are numbered. But the FDP managed to survive during the Adenauer era, thanks to the principle of proportionality embodied in the electoral system. Although in 1961 the party did "abnormally" well, receiving 13 percent of the votes and 67 seats in the Bundestag, the aggregative character of the CDU/CSU and the efforts of the SPD to develop an appeal broadly among the electorate constantly threatened to submerge the programmatic identity of the FDP. As a result, the Free Democrats stressed the *functional* contribution which their party could make as the "third force" in West German politics.

Central to the third force idea is the assumption that a party and electoral system which allows a single party to have majority control of the Bundestag is ill suited to parliamentary democracy in the Federal Republic. To those who question this assumption by pointing to the example of the British system, the FDP responds that the political culture in West

Germany has not sufficiently matured for the reception of the British model. Thus, the inner checks and conventional restraints which constitutionalize and limit the power of the majority party in the British setting, it is argued, are not securely anchored in the West German environment. Only through an arrangement in which the FDP can serve as the "balance wheel," as a coalition partner, can restraints and moderation be imposed upon the dominant party and the government.[15]

If the FDP is to implement the third force idea, it must overcome a number of formidable problems. The starting point is to try to preserve the existing electoral system of proportional representation. Then, second, the party must win at least 5 percent of the popular vote in the Bundestag election to qualify for its proportionate share of the seats.[16] Third, it must frame an electoral appeal that will cut into the votes which either of the two major parties might otherwise obtain, for the third force idea assumes that no single party will have an effective majority of the Bundestag seats. Finally, to

[15] The third force idea is developed in Karl-Hermann Flach, *Dritte Kraft, der Kampf gegen den Machtmisbrauch in der Demokratie* (Bonn, 1957). Cf. also Uwe W. Kitzinger, *German Electoral Politics* (London, 1960), 151–69.

[16] Although the system used in electing delegates to the Bundestag is sometimes described as a mixed system of proportional representation and plurality vote, it is in fact a genuine system of proportional representation. Within the proportionality arrangement, half (since 1953) of the Bundestag membership was selected in single-member constituencies by plurality vote, the remaining half of the membership was drawn from *Land* lists. The point is that the total representation of each party in the Bundestag was proportionate to its popular vote won on the *Land* lists or second ballot. However, no party could share in the distribution of of seats in the Bundestag unless it won three single-member constituency seats or 5 percent of the votes cast throughout West Germany on the second or party list ballots. Since the FDP was unable to win any single-member constituencies, the 5 percent barrier was the one that had to be overcome by the party if it was to qualify for representation in the Bundestag. A reliable explanation of the electoral system, as used in the 1957 Bundestag election, is found in Kitzinger, *German Electoral Politics,* 17–37.

strengthen its bargaining power in forming the coalition the FDP must also be sensitive to the electoral appeal of other minor parties and in its electoral strategy attempt to prevent a rival minor party, as an alternative coalition partner, from winning seats in the Bundestag.[17]

Even if these conditions were met, the area of maneuverability open to the Free Democrats in negotiating the terms of the coalition was restricted by the probability that in choosing between the two major parties the Free Democrats would have to opt for the Christian Democrats. Although the SPD, from time to time, coalesced with the FDP in forming various *Land* governments, the SPD had been reluctant to make the kind of concessions to the FDP that would permit an SPD-FDP coalition at the national level. In addition, the economic liberalism of the FDP and the financial dependency of the FDP upon business contributions made it difficult for the FDP to be a party to an arrangement that would allow the Socialists to be the dominant partner in a national government.[18]

The probability that the Free Democrats would have to opt for the CDU/CSU had certain implications for the FDP's

[17] Thus arises one of the many dilemmas for the FDP: how far should it go in attempting to counter the electoral appeal of the rightist minor parties, in advocating the policies and embracing the slogans of nationalist elements? The emergence in 1964 of the National Democratic Party (NPD), its apparent success, at least temporarily, in bringing together into a single party the remnants of the far right in West German politics, and the successes of the NPD in *Land* elections in 1966 in winning 7 to 8 percent of the popular votes (e.g., in Hesse and Bavaria) suggest that the Free Democrats may not be successful in the future in preventing additional minor parties from securing representation in the Bundestag. In competing against such minor rightist parties, the FDP may be placed under additional pressure to emphasize the theme of reunification and national unity.

[18] On the financing of the West German parties, including the FDP, see Ulrich Dübber, *Parteifinanzierung in Deutschland* (Köln and Opladen, 1962), and Ulrich Dübber and Gerard Braunthal, "West Germany," in Richard Rose and Arnold J. Heidenheimer (eds.). *Comparative Political Finance,* special issue of *Journal of Politics,* XXV, (1963), 774–89.

electoral and coalition strategy. Why vote for the FDP if in fact it merely supplies the additional margin of votes necessary to ratify CDU/CSU proposals? To avoid this "deadly embrace," the Free Democrats would have to insist upon a coalition relationship in which they received from the CDU/CSU genuine concessions in both ministerial assignments and policy questions. This paradoxical position, that of maintaining a separate identity within a framework of dependency on the larger coalition party, more than once erupted into open warfare between the CDU/CSU and the FDP.

The most dramatic example of the uneasy alliance between the two groups, prior to the cabinet crisis induced by the *Spiegel* Affair, is found in the "Düsseldorf Revolt" of early 1956 in which the FDP withdrew from the *Land* coalition government in North Rhine-Westphalia, forcing the CDU to become the opposition party in the *Land* while the FDP then aligned with the SPD to form a new government. Although the incident occurred at the *Land* level, the causes of the split developed out of the dissatisfaction among FDP elements with the refusal of Adenauer to favor a relaxation of West Germany's trade restrictions with Eastern Europe and Adenauer's decision—which he later reversed—to support the French plan to place the Saar under international control. The breach was widened by Adenauer's periodic threats to seek a revision in the electoral system which, if effected, would have eliminated the FDP from future representation in the Bundestag.[19]

[19] On the probable effects of a purely single-member, plurality vote system on the Bundestag representation of the FDP, see Michael Steed and Nermin Abadan, "Four Elections of 1965," *Government and Opposition,* I (May, 1966), 321–23. As early as 1953 the CDU announced its support of the single-member, plurality electoral system for determining representation in the Bundestag. See the *Hamburger Programm vom 22. April 1953,* in Flechtheim, *Dokumente,* II. 95. By 1967 the SPD was reportedly prepared to join with the CDU/CSU to convert the electoral system into a single-member system, comparable to that used

Out of the 1956 Düsseldorf Revolt emerged a new leader-ship cadre which directed the FDP's campaign in the 1957 Bundestag election. These "Young Turks" included Wolf-gang Döring, who would play a key role in devising the FDP strategy during the *Spiegel* Affair. But as a result of the 1957 election the FDP was temporarily isolated from the national government, formed out of a coalition of the CDU/CSU, which had won an absolute majority of the seats, and the relatively insignificant German Party. In formal opposition to the government between 1957 and 1961, the FDP Bundestag *Fraktion* enjoyed greater freedom in criticizing Adenauer's policies, but its role as a third force was nullified.

During the 1961 Bundestag election campaign the FDP returned to a strategy of the third force.[20] Under the chairmanship of Erich Mende, the FDP promised to enter a national coalition with the CDU/CSU, assuming "appropriate" concessions were made in negotiating the terms of the coalition. Among these concessions was that Konrad Adenauer retire from the chancellorship. The *ohne Adenauer* (without Adenauer) strategy was motivated by a prevailing mood within the FDP that he was too inflexible in his policies toward the East and that, in general, he could not be trusted to abide by any agreement into which the CDU/CSU entered with the FDP in the formation of a coalition government. But such a move was also premised on the hope that the FDP could capitalize upon the Chancellor's declining prestige by attracting votes from former CDU/CSU supporters who, while agreeing with the economic policies of the Adenauer

in Britain. However, the SPD appeared unlikely to approve the proposal unless its going into effect were delayed until 1973.

[20] See Bernhard Vogel and Peter Haungs, *Wahlkampf und Wähler-tradition, Eine Studie zur Bundestagswahl von 1961* (Köln and Opladen, 1965), 325–28; and Samuel H. Barnes *et al.,* "The German Party System and the 1961 Federal Elections," *American Political Science Review,* LVI (December, 1962), 899–914.

government, were becoming dissatisfied with Adenauer's leadership, particularly in foreign policy. To some extent the FDP campaign strategy succeeded, with an unexpected assist from Adenauer's hesitant reaction to the Berlin Wall crisis of August, 1961. Its 1961 resurgence of strength in the Bundestag, plus the elimination both of all other minor parties from the Bundestag and of the absolute majority of the CDU/CSU, seemed to have vindicated the FDP's emphasis on the third force notion.

During the protracted negotiations in the fall of 1961 over the formation of a new government, however, the FDP was outmaneuvered by Adenauer.[21] He quickly isolated the opposition to him within his own party and won the support of the overwhelming majority of his party's *Fraktion* for the chancellorship. After complex negotiations, during which both parties made halfhearted overtures to the SPD, the FDP capitulated by accepting Adenauer as his own successor. Adenauer promised, without fixing a precise date, to retire sometime prior to the next (1965) Bundestag election. The FDP was assured by the CDU/CSU that it would make no effort to modify during the life of the coalition government the principle of proportionality in the system for electing Bundestag deputies.

It is against the background of these events that one must consider the role of the FDP during both the formative and bargaining stages of the *Spiegel* Affair. Although several *Land* organizations of the FDP immediately voiced complaint against federal authorities for an apparent failure to follow proper administrative procedures in alerting the Hamburg and North Rhine-Westphalia governments of the impending use of federal police in carrying out the raids in

[21] Peter Merkl, "Equilibrium, Structure of Interests and Leadership: Adenauer's Survival as Chancellor," *American Political Science Review,* LVI (September, 1962), 634–50.

Hamburg and Bonn, the national leaders of the FDP seemed uncertain at the outset about the response they should make to the *Spiegel* investigation.[22] While they were not insensitive to the complaints, they also recognized that as coalition partners in the national government they were not entirely free to criticize the action. The Cuban missile crisis, still potentially dangerous, warned against any unnecessary disruption in the national coalition, and the various doctrinal strands represented within the FDP's leadership group also caused initial disunity in formulating a position. While the libertarians were disturbed by what appeared to be violations of individual and press freedoms, the more conservative elements within the FDP were concerned by apparent leaks in the security system of the federal government and did not wish to be cast in the role of defending traitors.[23] Finally,

[22] On October 28, 1962, Willi Weyer (FDP), Interior Minister and Deputy Premier-President of North Rhine-Westphalia, formally asked Federal Interior Minister Hermann Höcherl (CSU) to explain fully to all *Land* interior ministers the reasons for the apparent violation of accepted norms of administrative relations between the federal and *Land* levels in the enforcement of federal criminal law. (*Hamburger Echo,* October 29, 1962) Höcherl replied that he was in no position to reveal the particulars of the methods employed in the *Spiegel* raids. This position was rather astounding in light of the fact that the Security Group of the Federal Criminal Office, which assisted in the Hamburg raids and arrests, is under the supervisory jurisdiction of Höcherl's ministry. Alfred Frankenfeld, chairman of the FDP *Fraktion* in the Hamburg Assembly *(Bürgerschaft),* announced on October 29 that in behalf of his *Fraktion* in Hamburg he was urging the FDP Bundestag *Fraktion* to reconsider its earlier support for the government-sponsored emergency laws. (*Frankfurter Allgemeine Zeitung,* October 30, 1962) Frankenfeld also revealed that as leader of the FDP group in the Hamburg Assembly he planned to submit on November 7, 1962, a set of parliamentary questions to elicit from the Hamburg *Land* government information on the propriety of Hamburg's involvement in the *Spiegel* raids. From Hesse also came word that its FDP *Land* organization was displeased with the manner in which the *Spiegel* investigation has been handled. (*Frankfurter Rundschau,* October 29, 1962)

[23] FDP Bundestag deputy Oswald Kohut from Hesse wired Stammberger: "Our supporters have not elected us in order to permit the introduction of conditions in the Federal Republic which when the CDU/

the FDP's leaders, particularly national chairman Erich Mende, were sensitive to the criticism that the party was opportunistic and unprincipled. An ill-considered and hasty condemnation of the handling of the investigation might easily be interpreted as an irresponsible act, designed more to firm up the Free Democrats' position within the coalition government than to clarify the controversy. The key to the FDP response to the *Spiegel* investigation was provided by Federal Minister of Justice, Wolfgang Stammberger, one of five FDP members of the coalition cabinet.

The relationship between the Federal Prosecutor's Office and the Federal Ministry of Justice is governed by the general premise that the investigation of suspected violations of federal law is a nondiscretionary and nonpolitical function, immune from binding instructions from the "political" executive, the government. It is thus not the responsibility of the Minister of Justice to initiate investigations of federal crimes. This role is assigned to the state's attorneys, within each *Land,* and to the Federal Prosecutor's Office in cases of such suspected federal crimes as treason. The public attorneys, in turn, are to work closely with the examining judges of the appropriate courts in securing the warrants necessary for implementing an investigation.[24]

Nevertheless, the Justice Ministry has a quasi-supervisory relationship with the Federal Prosecutor's Office. The director of the Federal Prosecutor's Office *(Generalbundesanwalt)* is appointed by the President of the Federal Republic upon the recommendation of the Minister of Justice. The *Generalbundesanwalt* may also be dismissed for legal cause by the President of the Federal Republic, upon the recommendation

---

CSU had an absolute majority were not possible." (*Frankfurter Rundschau,* October 29, 1962)

[24] *Strafprozessordnung vom 12 September 1950, Bundesgesetzblatt 455,* paragraphs 36, 98, and 152.

of the Chancellor and Justice Minister. The Ministry of
Justice is authorized to "recommend" to the Federal Prosecutor's Office the need for a particular investigation, although
the final decision to initiate the investigation remains with
the attorneys. Finally, the relevant statute (*Gerichtsverfassungsgesetz,* paragraph 147) explicitly obligates the Federal
Prosecutor's Office to advise the Federal Ministry of Justice
of investigations that have "a particular public importance."[25]

Minister of Justice Stammberger had gone to Munich on
October 26 to address a group of Bavarian lawyers on the
need for reform in the German penal code. On Saturday
morning, while eating breakfast in a Munich hotel, he learned
from the newspapers of the police actions of the previous
evening against *Der Spiegel.* In interviews that day with

[25] Relevant is the following segment of a November 2, 1962, radio
interview with Dr. Max Güde (CDU), who prior to his entry into the
Bundestag served as the director of the Federal Prosecutor's Office:

Interviewer: To what extent is the Federal Prosecuting Attorney
obligated to inform the Justice Minister or Ministry about a contemplated or projected investigation?

Güde: Now I have always taken the position that the Federal
Prosecuting Attorney operates a law office and not a government
agency. Thus I have always been of the opinion that he has the
final authority to issue orders in legal matters. . . . But in questions
of law which have apparent political implications, I believe the
Federal Prosecutor's Office is to inform the Federal Justice Minister,
not for the purpose of involving him in the decision, but to inform
him as to what results he can expect and perhaps in a high policy
matter, in addition, to inform in advance the cabinet.

Interviewer: May I conclude that you believe the *Spiegel* matter is
one of high policy?

Güde: It has obviously become one . . . whether it could have been
foreseen as one I cannot pretend to know . . . if one could have
anticipated it being so, the Justice Minister and cabinet should have
been brought into confidence. . . . *(BPA Abt. Nachrichten—Rundfunkaufnahme, Deutsche Gruppe West—SDR/2.11.62/Lg).*

The reporting obligation of the public attorneys to the justice ministers
is also commented upon in Otto Schwarz and Theodor Kleinknecht,
*Strafprozessordnung, Gerichtsverfassungsgesetz, Nebengesetze und ergän-
zende Bestimmungen, Beck'sche Kurz-Kommentare* (München and Berlin,
1963, 24th edition), Vol. VI, 767.

newspaper reporters he stressed that he had not been informed in advance of the raids and initial arrests.[26] He added however that the investigations were under the sole jurisdiction of the Federal Prosecutor's Office. Instead of returning promptly to Bonn he proceeded from Munich to Stuttgart and spent Saturday evening with relatives. As originally planned, he returned to Bonn on Sunday. The following day he submitted to an interview with a reporter of the Hesse Broadcasting Network. His responses to the questions confirm the impression that, as yet, Stammberger assumed that, in spite of mounting public criticism, neither he nor the FDP had any reason to question the procedures used in the investigation:

Question: Has the Federal Prosecutor's Office received any instructions from you?

Stammberger: No! The Federal Prosecutor's Office is in no way affected by instructions from me, but rather it has the independent responsibility of determining violations of this type. In this particular case, then, I gave no instructions. . . .

Question: There is mention also of active bribery in the charges against *Der Spiegel's* staff. . . . However, one has not heard of any actions yet against officials in the Defense Ministry.

Stammberger: [Because the case is a pending juridical matter]. . . . I am not free to give you any details. But I may say that in any event all those responsible and guilty will be brought to justice, quite irrespective of where or who they are.

Question: Another basic question. [The Federal Prosecutor's Office has said that in many instances it has to examine a wide range of publications to see if state secrets are illegally published.] Is that not a form of precensorship and how is this to be reconciled with the Basic Law?

Stammberger: No, in no sense is that precensorship, but it is quite simply a result of the Federal Prosecutor's Office's duty to seek out violations of this kind. . . .

[26] *Stuttgarter Nachrichten,* October 29, 1962, and *Süddeutsche Zeitung,* October 29, 1962.

Question: . . . In the public media there has been conveyed the unfortunate impression that this action might be a retaliation by the Defense Minister against *Der Spiegel.* Could you comment. . . .

Stammberger: . . . I believe such an impression is unfounded. There is . . . a coincidental conjunction between the action, which was initiated on the authority of juridical decisions, and the termination of the so-called Fibag Affair. But both matters undoubtedly stand separate from each other.[27]

However, by Tuesday, October 30, both the Free Democrats and Stammberger were beginning to feel the heat generated by the *Spiegel* action. Press criticisms were now widely circulating in both West Germany and abroad. Complaints were flowing into Stammberger's office, including those of his party colleagues in the various *Länder.*[28] The FDP *Fraktion* in the Hamburg assembly had already introduced a resolution asking the Hamburg government to explain its role in the police action.[29] *Der Spiegel* announced it was receiving wires

[27] *BPA Abt. Nachrichten, Rundfunkaufnahme, Deutsche Gruppe West, Hessischer RF 29.10.62/1905 Anhang I.*

[28] *Frankfurter Rundschau,* October 29, 1962; *Frankfurter Allgemeine Zeitung,* October 31, 1962; *Der Spiegel,* November 7, 1962, 52.

[29] *Hamburger Abendblatt,* October 30, 1962. Hamburg has traditionally supported a tolerant attitude toward press criticism. Relatively good relations had also existed in Hamburg between the police authorities and the public. Thus the index of chagrin on the part of the Hamburg authorities steadily mounted as the federal government seemed incapable of satisfactorily explaining the manner in which the *Spiegel* raids were carried out in Hamburg. Compounding the strained relations between the Hamburg government and the federal authorities was the continuation in Hamburg of the searching of *Der Spiegel's* offices. Hamburg Mayor Neuermann (SPD) wired Adenauer on November 2: "For more than a week now the still uncharged editorial and publishing offices have been hindered in their work in the most extensive manner. The preparation of the next issues of *Der Spiegel* appears to be jeopardized. I see in this a possible danger of illegally limiting press freedom and therewith a violation of the Basic Law. . . . The last issue of *Der Spiegel* was apparently subjected to precensorship. That would mean a violation also of the Basic Law. . . ." *Die Welt,* November 3, 1962, p. 1. Adenauer replied to Neuermann by warning him that the Hamburg authorities were in danger of interfering with the impartiality of a pending juridical matter.

and letters of sympathy at the rate of two thousand a day.[30] Student demonstrations, initiated at Hamburg University, quickly spread to Frankfurt, Bonn, West Berlin, Munich, and Freiburg.

The FDP was clearly faced with a dilemma. How, and to what extent, could it disassociate itself from the *Spiegel* investigation? An unexpected answer was provided by Stammberger. From both his state secretary, Walter Strauss (unrelated to Franz Josef Strauss), and officials in the Federal Prosecutor's Office he learned on October 30 of several curious circumstances surrounding the investigation. Walter Strauss had been taken into full confidence by the planners of the police action; yet he had not passed on this information to Stammberger. Stammberger had simply learned from a letter dated October 18, that an investigation had been initiated in the Federal Prosecutor's Office. The letter, for still unexplained reasons, did not reach Stammberger's desk until October 24.[31] It did not mention the course of action the attorneys were planning against *Der Spiegel.* Stammberger learned also on October 30 that Walter Strauss had been advised by his counterpart in the Defense Ministry, State Secretary Wolfgang Hopf, to keep the planned police actions in "strictest confidence." Why had Stammberger been kept in the dark about the planned police raids? Who had authorized State Secretary Hopf to advise State Secretary Strauss? Had Hopf specifically warned Walter Strauss against informing Minister Stammberger of the planned action? Was Franz

---

Nevermann responded by terming Adenauer's attitude "grotesque" and by concluding that Adenauer had missed entirely the point of the objections from Hamburg. *Der Tagesspiegel,* November 4, 1962, and *Die Welt,* November 5, 1962.

[30] *Frankfurter Rundschau,* October 31, 1962, and *Kölner Stadt-Anzeiger,* November 5, 1962. The latter reported that by November 4 *Der Spiegel* had received more than thirty thousand letters of support from both West Germany and abroad.

[31] *Der "Spiegel"-Bericht,* 195.

Josef Strauss the central figure in this "conspiracy of silence"? Of what significance was it that Walter Strauss belonged to the CDU?

On October 31 Stammberger was prepared to act, with or without support of his party's colleagues. In a conference that afternoon with FDP Bundestag leaders Stammberger announced that he would ask to be released from his ministerial post, unless the Chancellor supported his effort to explore fully the responsibility for this affront to the authority of the Minister of Justice. Whatever the legal obligations of the Federal Prosecutor's Office *vis-à-vis* the Minister of Justice concerning impending investigations, Stammberger reasoned, a serious transgression had been committed against him as minister by the failure of his state secretary to have kept him informed. With Wolfgang Döring taking the lead in the discussions, Erich Mende and others who had cautioned against disrupting the coalition were finally persuaded that the FDP could not ignore the implications of the Stammberger episode for the coalition relationship. They thus decided not only to support Stammberger in his demands but also to extend them: (1) Stammberger must be retained as Minister of Justice; (2) Stammberger must be permitted to conduct an inquiry into the planning of the *Spiegel* action and to locate the responsibility for his being circumvented by his own state secretary; (3) those "directly responsible" for the circumventing of Stammberger must be brought to "account," regardless of who they are; and (4) the chancellor must provide assurances that in the future the coalition party would be more "fully integrated" in the governmental decisions processes.[32]

Following the FDP conference, Mende contacted Adenauer, advised him of the FDP position, and requested an immediate meeting between the Chancellor and the party's leaders.

[32] *Die Welt*, November 5, 1962, and *Der Spiegel*, November 14, 1962, p. 48.

During the meeting, later that day, Stammberger repeated to the Chancellor his intention to submit his resignation, unless he was supported in an attempt to explore the handling of the *Spiegel* investigation. Mende reminded the Chancellor of the need for mutual confidence between the coalition parties. Adenauer asked for time to consider the Free Democrats' demands. It was decided among the FDP leaders that until Adenauer made his decision, no FDP minister should attend the cabinet meeting which, having recessed earlier that day, reconvened at 7 P.M.

At the evening session of the cabinet, Adenauer, who had made no public statement on the *Spiegel* controversy, committed what must be regarded as a serious tactical error. After indicating to his Christian Democratic colleagues that he anticipated no disruption in the coalition government, he permitted a consideration of the two policy items in which his unrepresented coalition partners were vitally interested— the social welfare proposals and the 1963 budget recommendations. Upon hearing of this brazen affront to the FDP, Mende alerted all members of the FDP national committee and FDP Bundestag deputies that a caucus would be held on November 2 to decide future strategy in the *Spiegel* Affair.

Chapter V

POLITICAL
BARGAINING, I

By November 2, 1962, the *Spiegel* Affair threatened to un-hinge the CDU/CSU-FDP coalition that had been so adroitly constructed by Adenauer in the fall of 1961. As a result of the FDP insistence that Stammberger be retained as Minister of Justice, that Adenauer give assurances the FDP would be more fully integrated into the cabinet decision processes, that Stammberger be permitted to inquire into the handling of the *Spiegel* investigation, and that all persons "directly responsible" for the circumventing of Stammberger be brought to "account," the Chancellor was faced with a dilemma. At the Free Democratic caucus on November 2 it was decided that if the foregoing conditions were not satisfied the FDP would withdraw from the cabinet. The collapse of the FDP-CDU/CSU coalition, assuming that the Free Democrats did not then coalesce with the Social Democrats to replace Adenauer altogether, would deny in the months ahead the certainty of the 67 FDP Bundestag votes badly needed by Adenauer for majority support of his government's policies, and particularly the 1963 budget proposals. On the other hand, a complete capitulation to the FDP terms was personally objectionable to Adenauer and, as a practical matter, might alienate the Strauss-led CSU deputies, whose support Adenauer also re-quired for majority control of the Bundestag. After five days of hectic and sometimes confused political bargaining, a solu-tion seemed to have been found that would both release Adenauer from his dilemma and preserve the coalition.

An Irrelevant Solution

During their discussions immediately prior to their confrontation with Adenauer at the beginning of November, and particularly upon the urging of FDP *Fraktion* deputy chairman Wolfgang Döring that a "hard" line be taken with the Christian Democrats, the FDP leaders agreed that the circumvention of Stammberger represented not only a personal affront to one of their colleagues but also a violation of the spirit of the coalition relationship. Perhaps as persuasive to the FDP leaders, however, was the argument that if the FDP could be so easily ignored by the dominant party of the coalition its claim as the "third force" or "balance wheel" in the Bonn system might be interpreted as farcical by the voters.

Adenauer did not immediately capitulate to the FDP. Although it is a matter which defies tight empirical verification, his strategy during the early days of November seems to have been intertwined with various considerations. A full acquiescence in the conditions stipulated by the Free Democrats implied an admission by Adenauer that serious indiscretions had indeed been committed by politically responsible persons in his government. Adenauer simply did not believe this interpretation to be valid. In preliminary discussions Adenauer informed the FDP leaders that Stammberger was on weak ground in insisting that he should have been informed in advance of the October 26 police action. The Chancellor reasoned that the entire investigation was under the control of the "non-political" organs of the national government, the Federal Prosecutor's Office and the examining judges of the Federal High Court. Neither of these agencies, Adenauer added, was legally bound to consult with or solicit advice from the Justice Minister in instigating criminal proceedings against suspected violaters of federal law. It was also likely that the CSU encouraged Adenauer to resist the FDP demand that Stammberger be allowed to inquire fully into the planning and implementation of the *Spiegel* action. Whatever Strauss's involvement in the action—and at this stage of the Affair perhaps only Strauss and a few of his closest associates knew the particulars—the CSU Bundestag deputies had no intention of exposing unnecessarily their leader to harsh criticisms for his assisting in the apprehension in Spain of a suspected traitor. While Adenauer probably was not prepared to shield Strauss at all costs, he preferred to avoid a course of action that might satisfy the FDP but simultaneously jeopardize the close relationship between the CDU and CSU, which represented a bloc of votes in the Bundestag upon which the Adenauer government depended for a positive majority.

The Chancellor was also personally outraged by the demands of the Free Democrats. At the heart of this indignation was his belief that in fact no serious affronts had been committed against the FDP and that the critics were blinded by trivia as compared with the gravity of the charges against *Der Spiegel*. In light of the efforts of the FDP in 1961 to replace him with Erhard as chancellor, coupled with the rumors in the press that the party might ultimately exploit the *Spiegel* controversy to revive its move to oust Adenauer, the Chancellor may have concluded that elements within the FDP were motivated by narrow, anti-Adenauer considerations which must be resisted. In addition, Adenauer was stylistically ill equipped to make the sort of concessions demanded by the FDP.[1] His leadership style since 1949 had essentially

[1] For estimates of Adenauer's leadership style, see Rudiger Altmann, *Das Erbe Adenauers* (Stuttgart, 1960), particularly at pp. 34 ff. and 131 ff.; Klaus Bölling, *Republic in Suspense* (New York, Washington and London, 1964), 154–69; Karl D. Bracher, *Deutschland zwischen Demokratie und Diktatur* (München and Bern, 1964), 124–30; and Arnold J. Heidenheimer, *Adenauer and the CDU* (The Hague, 1960), particularly pp. 230–44.

rejected the reliability of "transitory" public opinions and press criticisms as guides to important policy decisions. The Free Democrats' argument that public reactions to the *Spiegel* Affair could not be ignored may have stiffened his determination not to be stampeded into a hasty capitulation to their ultimatum. Finally, Adenauer and his advisors had reason to believe that the FDP was amenable to compromise. The rather temperate and conciliatory statements from Free Democratic leader Erich Mende suggested that his party was attempting to respond at least modestly to public opinion and press criticisms and affirm to the public its credentials as a moderating force within the Adenauer government. Both of these aims, Mende seemed to be saying, could be obtained by the FDP without having to dissolve the coalition relationship.

During the first cabinet crisis, however, a central question of the *Spiegel* Affair was skirted by both the FDP and the CDU/CSU. It concerned only indirectly the circumventing of Stammberger and focused on the possibly improper intervention of Franz Josef Strauss in the implementation of the raids and arrests, especially of Ahlers in Spain. If, as Adenauer and his advisors argued in their talks with the FDP leaders, the Legality Principle *(Legalitätsprinzip)* had governed the *Spiegel* investigation, then Strauss had no greater claim than did Stammberger to an independent role in the investigation.

What, so far, had Defense Minister Strauss admitted about his role in the *Spiegel* action? Strauss's first public statement was contained in an interview published in the October 30 issue of the *Abendpost* (Frankfurt). To the question, "Did you or did you not cause this [investigation]?" Strauss replied: "I have other interests than—let me use the vulgar expression —to dirty my own nest, and I can say neither I personally nor my office had absolutely anything to do with the instigation of this action." The qualifying word, "instigation," should be noted, since the suspicion against Strauss by this time rested not so much on the presumption that he instigated the investigation as on the report that he improperly and independently *intervened after* the investigation was under way. Thus the October 30 statement by Strauss was not addressed precisely to the central issue. On November 1 Strauss refused to elaborate for reporters his role in the action, saying that any statement by him might be "construed as a deliberate attempt to influence the course of a juridical matter." However, on November 3 he departed from the no-comment policy by submitting to an interview with the *8-Uhr-Blatt* (Nürnberg). The relevant segment of the interview reads:

8-Uhr-Blatt: It is not important what we do or do not believe. It is a matter of simply getting an answer to the question whether the action against *Der Spiegel* was an act of revenge on your part.

Strauss: It was no revenge on my part. I have had nothing to do with the matter. In the truest sense of these words, nothing to do!

8-Uhr-Blatt: Did you know of it, that this action was planned?

Strauss: When I came back from vacation [on October 16], the Federal Prosecutor's Office had already requested an opinion from the Defense Ministry whether certain published material in *Der Spiegel* satisfied the condition of treasonable publication. I approved, of course, the complete cooperation of my office, but at the same time decided that two particular experts should be appointed, rather than my ministry generally, to prepare the opinion.

8-Uhr-Blatt: The mere promise of official cooperation, however, might be attributed to you as an act of retaliation against Augstein?

Strauss: I proceeded with this in mind. For this reason I asked State Secretary Hopf to come to me—he is not a party colleague of mine but subscribes to the tenets of another party—and laid the matter before him. I brought to Herr Hopf's attention our precarious situation with these words: If we do nothing, the Ministry will be placed in the position of contributing to the act of treason. If we do something, it will be said that Strauss wanted revenge against Augstein. State Secretary Hopf took the position that regardless of the consequences we could not refuse our official cooperation with the Federal Prosecutor's Office. We both agreed and decided that the entire *Spiegel* matter would be handled [insofar as the Defense Ministry was involved] by State Secretary Hopf. In this case I therefore assigned to the State Secretary the full powers of the Minister and authorized him to deal in complete freedom with the matter and in making the decisions. If you will, in this instance Herr Hopf was for the moment the head of the ministry.

On November 5 the chancellor's office announced that the FDP-CDU/CSU dispute had been resolved without the need for any changes in cabinet posts. The official communique read:

> Under the chairmanship of the Federal Chancellor, representatives of the CDU/CSU *Fraktion* and the FDP *Fraktion* met today. They have asked the Federal Minister of Justice to withdraw his resignation offer. The Federal Minister of Justice agreed to this request.
> Moreover, the consensus concluded that State Secretary [Walter] Strauss would be relieved of his duties as State Secretary of the Ministry of Justice. State Secretary Hopf has proposed that he go on an indefinite leave of absence. The Federal Defense Minister has granted this request. The participants were unanimously agreed that particularly because of the present political situation [the Cuban missile crisis] the existing coalition should continue without any changes.[2]

The FDP's conditions for remaining in the cabinet had been partially, but not entirely, fulfilled. One was obviously met: Stammberger would be retained as Justice Minister. One was implicitly accepted: Stammberger would undertake

---

[2] *Die Welt,* November 6, 1962. Federal President Heinrich Lübke apparently employed whatever persuasive powers he and his office possessed to prevent a rupture in the CDU/CSU-FDP coalition. On Friday, November 2, he conferred with Adenauer; the following day he invited Mende to a conference.

an inquiry into the conduct of the *Spiegel* investigation. How far he might go in uncovering the particulars was left in doubt. Nothing was said about a third condition, that the FDP be more fully integrated in the governmental decisions processes. Presumably the FDP felt it had demonstrated over the past few days that it would no longer tolerate the kind of treatment it had received in the *Spiegel* case.

The fourth condition, that "all persons directly responsible" for the circumvention of Stammberger be brought "to account" presented the greatest difficulty. Here the "solution" left unanswered as many questions as it resolved. The granting of leaves to state secretaries Hopf and Walter Strauss could only be a credible solution if, in fact, these two civil servants had acted during the *Spiegel* controversy upon their own initiative in circumventing Stammberger. To many critics this conclusion seemed incredible. Ignoring for the moment the reputations of both Hopf and Walter Strauss as discreet and experienced civil servants, what possible motive could they have had in presuming on their own authority to carry out this intrigue against Stammberger?

The Hopf-Strauss formula was also irrelevant in explaining Ahlers's arrest in Spain. The West German public still did not know who had authoritatively requested the Spanish authorities to arrest Ahlers. Rumors persisted that Franz Josef Strauss must have initiated the request, since it was reasonably well established by now that the West German military attaché, upon the instructions of someone, had requested in Madrid on the night of October 26 that the Spanish police assist in locating Ahlers and returning him to West Germany. The Ahlers episode was also causing some embarrassment to the Spanish government, which through a spokesman in Madrid explained that the Security Group of the West German Federal Criminal Office had officially requested the arrest of Ahlers.[3] In Bonn spokesmen for the West German government promptly denied that the Federal Criminal Office had initiated the request.[4]

Why had the FDP accepted the dubious Hopf-Walter Strauss formula in fixing responsibility for the circumvention of Stammberger? The party could hardly have wanted to shield Franz Josef Strauss, at all costs, from further embarrassment. To the contrary, relations between the Defense Minister and the party had been strained during the past few days, particularly as a result of the criticism Strauss was now making of the FDP in the Bavarian *Landtag* campaign which was in progress. A partial answer might be found in the position which Hopf himself had taken. In meetings with the FDP he assumed responsibility for the short-circuiting of Stammberger by acknowledging that he had instructed State Secretary Walter Strauss to keep in "strictest confidence" the impending police raids. Hopf added, however, that it was a misunderstanding if Walter Strauss concluded that Stammberger was also to be excluded from the group entitled to know of the plans. Hopf refused to implicate his own minister, Franz Josef Strauss, in the matter. More importantly, the FDP may have reasoned that if the Defense Minister had played an improper role it would presumably be uncovered eventually by Stammberger's inquiry. The tension created by the Cuban missile crisis and Adenauer's impending trip to Washington to confer with President Kennedy, coupled with the lack of firm evidence that Defense Minister Strauss was at fault, possibly persuaded the cautious Erich Mende to use his moderating talents to secure a quick termination of the

[3] *Die Welt,* November 7, 1962; *Süddeutsche Zeitung,* November 7, 1962.

[4] *Frankfurter Allgemeine Zeitung,* November 8, 1962, p. 1. Cf. the transcript of the second day of debate on the *Spiegel* Affair, *Stenographischer Bericht, Deutscher Bundestag, 4. Wahlperiode, 46. Sitzung* (November 8, 1962), 2015–2020.

cabinet dispute. There still remained, however, the question of the Ahlers arrest. The FDP seemed contented to ignore this issue, at least for the moment.

But what if the FDP had rejected the CDU/CSU terms for settling the dispute? What options were available to the FDP? It could have simply withdrawn from the cabinet and, without joining the SPD in an effort to unseat Adenauer, reverted to its earlier role (1957–61) as an independent *Fraktion* in the Bundestag. However, Mende had consistently warned his colleagues of the futility of the FDP's isolating itself in the Bundestag. Excluded from the formulation of cabinet decisions and hopelessly overshadowed in the Bundestag by the SPD as an oppositional party, the FDP would jeopardize whatever remaining electoral appeal it had and invalidate its functional importance as a third force in the bipolarizing party system.

Alternatively, the FDP could withdraw from the Adenauer cabinet and then regain its position as a third force by entering a coalition with the SPD.[5] Even if the FDP could overcome the formidable opposition within its own circles to a Socialist-dominated coalition, the SPD cancelled this option on November 5 by deciding to refuse to discuss seriously an FDP-SPD coalition and to utilize instead the parliamentary

[5] Under the "constructive vote of no confidence" provision (Article 67) of the Basic Law, Adenauer could not be compelled to resign unless a majority of the entire membership or, in this case, 250 deputies first agreed to a successor. Together the FDP and the SPD had a majority, with a combined total of 257 of the 499 voting members of the Bundestag (West Berlin's delegation of 22 deputies were not entitled to vote on substantive matters). However, one of several reasons for the reluctance of the SPD to consider seriously the strategy of coalescing with the FDP to dislodge Adenauer was the marginality of the majority such a coalition would have in the Bundestag. With a scant margin of seven votes in the majority and with the unpredictability, so the SPD reasoned, of several FDP deputies in their voting behavior, a SPD-FDP coalition appeared numerically tenuous and unreliable for a sustained period of cabinet stability.

questioning techniques to explore the unanswered questions surrounding the *Spiegel* Affair.

A final option, that of remaining in coalition with the CDU/CSU but without Adenauer as chancellor, who seemed to be obstructing any greater concessions during this stage to the FDP, did not present itself. None of the factions within the CDU/CSU construed the dispute as essentially involving Adenauer's leadership and none was willing to collaborate with the Free Democrats in displacing Adenauer as chancellor.

Questions and Answers: The Bundestag Debate

By November 5 the tentative strategy of the Social Democratic Bundestag *Fraktion* had been decided. It could not accept the CDU/CSU argument that the central issues of the *Spiegel* controversy were juridical, best left to the appropriate courts for eventual determination. Questions concerning precensorship, the prolonged search of *Der Spiegel's* archives, and the guilt of Augstein and his associates of treasonable publication, the SPD acknowledged, required juricial processing. But the clarification of and the location of responsibility for violations of political norms did not lend themselves to adjudication. Had the *Spiegel* investigation been politically inspired? If so, by whom? Had the seizure of Ahlers in Spain been initiated improperly by political, not legal, officers of the West German government? If so, by whom? Had state secretaries Hopf and Walter Strauss deliberately circumvented Justice Minister Stammberger as a result of instructions from a politically accountable official? If so, upon whose instructions? Of the various techniques available to the opposition party in the Bundestag—committee of inquiry, written questions, oral questions, and the question hour—the question hour had the advantage of quickly confronting the government with the responsibility of answering these questions. Thus on November 5 Karl Mommer, executive secretary of the SPD Bundestag *Fraktion,* submitted eighteen questions to Bundestag President Eugen Gerstenmaier, with the request that the Bundestag be convened at the earliest moment to receive them in formal Question Hour. Anticipating that the FDP and the CDU/CSU were about to resolve their coalition dispute, Mommer added that the questions would be pursued regardless of the decision of the FDP about remaining in the cabinet.[6] Gerstenmaier announced that the questions would be taken up on November 7.

The November 7 Question Hour in the Bundestag produced little new information that could clarify the major areas of dispute.[7] Why did the Federal Interior Ministry fail to contact, immediately prior to the raids, the *Land* Interior Minister in North Rhine-Westphalia? Why did it, instead, contact Ludwig Adenauer, state secretary of the *Land* Ministry? Federal Interior Minister Höcherl had no explanation. He simply declared that his ministry "assumed" that State Secretary Adenauer would notify his ministerial superior. Why did State Secretary Walter Strauss fail to inform his superior, Stammberger, of the impending action? Höcherl, reading the answers supplied to him by Stammberger (who had excused himself because of sickness), "did not know." Who had placed the phone call initially to Madrid that led Military Attaché Oster to ask the Spanish police to take Ahlers and his wife into custody? Höcherl ruled out the Justice Ministry, the Federal Prosecutor's Office, and Interpol. He alluded weakly to an official, out of the country at the

[6] Mommer explained the position of the SPD and its reasons for submitting the parliamentary questions in a television interview on November 5. *BPA/Abt. Nachrichten, Rundfunkaufnahme, Deutsche Gruppe West, Deutschlandfunk/ 5.11.62/1900/Vt., Anhang VIII.*

[7] The first day of debate in the Bundestag on the *Spiegel* Affair is transcribed in the *Stenographischer Bericht, Deutscher Bundestag, 4. Wahlperiode, 46. Sitzung* (November 7, 1962), 1949–2011. The eighteen questions submitted by the SPD *Fraktion* are printed separately in *Drucksache IV/708, Deutscher Bundestag, 4. Wahlperiode.*

moment, of the Security Group of the Federal Criminal Office who "might" supply the information needed for his answer.

If the first day's question period failed to supply answers to key questions, it was nevertheless one of the stormiest sessions in the history of the Bonn Republic. The sensation occurred technically after the Question Hour had been ended. From the Question Hour the agenda moved to a 90-minute reading by Finance Minister Heinz Starke of the 1963 budget proposals. Following Starke's report, SPD Deputy Heinrich Ritzel read a statement clarifying the motives of the SPD in initiating the *Spiegel* debate.[8] He disavowed any lack of interest by his party in uncovering treason where it existed, but, he added, the SPD also insisted that the authorities, including the public attorneys, use procedures consistent with constitutional and legal norms. Following Ritzel's statement, Chancelor Adenauer took the floor and admonished the chamber:

Ladies and gentlemen, from my knowledge of the matter I extent to all officials . . . my thanks and my respect. (Applause from the CDU/SCU.—Protests from the SPD.)

I would like here to direct to all parties and to the German people a request. (Incessant, lively protests from the SPD.)

Treason has been committed—that is very probable—(Prolonged protests from the SPD.)—by a man who had in his hands a power, a journalistic power. I take the position: the more power, including journalistic power, anyone has in his hands . . . the more he is obligated . . . to remain true to the limits, which the love of the people—(Lively protests from the SPD. Calls returned by the CDU/CSU. Deputy Dr. Schmidt (Wuppertal): Spiegel-Party!)

Bundestag President Dr. Gerstenmaier: Please allow the Herr Chancellor to continue. (Deputy Wehner: But any pimp may slander the SPD!—Further protests from the SPD.)—Permit the Chancellor to continue! (Calls of "Oho" from the SPD.)—The

[8] *Stenographischer Bericht, Deutscher Bundestag* (November 7, 1962), *ibid.*, 1980.

President of this House also must protect the freedom of speech of the Chancellor. (Applause from the CDU/CSU.)

Federal Chancellor Dr. Adenauer: Ladies and gentlemen, is it therefore not disturbing (Very true! and applause from the SPD.), it is therefore not disturbing (Calls from the SPD: Yes!)

when a colonel of the Bundeswehr, after he hears that an investigation might be initiated against Augstein and the editors of *Spiegel,* goes out and tells them that, enabling them to cover up the evidence? (Calls from the middle: Scandalous.—Deputy Seuffert [SPD]: Has anyone said anything here about that?)

Yes, just read through what you have said (Deputy Seuffert: About entirely different things!)

and then wait for the results of further revelations! Then you will regret that you have even placed these questions. (Applause from the CDU/CSU.)

I declare again, ladies and gentlemen: I think as chancellor I am obligated to do it (Calls from the SPD:—to investigate!)

to thank the Federal High Court and the offiicals of the Federal Prosecutor's Office and of the Federal Criminal Office for having pursued this case with such intensity. (Applause from the CDU/CSU and the FDP.—Protests from the SPD.)[9]

SPD *Fraktion* chairman Fritz Erler moved quickly to respond to Adenauer's remarks:

Herr President! My very respected ladies and gentlemen! The intervention of the Herr Chancellor makes me extraordinarily unhappy. It makes me unhappy because with it unfortunately— unfortunately!—while one questions with concern the constitutional conduct of our authorities he adds to that concern by creating an environment which arouses further doubt about the strength of constitutional-legal principles in this country. (Applause from the SPD. "Pfui" calls, protests, and great commotion from the CDU/CSU. . . .)

Where treason is committed, it must be uncovered. (Prolonged and lively commotion and catcalls from the CDU/CSU.)

But at the same time an investigation of suspected treason does not suspend the constitutional-legal norms of the Basic Law. . . .

[9] *Ibid.,* 1981–1982.

A parliament which did not respond to the obligation to see that in an investigation of treason, which has been initiated, the residual constitutional and legal norms do not get trampled would not fulfill its controlling function. This is today what is involved and nothing else. (Applause from the SPD.—Commotion from the government parties.)[10]

Adenauer took up the argument again by repeating certain phrases in Ritzel's original statement and added:

Ladies and gentlemen, in the declaration which Herr Ritzel read (Sustained protests from the SPD.), or in those which he added, stands the following: on one side treason, but on the other side the protection of citizens before the abuses of ministers, state secretaries and—(Approval from the CDU/CSU.—Lively protests from the SPD.)

And then, ladies and gentlement, he declared: The concern about the methods which have been used—(Lively calls from the SPD: Very true!—Deputy Seuffert: Have you no concern? Has the Justice Minister no concern?—Calls from the SPD: Why did the Justice Minister want to resign?—Deputy Hermsdorf: He doesn't understand, he no longer understands!)

Now, ladies and gentlemen (Sustained protests from the SPD), we have (Continuous protests from the SPD.)

an abyss of treason in the land. (Deputy Seuffert: Who says so?)

—I say so. (Loud calls from the SPD: "Aha!" "So?"—Deputy Seuffert: Is this a pending juridical matter or not?)

For, ladies and gentlemen, . . . when a sheet which has a circulation of 500,000 copies systematically commits treason for money—(Excited calls from the SPD: Pfui! Huh!—Whistling and sustained protests from the SPD, among them Deputies Seuffert and Hermsdorf). . . .

Bundestag President Dr. Gerstenmaier: Ladies and gentlemen, I beg you to maintain order, which is necessary to permit the discussion to continue. There is no purpose—Herr Deputy Hermsdorf!—Herr Deputy Hermsdorf, be quiet! (Prolonged, continuous loud calls from the SPD.)

Federal Chancellor Dr. Adenauer: I am quite surprised. You

[10] *Ibid.*, 1983.

don't want to look at *Der Spiegel.* (Applause from the CDU/
CSU.—Prolonged, lively calls from the SPD.)

You merely want to look at the methods with which a case of
treason has been exposed,—they do not please you. That you
have just said. (Continuous commotion.)

Ladies and gentlemen, I repeat: I am bound by my conscience
to say that the officials of the Federal High Court, the Federal
Prosecutor's Office, the Criminal Office, and the cabinet deserve
our fullest support and the thanks of the German people. (Applause from the CDU/CSU.—Deputy Seuffert: Why did you
dismiss the state secretaries?—Additional, excited calls from the
SPD.)[11]

For the first time during the debate Erich Mende of the
Free Democratic Party took the floor. Obviously disturbed by
the tone of the proceedings, Mende cautioned the chamber
that it was in danger of interfering with a pending juridical matter. "The House does itself a disservice and parliamentary democracy a disservice if this matter is further discussed in this
atmosphere." Mende explained briefly that the dismissals of
Hopf and Walter Strauss had been prompted by their failure
to properly inform a superior and had thus "called into question the political bases of confidence between the competent
minister and his state secretary." Mende, in short, was cling-
ing to the view that the state secretaries were entirely responsible for the circumvention of Stammberger. He moved
that the *Spiegel* debate be immediately ended and that other
techniques be used to inquire into the various aspects of
the case.[12]

After disposing of Mende's motion, which was opposed by
the CDU/CSU as well as the SPD, the debate continued.
At one point SPD deputy Herbert Wehner was called to order
for unparliamentary language.[13] Adenauer, refusing to remain silent, again took the floor:

[11] *Ibid.,* 1984.
[12] *Ibid.,* 1987–1988.
[13] *Ibid.,* 1990.

. . . in the person of Augstein we have two complexes. . . . On the one side he makes money from treason; and that I find vulgar, pure and simple. (Call from the SPD: Is that proved?—Deputy Wehner: Hear! Hear!—Further calls from the SPD: Unbelievable!)

and second, ladies and gentlemen, he makes money from attacks generally on the coalition parties; and that pleases you, which you cannot deny. (Commotion and applause from the CDU/CSU. Call from the SPD: Infamous!) . . . I never read *Der Spiegel,* I would like to add here. (Approval from the CDU/CSU.)

I have better things to do.—(Approval and applause from the CDU/CDU.) . . . God, what is Augstein to me! The man has made money with his methods.

There are those who have helped him in this by subscribing to *Der Spiegel* and placing advertisements in it. These persons are not very high in my esteem, those who have given so many advertisements. (Applause from the CDU/CSU.) But he has made much money, he has made a great deal of money. In my view that is no measure of his moral worth; I can not help myself. (Jeers from the SPD.)[14]

Adenauer's remarkable and reckless performance was too much for FDP *Fraktion* deputy chairman Döring, who was reported to have been disappointed that his party had capitulated so easily on November 5 to Adenauer and the Christian Democrats. Döring took the floor and lectured the Chancellor:

. . . Herr Chancellor, it is very difficult for me to say what I believe I am now obligated to say. I think I need say to no one in this House that for years I have been a friend of Herr Augstein. I think I need tell no one in this House that no one would be more upset than I if, according to law and justice, the objective fact of treason is established in this case.

But, Herr Chancellor, I am obligated not only to my friends but also to citizen Augstein and all others to protest what you have said here: Herr Augstein makes money from treason. For then you have already rendered a judgment which falls only to the competence of the court. (Stormy applause from the FDP and the SPD.)

14 *Ibid.,* 1993–1994.

Herr Chancellor, I know what I am talking about. I am not prepared—and it is not a problem of coalition politics here—to accept without protest . . . that persons can be convicted before they have even seen a courtroom. (Applause from FDP and SPD deputies.)

. . . I say to you this: As little as I am prepared to defend a judicially ascertained mistake of my friend Augstein or his editors, I equally feel constrained to say as a member of the coalition that on the day the charges were first announced and alleged to be justified some things did not seem to be in order, that many people were disturbed, and among them was the one closest to me: my wife, of whose 26 family members 22 were placed in German concentration camps, a woman who found it difficult to return to Germany, to whom for weeks and months I had to explain that all of her fears and doubts, which she might still find justified here and there, were substantially unwarranted, a person who now asks me: Is it possible that when a mere suspicion exists improper procedures can be used, is there somewhere a control that can be invoked to clear up this matter.

Ladies and gentlemen, I swear now to my own coalition friends: We must not create the impression that a simple question of coalition politics or power politics is involved here! Read the foreign newspapers![15]

Press reaction to the first day of the *Spiegel* debate was critical.[16] The respected *Süddeutsche Zeitung* editorialized that "when it is the Government that decides what a constitutional state is, it might be questioned whether we live in one." The cautious *Frankfurter Allegmeine Zeitung*, long a supporter of Adenauer's policies, concluded: "The Federal Government has apparently decided to sail through the growing storm of the *Spiegel* matter with full sheets. . . . The

[15] *Ibid.*, 1995–1996. Two months later, Döring died of a heart attack.
[16] Of the twenty-four daily West German newspapers whose November 8, 1962, editorials on the first day of the debates are contained in the *Spiegel* Affair files (Code 700-2/0, Box 6) of the Press Evaluation Section of the Bundestag Library, twenty-one are critical of the manner in which the federal government presented its case to the Bundestag; only three are either "mixed" or favorable toward the Government.

course which the head of the Government has taken is reckless." Less restrained was the *Neue Rhein Zeitung:* "This
is a black day, if not the blackest day, in parliament of the
young German Federal Repubic. . . . This must be unique
in the history of our young parliament; no, in the history of
parliamentarianism anywhere: from the speaker's podium of
the revered house the head of the Government intervenes in
a judicial proceeding!" The *Westdeutsche Rundschau* called
for Adenauer's resignation. *Der Spiegel* announced it was
filing a complaint with the courts requesting a restraining
injunction against the Chancellor from repeating in public his
charges of treason against Augstein and his associates. The
bitterest comment came from the SPD-oriented *Frankfurter
Rundschau,* which from the outset had taken a harsh line
against the authorities for the *Spiegel* fiasco: "Fully aware of
what we are saying, we declare quite advisedly that against a
person to whom the methods of the investigation of a suspect
are neither here nor there the judgment must be rendered that
temperamentally he is a Fascist."

On November 8 Defense Minister Strauss finally took the
floor to respond to questions concerning the arrest of Ahlers
in Spain.[17] Following a circuitous route of questions and
answers, Strauss officially confirmed what the press had reported for several days: West Germany Military Attaché
Oschim Oster on the night of October 26 was asked through
a phone call from the West German Defense Ministry to request the Spanish police to take Ahlers into custody. Who
personally placed the call? Strauss evaded the question by
repeating his original response, that his Ministry had placed
the call since it had reason to believe that Military Attaché

[17] The transcript of the second day's debate is contained in the
*Stenographischer Bericht, Deutscher Bundestag, 4. Wahlperiode, 46.
Sitzung* (November 8, 1962), 2013–2026.

Oster knew of Ahlers whereabouts and thus ought to be requested to help locate Ahlers. As Strauss explained it:

During the execution by the public attorneys of the court issued search, seizure, and arrest orders the Defense Ministry did not know of any arrests or of any arrest attempts outside the one quite specific instance in the Ahlers case, and in this one instance [it was informed] because as a result of the unsuccessful attempt to have this arrest carried out the Security Group of the Federal Criminal Police learned that Herr Ahlers was not here, that Herr Ahlers was in another country—for us this bit of information would have been irrelevant,—that is, that Ahlers was in Spain—, except that he was in Spain and the German Military Attaché knew about it. The Security Group of the Federal Criminal Office did not communicate [with the Defense Ministry] merely out of . . . technical requirements in this instance, but because the Security Group wanted to know in the course of official assistance—Article 35 of the Basic Law: What is going on here? We have an arrest warrant issued by the highest court and the author of the incriminating article involved centrally in the investigation is, if you will, with the knowledge of the Defense Ministry in another country. . . . The German Military Attaché, who knows Herr Ahlers from the time of their both working with the Blank Office—one of them was a press aide; this is generally known of course and there is nothing new in revealing it; the other had been an intelligence officer—was contacted in the night [of October 26, 1962] and asked whether he knew anything about the trip. For if Herr Ahlers—and this was by all means not to be excluded from the realm of possibility, particularly at nighttime—were to travel on to Morocco, a vacation destination which he had given, and not return—which would hinder the success of the investigation—, then the shadow of suspicion would be cast that with the assistance of an agency or of a person in the service of the Defense Ministry a man had been permitted to escape having to testify, one who according to our best information was best informed about the security leaks [in the Ministry and through which the Foertsch article was developed. . . .[18]

In light of Strauss's admission that his ministry had contacted Oster and asked him to have Ahlers arrested, SPD

[18] *Ibid.,* 2019.

Deputy Metzger inquired in a supplementary question whether the government was still of the opinion that in all instances the law had been observed:

Interior Minister Höcherl: Herr Metzger, have you put the question to me?

Metzger: To the Federal Government! (Deputy Wehner: How can anyone know who is responsible? Calls of Huh! from the CDU/CSU.)

Höcherl: . . . Morally seen, everyone has cooperated in bringing back a traitor and placing him before the prosecutor. . . . The Federal Government naturally takes the position that the regulations should be respected. But in such a situation one should not apply too trivial a standard.[19]

The second day of the debate ended with Strauss in the midst of trying to justify his ministry's involvement in assisting with the investigation. In alluding to the expert opinion which his ministry prepared and completed on October 19 for the Federal Prosecutor's Office, Strauss was interrupted by FDP deputy Dr. Kohut, the only member of the FDP *Fraktion* who participated in the questioning:

Herr Minister, are you prepared and in a position to repudiate the rumor that the person who drafted the expert opinion in your office earlier held a high rank in the [Nazi] SS? (Call from the center: Ah, now it gets primitive!)

Strauss: I certainly do not want to dodge any questions, but please understand that I can not answer such a question. . . .

Kohut: Herr Minister, do I understand then that questions concerning earlier activities in the SS may no longer be asked in the German Federal Republic under the Adenauer government? (Applause from the SPD.—Vigorous jeering from the CDU/CSU: Scandalous! Unheard of! Persistence commotion from the center.)

Strauss: . . . You do German democracy a great disservice. . . .

Kohut: Do not constantly dodge the question, Herr Minister, whenever it is unpleasant. . . .

[19] *Ibid.,* 2020.

Strauss: Herr Colleague Kohut (Prolonged disturbances and commotion), I am being courteous to you and also candid and I ask you to refrain from playing the role of the prosecutor with me (Laughter and jeers from the SPD). . . . I do not know the background of those (Jeers), who have prepared the expert opinion and I have not troubled to find out. At the moment someone is admitted as a civil servant or as an officer, I cease looking into his past and conducting a second or third denazification. (Bravocalls from the center and applause from the center.—Deputy Dr. Kohut: I then conclude that SS people now write expert opinions concerning democrats!). . . .[20]

Dr. Kohut's line of questioning must have disturbed his Free Democratic colleagues who were still seeking to maintain a semblance of harmony with the CDU/CSU and ride out the *Spiegel* controversy with the coalition intact. At the request of the FDP leaders, Kohut read into the record of the day's proceedings a statement toning down considerably his insinuation: "I regret that from my questions to the Herr Federal Defense Minister there might arise a suggestion of collective guilt involving the person who prepared the expert opinion. In common with my political friends I oppose, true to the liberal tradition, every collective indictment and acknowledge individual responsibility in a constitutional system; similarly I stress the demand for all citizens the protection of law so that no injustice is inflicted on anyone."[21]

One thing was clear from the second day's questioning. Strauss was adept at evading the central issues around which the controversy had clustered: who, and by what authority, placed the phone call to Spain asking for the police arrest of Ahlers and who had instructed state secretaries Hopf and Walter Strauss to ignore Stammberger in assisting with the investigation against *Der Spiegel?*

After several diversionary questions and answers, SPD

[20] *Ibid.,* 2024–2025.
[21] *Ibid.,* 2067 (*Anlage* 2).

Fraktion Chairman Fritz Erler returned the third day's questioning to a key issue by asking Strauss pointedly whether he personally talked with Military Attaché Oster and asked Oster to bring in the Spanish police for the arrest of Ahlers.[22] Strauss finally admitted that he did:

Since the military attaché . . . did not want to know the circumstances but said: "I recognize only the voice of the Minister," I was connected with him and I repeated to him the nature of the situation: (Calls from the SPD: Aha!) The Security Group of the Federal Criminal Office has called and maintains that Colonel Oster knows of this trip, Herr Ahlers is being sought because of the suspicion of treason, a court warrant for his arrest has been issued, it is based on the danger of his fleeing and obstructing justice, what goes on here?

Strauss was then asked, after several supplementary questions, whether he or his ministry had also asked the Security Group of the Federal Criminal Office to send by teletype a copy of the arrest warrant to the Spanish police. The question was important in establishing whether the initiative for the seizure of Ahlers came really from the Federal Prosecutor's Office or some other appropriate agency or inappropriately from the Defense Ministry. Strauss evaded the question. When pinned down, he said, "Nothing is known to me of this."[23]

Erler returned the questioning now to a second crucial area of controversy by asking Strauss whether he had taken part in any discussions between October 16 (when Strauss returned from vacation) and October 26 with state secretaries Hopf and Walter Strauss about any aspect of the *Spiegel* investigation. Strauss first equivocated, then concluded with

[22] The transcript of the third day's debate is contained in the *Stenographischer Bericht, Deutscher Bundestag, 4. Wahlperiode, 47. Sitzung* (November 9, 1962), 2075–2089. Erler's supplementary question and Strauss's response appear on pp. 2077–78.

[23] *Ibid.,* 2080.

this statement: ". . . I am informed on October 16 because a few persons in my ministry, including State Secretary Hopf, came to me and gave me information about the events of October 9 to October 16. From October 16 to October 26 . . . I took part in no conference. However, obviously I was told by the appropriate personnel in my office that this matter was in progress. More I did not know. I did not know what was coming; I did not know when it was coming; I did not know against whom it was coming, etc."[24] The closing words of this statement should be kept in mind in any final assessment of the accusation that Strauss lied to the Bundestag.

Strauss ended the third day's discussion by reading into the record a formal denial that the expert opinion prepared in his ministry had been written by anyone with a former SS background. Mende, apparently miffed that his colleague Kohut had circulated the charge, acknowledged that the story had originated with the East German and Moscow radio networks and announced that the *Fraktion* has made sure that "Kohut would not spread such rumors about in the future."[25]

If the government had a strong defense against the criticisms which had been aroused against it by the *Spiegel* Affair, it seemed peculiarly inept in presenting it. The contradictions uttered by various press officers during the previous ten days had been fully exploited by the press. During the *Spiegel* debates the government once again seemed to have done publicly its position more harm than good. An opinion survey conducted shortly afterwards reveals that out of a representative population sample (sixteen years of age and over) 59 percent had "followed" the debates. Of those who had followed the debates, only 16 percent felt that "Adenauer and the Government" had made "a good impression." A clear majority (54 percent) felt that Adenauer and the Gov-

[24] *Ibid.*, 2084.
[25] *Ibid.*, 2089.

ernment had "*not* made a good impression" and the remaining 30 percent were "undecided."[26] Moreover neither the irrelevant solution devised by the coalition parties nor the attitude of the government as evidenced by the remarks of Adenauer and Höcherl during the Bundestag debates was designed to satisfy the critics. Immediately after the debates, therefore, the dissident groups returned to the offensive and, in certain instances to be examined in the next chapter, sharply escalated their attacks.

[26] Neumann, "Die Spiegel-Affäre in der Öffentlichen Meinung," 19.

Chapter VI

POLITICAL BARGAINING, II

The FDP's acceptance of the Hopf-Walter Strauss formula tentatively suggested that Adenauer's government would be able to survive the *Spiegel* controversy with its coalition intact. However, events soon proved the premises of the formula to be untenable and in mid-November the FDP repudiated its earlier agreement to remain in the cabinet. This time the FDP made good its threat to withdraw and presented Adenauer with his second and more serious cabinet crisis. During the remaining days of November, and against the backdrop of both the *Landtag* election campaign in Bavaria and the intensification of criticism from certain groups outside the governing circles, all three parties in Bonn were involved in a series of negotiations in which various national coalition possibilities were explored. In early December the Chancellor finally found a solution for ending the political crisis; with it, however, the end of the Adenauer era was also definitey fixed.

The "Truce"

In a November 9 meeting with the leaders of the CDU/CSU, the SPD, and the FDP, Chancellor Adenauer had secured an agreement that a truce would be observed during the next seven days, permitting Adenauer and his advisors to prepare for their trip to the United States where he would discuss with President Kennedy the recent Cuban missile crisis and its implications for West Germany. Already postponed once because of the *Spiegel* Affair, the trip would take

Adenauer to Washington on November 14 and was expected to keep him there for two or three days. During the truce the Social Democrats agreed to withhold additional parliamentary questions concerning the *Spiegel* controversy.

Although spokesmen for the FDP voiced concern about the general tone of the *Spiegel* debates in the Bundestag, the FDP's basic response offered no immediate threat to the November 5 coalition agreement. From the beginning the Free Democrats had maintained that procedural errors in the *Spiegel* investigation could be ferreted out and corrected, if necessary, without disrupting the coalition. The deliberate exclusion of Stammberger from the circle of officials who had prior knowledge of the police actions did have implications for the coalition. When on November 5 it was decided to relieve state secretaries Hopf and Walter Strauss of their duties, the responsibility for this apparent violation of the spirit of the coalition had been fixed and the punishment exacted. Thus, even though Franz Josef Strauss seemed to have admitted in the subsequent Bundestag debates a role in the affair greater than he had previously acknowledged, the FDP refused to regard this new information as requiring a reconsideration of the November 5 settlement.

There were two weaknesses in the FDP's position. It was premised on the assumption that the state secretaries were entirely responsible for the circumvention of Stammberger, and it failed to satisfy the public's doubt about the propriety of Strauss's conduct in the arrest of Ahlers. FDP leaders were aware of these weaknesses in their position, but seemed unable to find a strategy that would overcome them. Siegfried Zoglmann, executive secretary of the FDP Bundestag *Fraktion,* suggested on November 9 that, whatever the remaining questions presented by the *Spiegel* controversy, the "legitimate" freedom of the press clearly had not been endangered by the

Spiegel case.[1] His party colleague, Hermann Busse, a former judge with the Constitutional Court of North Rhine-Westphalia, confirmed Zoglmann's impression and added that perhaps a parliamentary committee of inquiry should now be constituted to explore "calmly" the remaining issues in the affair.[2] Even Justice Minister Stammberger refused to say, in an interview on November 11, whether Strauss had acted improperly and warned that whatever the defects in the procedures no reasonable analogy could be drawn between the *Spiegel* action and "Gestapo techniques."[3]

The most reliable index of the FDP's position during the "truce" is found in Mende's extended comments of November 11.[4] He announced that his *Fraktion* believed the Bundestag standing committee on law should inquire now into possible legal errors in the *Spiegel* investigation and the standing committee on defense should inquire into questions with "military implications" arising out of the *Spiegel* Affair. Mende chided the SPD for having unnecessarily diverted the *Spiegel* controversy and asserted that the party must assume responsibility for delaying the procedures for discovering the truth. In Mende's opinion, if the SPD had refrained from invoking the question hour technique, a special committee of inquiry could have already begun receiving testimony that would "clarify" the Ahlers episode. Mende admitted that in light of Strauss's statements before the Bundestag it would have been "better" if Strauss had rendered appropriate assistance in the Ahlers case three days prior to the actual arrest, thus avoiding the hasty improvisations of the night of October 26. Mende concluded, most significantly, with the warning that, whatever the

[1] *BPA Abt. Nachrichten, Rundfunkaufnahme, Deutsche Gruppe West, Deutsche Welle 9.11.62.*

[2] *BPA Abt. Nachrichten, Rundfunkaufnahme, Deutsche Gruppe West, SDR 9.11.62 / 22.00/Mei "Woche in Bonn."*

[3] *Deutsche Zeitung,* November 12, 1962.

[4] *Ibid.*

merits of the continuing criticisms against Strauss and the authorities, the Defense Ministry could not recall State Secretary Hopf to active duty without prior approval of the FDP Bundestag *Fraktion.* Defense Minister Strauss was apparently unimpressed with Mende's warning. Later that day on a radio interview, Strauss explained that Hopf was simply on sick leave and implied that Hopf would soon return to his duties.[5]

The position of the SPD after the Bundestag debates differed markedly from that of the FDP. According to its spokesmen, the answers given by the government left the basic issues unresolved. Responsibility for Ahlers's arrest had not been fixed. Strauss had lied to the public concerning his role in the *Spiegel* case. As to the FDP suggestion that parliamentary committees be utilized in exploring the remaining issues, the SPD discounted their usefulness, both because of the time-consuming nature of their processes and the control of the committees by the government's majority coalition.[6]

Publicly the CDU/CSU spokesmen continued a show of unity, insisting that the charges against the authorities had not been proved. Alluding to the rumor that *Der Spiegel* had

[5] *BPA Abt. Nachrichten, Rundfunkaufnahme, Deutsche Gruppe West, Hessischer RF/6.11.62/21.00/He, Anhang A.* In response to a question about State Secretary Hopf's impending "leave" from the Defense Ministry, Strauss explained: "Herr Hopf this year has a major surgical operation behind him. He had to interrupt post-operative treatment because of the workload in the Defense Ministry, the tense international situation, and the NATO maneuver exercises have not permitted for three years an extended absence for the State Secretary. We hope that the international situation is lessening. The duties in this connection have been especially heavy concerning NATO [but] they have now been carried to the point that Herr Hopf is at present able to take an uninterrupted vacation."

[6] *SPD Pressedienst, P/XVII/227,* November 9, 1962. See also the radio comments of SPD *Fraktion* chairman Erler in *BPA Abt. Nachrichten, Rundfunkaufnahme, Deutsche Gruppe West, Deutsche Welle, 9.11.62* and the radio remarks of SPD Bundestag *Fraktion* executive secretary Friedrich Schäfer in *BPA Abt. Nachrichten, Rundfunkaufnahme, Deutsche Gruppe West, NDR, 10.11.62/19.45, "Der Standpunkt."*

obtained security information from SPD deputies, they suggested that a more fruitful line of inquiry for those interested in the truth would be to take up the question of security leaks.[7] Behind the scene, however, there appeared to be a growing uneasiness about the vulnerability of Franz Josef Strauss to criticism. At a November 12 meeting of the executive committe of the CDU/CSU Bundestag *Fraktion*, Foreign Minister Gerhard Schröder, potential rival of Strauss for eventual leadership of the CDU/CSU, revealed a memorandum from the German Ambassador in Madrid showing that Strauss phoned not once but twice on the night of October 26. This bit of information contradicted Strauss's account before the Bundestag and suggested that Strauss had taken the initiative in involving the Spanish police in arresting, contrary to the accepted procedures, a German citizen.

It is possible also that the electoral significance of the *Spiegel* Affair was beginning to assert itself and to cause the Christian Democrats to reconsider their position. On November 11, in the Hesse *Landtag* election in which the *Spiegel* Affair became one of several major issues, both the Free Democrats and the Social Democrats increased their popular vote and representation in the assembly. In the 1958 *Landtag* election the SPD received 46.9 percent of the valid votes; in the 1962 election it received 50.9 percent. The FDP had received 9.5 percent of the votes in the earlier election; now it received 11.4 percent. The CDU slipped from 32 percent to 28.8 percent. Whether the *Spiegel* Affair had any substantial effect on the results is uncertain; a number of major newspapers concluded that it had been of significance and CDU/CSU Bundestag *Fraktion* chairman von Brentano in the November 12 meeting of the CDU/CSU leaders warned that the

[7] *DUD* [Deutschlands-Union-Dienst], *CDU/CSU Bundestagfraktion* *14.11.62.*

electoral significance of the *Spiegel* Affair could no longer be ignored.[8]

At this point Chancellor Adenauer introduced publicly a comment that confirmed Strauss's view that Hopf was soon to return to the Defense Ministry. In an interview with a group of American journalists just before his departure for Washington, Adenauer, when questioned about the *Spiegel* Affair, remarked that had he been "Herr Strauss . . . I would have promptly revealed that I had personally intervened in the Ahlers case." Then he added: "Herr Hopf will return to his duties as soon as his health permits. And I am myself pleased that Herr Hopf will be returning."[9] In one sentence the Chancellor had exploded the myth of the Hopf-Walter Strauss formula on which the FDP had staked its reputation as the third force in the Bonn system. And he had done it without giving the FDP advance warning. Caught completely by surprise, Mende hurriedly called a meeting the same night of his *Fraktion* colleagues.

Mende's cautious approach during the *Spiegel* Affair, contrary to that preferred by Döring, was now discredited. He had apparently already lost some support within his own *Fraktion*. During a routine re-election of the FDP *Fraktion's* executive committee members, just after the *Spiegel* debates, Mende had received fewer votes (44 of 62) than had Döring (51 of 59) for the chairmanship and vice-chairmanship, respectively. Mende now accepted the "hard" line. After a nine-hour session, the Free Democratic leaders agreed that with the recall of Hopf the settlement of November 5 was untenable. Franz Josef Strauss would have to go. The FDP

[8] *Der Spiegel*, November 21, 1962, p. 46; *Die Welt*, November 13, 1962; *The Times* (London), November 14, 1962. However, cf. Klaus Kamphöven, "Landtagswahlen ohne Schema," *Die Politische Meinung*, VI (Dec., 1962), 3–5.

[9] *Deutsche Zeitung*, November 13, 1962; *Frankfurter Allgemeine Zeitung*, November 13, 1962; and *Der Spiegel*, November 21, 1962, p. 46.

ultimatum was transmitted on November 15 to Minister of Special Affairs Heinrich Krone, who had been left in charge of the *Spiegel* problem while Adenauer was in Washington. Krone phoned Adenauer in Washington and urged the Chancellor to return as quickly as possible. Adenauer rescheduled his flight twenty-four hours earlier than originally planned.

But once again the SPD had taken the initiative away from the FDP. On the previous day the SPD *Fraktion* announced that it was preparing a resolution for immediate introduction in the Bundestag that would call upon Chancellor Adenauer to recommend to Federal President Lübke the dismissal of Strauss from the cabinet.[10] The press release added: "In any other democratic state in the world such a person would have been dismissed for only a tenth of the affairs which are associated with the name of Minister Strauss."[11] For both the FDP and the SPD the "truce" had ended.

Judgment at Nürnberg

The Bavarian *Landtag* election was entering its final phase when the FDP demanded Strauss's dismissal. At the Bavarian rallies Strauss vigorously defended his conduct and warned his audiences that those who wanted to remove him from the Defense Ministry were following the line of the East German communists. Strauss stressed that no less a crime than treason was involved in this dispute. To the charge that he had lied, both in public and in the Bundestag, about his involvement in the *Spiegel* investigation, Strauss replied in an interview with a reporter of the *Dortmunder Ruhr-Nachrichten* (November 15, 1962): ". . . I am very happy to have the oppor-

---

[10] *Pressemitteilungen und Informationen, SPD 14/11/62,* No. 308/62. Constitutionally accountable directly to the Chancellor, federal ministers are dismissable only through a request lodged by the Chancellor with the Federal President. A motion, even if approved by the Bundestag majority, calling upon the Chancellor to dismiss a minister is not formally binding upon the Chancellor.

[11] *Ibid.*

tunity to say once again that here one has been dealt a stacked deck. I have never maintained I had nothing whatsoever to do with the whole matter and that I knew nothing of the whole matter. I have simply maintained—and this represents the whole truth—that neither the Defense Ministry nor myself had anything to do with the initiation of the proceedings." Writing in the November 23 issue of the *Münchner Merkur* Strauss continued to argue his case:

I have fulfilled my duty and in full approval of the Federal Chancellor. Where the betrayal of military secrets is concerned, the Defense Minister is involved and responsible. I have not set in motion the investigation. The Federal Prosecutor's Office decided the facts were sufficient for it on its own authority and without drawing in anyone else to initiate the measures. It is the obligation and responsibility of all governmental agencies to lend official assistance insofar as feasible. Nothing other than this was done by my ministry. Those who try to ensnarl me in the matter should first reveal frankly their motives and the background. . . . In this hour the people want no government crisis and certainly not a state crisis induced by partisan politics and electoral tactics. For six years the Moscow propagandists have worked for the downfall of the Adenauer government. In recent weeks they have intensified their propaganda.

On November 14 the Bavarian leadership of the CSU had rallied to Strauss's support. They contacted Bonn and insisted that the national leadership of the CDU not abandon Strauss. The Bavarian FDP leadership issued a statement that it stood united behind its national party leadership in the *Spiegel* controversy, although it carefully added that it was not renouncing in advance the possibility of entering a coalition in Bavaria with the CSU after the November 25 election.[12] As late as November 16 Mende emphasized that while the FDP could no longer work with Strauss, he hoped an "appropriate" solu-

[12] *Süddeutsche Zeitung*, November 16, 1962.

tion could be found without forcing the FDP to withdraw formally from the government.[13]

The personal rivalry between Adenauer and his Minister of Economics Ludwig Erhard, intensified since 1959 by the succession question, precluded Erhard from playing a direct role in attempting to arbitrate the CDU/CSU-FDP dispute. Had he been chancellor at the time, Erhard may have reacted differently than Adenauer to the controversy. He had been one of the few Christian Democratic leaders to voice an early concern about Strauss's role in the *Spiegel* action. Urging repeatedly in public that "all the cards be laid on the table," Erhard resisted the temptation to construe the affair as simply a matter of partisan and petty politics. At a CSU voting rally in Hof, Bavaria, on November 18 he counseled the audience: "It is necessary that we not only reexamine our political style, but that we modify it. Only in this way will we avoid the confusion of ideals in which it is possible to mix together the highest and lowest values into a kind of potpourri and convey to the citizen the impression that the 'government' and the 'opposition' are merely matters of tactics and pacts."[14]

Adenauer still rejected a quick surrender to the FDP. Although he and his advisors finally recognized that Strauss would have to resign his ministerial post, this would now happen whatever the strategy of the CDU/CSU. Since Strauss would have to be jettisoned, Adenauer wanted concessions in return from the FDP. Primary among these was Adenauer's

[13] *Der Tag* (West Berlin), November 17, 1962.

[14] *Deutsche Zeitung,* November 19, 1962. The CDU President of the Bundestag, Eugen Gerstenmaier, also seemed to share Erhard's impatience with Strauss's equivocation in explaining his involvement in the affair. At the Congress for the Freedom of Culture on November 16 at the University of Cologne, Gerstenmaier is quoted as having remarked, in alluding to the *Spiegel* controversy, that "I would submit that it is much more dangerous to put the matter under the table. I shall not go into the matter here. But I believe that it would have been more correct and useful if from the beginning there had been a frank and candid discussion about it." *Neue Rhein Zeitung,* November 17, 1962.

being allowed to retain his own position, which seemed increasingly in jeopardy as the FDP began hinting that the unresolved question within the CDU/CSU of the successor to Adenauer was an unsettling and intolerable obstacle to contiued cooperation between the coalition parties. Strauss compounded Adenauer's difficulty by hinting in the Bavarian campaign that he had acted with the approval of the Chancellor. Had the Chancellor really known from the outset about the planned *Spiegel* action and specifically authorized the circumventing of Stammberger? On November 19 Adenauer's office denied that the Chancellor had expressly approved any of the questionable circumstances surrounding the *Spiegel* investigation, including the circumvention of Stammberger.[15] In any event, with no immediate solution in sight the FDP Bundestag *Fraktion,* called to a special caucus on November 19 in Nürnberg, finally made good its threat to withdraw from the government. A reporter for the *Kölner Stadt-Anzeiger* melodramatically described the event:

It is 11:10, Monday morning, as Erich Mende gets out of the car in front of the Grand Hotel Nürnberg. Ten, twelve young men hold up a long transparent banner. "Out with Strauss," it says. "Mende hold fast, think of your backbone."

Erich Mende laughs. If during this year of the Bonn coalition the time has come, then surely he believes it is now. Things will not continue as they are, so runs the betting. The FDP is after the head of Strauss, whatever the cost. Even if it means the subsequent resignation of their own five ministers. . . .

Much appears in fact already to have been decided. Yet the question persists in the smoke-filled, overcrowded foyer of the hotel. Will the demands of the *Fraktion* exceed those to which Mende is committed? Will the group around Deputy Chairman Döring demand not only the resignation of the Defense Minister but also that of the Chancellor? Will the five FDP ministers— Stammberger and Starke particularly—let themselves be sacrificed

[15] But see below, p. 172–73.

without fighting back? Will an ultimatum be issued to the CDU/ CSU?

The decision is to be made in the Marmorsaal of the hotel. It was formerly called the Richard-Wagner-Saal. Sculptures and frescoes adorn grotesquely the walls. The FDP deputies grin: Erich Mende sits just under the huge painting of Siegfried. In shining armor stands the renowned warrior under a German oak, surrounded by ten naked but voluptuous Rhine maidens. Will Mende today play the role of the valiant warrior?

The press is dismissed. The 90 men and woman of the executive committee and *Fraktion* of the Free Democrats want to make their most important domestic political decision since the creation of this Government among themselves. Reporters in the foyer order their first round of coffee. The long watch begins.

It lasts two and a half hours. Then the doors of the Marmorsaal open. . . . "It is decided," says Erich Mende. "My recommendation has been accepted. I shall now notify Adenauer. . . ." Outside, the banners have been lowered. One remains: "Out with Strauss." [16]

A Crisis of Confidence

Although speculation persisted that Adenauer would not make a decision about Strauss's future in the cabinet until after the Bavarian *Landtag* elections, it appears, at least in retrospect, that the tentative decision was made several days prior to the election. In effect, the advice being given Adenauer clustered around the following points: (1) the Chancellor should not attempt in the months ahead to maintain a government without majority support in the Bundestag; (2) the FDP, as a result of its decision on November 19, would not supply the margin of votes needed for majority support if Strauss remained in the government; (3) the Bavarian CSU, upon whom Adenauer also depended for votes sufficient in the Bundestag to give him a majority, was not prepared to obstruct the removal of Strauss, however strongly it asserted the contrary position in public; and (4) the SPD was just as

[16] Report filed by Klaus Bresser in the November 20, 1962, issue.

firmly committed as the FDP to Strauss's removal and it therefore represented at this stage no real alternative to the FDP as a coalition partner for the CDU/CSU. From every perspective, in short, Strauss's dismissal from the cabinet seemed unavoidable. Yet Adenauer still seemed to be playing for time, possibly to allow the CSU to exploit the Strauss issue in the Bavarian election against "those in Bonn," and, secondarily, to maintain some bargaining power when the time came to negotiate with the FDP over the terms of a new coalition.

Whatever the tactical merits of Adenauer's delay in resolving the issues, he and his government were badly exposed in the remaining days of November to the critics, and the patience of even the more dispassionate observers seemed to be wearing thin in view of the seemingly interminable controversy and the inability of the authorities to provide convincing responses to the criticisms. On November 13 Adenauer had requested the ministers of justice, interior, foreign affairs, and defense to prepare jointly a report indicating the nature of the involvement of their ministries in the planning and implementation of the *Spiegel* action. In vain the critics waited in November for the report. It did not become public until February, 1963, and even then not without prodding by the SPD Bundestag *Fraktion*. And the remarkably inept public information program conducted by the government during November compounded the embarrassment of the authorities. In the November 24 issue, for example, of the officially published *Bulletin des Press-und Informationsamtes* (No. 217) an article by Professor Hellmuth Mayer not only seemed to assume the guilt of Augstein and *Der Spiegel* but also represented a crude attempt to win legal support for Strauss in the Ahlers episode. Professor Mayer reasoned that:

There has been and there is frequently the case that rendition agreements do not exist, especially after wars. Nevertheless, rendition may still be performed. In such a case the juridical authorities which request rendition merely have no right to demand it. In addition, the tendency of international development is occurring on the basis of constitutionalism to view the system of justice in all countries as a unified organic whole. An arrest in a foreign country is accordingly, insofar as there is no right of rendition, permissible and valid according to German procedural law if it corresponds to German municipal law, that is, if it, undertaken in Germany, would have been proper according to criminal law and criminal procedures.

This is the case in *Landesverrat* (treason). At all times allied nations or those with common security interests have extradicted to one another their traitors, insofar as this lies in the common security interests. To assert these interests is the natural responsibility [*natürliche Aufgabe*] of the military authorities. . . .

The spurious legal reasoning characterizing Professor Mayer's argument was overshadowed, from the critics' perspective, by the professor's background. The SPD *Fraktion* questioned the government in the Bundestag about the propriety of printing in an official publication the legal opinion of a jurist who in 1936 had seemed so willing to cooperate with the Nazi system by writing a commentary on German criminal law in which he grafted onto German law the principles of national socialist dogma. Replying later for the government, Federal Press Secretary von Hase said: "The Federal Government is of the view that it is sufficient if the article is written by a chaired professor of the law and state science faculty of a German university."[17]

If Professor Mayer found it possible to support the government in the *Spiegel* controversy, this was not the case for a significantly large number of his colleagues throughout the Federal Republic. Prominent historian Professor Gerhard Ritter, in a letter on November 10 to the editor of *Frankfurter Allgemeine Zeitung*, had discounted the significance of

[17] *Deutscher Bundestag, 4. Wahlperiode, 50. Sitzung, Stenographischer Bericht* (December 5, 1962), pp. 2208–09.

the *Spiegel* Affair and complained of the "eternal fixation on the evils of Hitler's dictatorship." Professor Karl Dietrich Bracher, director of the *Seminär für Politische Wissenschaft* at Bonn University and a leading authority on modern German political history, responded to Ritter's letter by writing one of his own to the same newspaper on November 13. Developing a theme which was soon taken up and expanded by groups of academicians, Bracher lectured Professor Ritter: "Perhaps the parliamentary debates of last week have shown him in the meantime that the tactics of denying, of concealing accomplished facts signifies the scandal which has led to the state crisis. A federal chancellor who dismisses an irregular seizure action as a trifle and defames the accused before the hearing of evidence, a defense minister who denied his participation for two long weeks and permitted his state secretary to bear consequences of political responsibility without the revelation of his own involvement . . . that is the core of the crisis of confidence which could very well become a crisis of democracy."

Whether recalling charges that the German academic community had remained all too passive during the 1930's when the Nazis consolidated and abused their authority or responding more immediately to the student protests which erupted in late October and continued unabated throughout November, groups of university and technical college faculty members now entered the fray and warned of the crisis of confidence sweeping the country. The initiative was asserted by fifty-four professors at the University of Tübingen who released to the press on November 19 a "public declaration." Disavowing any attempt to pass judgment on individuals involved in the affair or to weigh the merits of the legal arguments surrounding the controversy, the signers stressed the crisis of public confidence facing the Bonn system. Their real concern was that in recent weeks "the Federal Government and the political system, of which we are citizens, has lost its credibility . . . that abroad, and particularly among our allies in the free world the return to methods of the German past will be suspected and confirmed, that many citizens of our country, among them especially our students, ask in growing uneasiness whether the principles of constitutionalism and the rules of the democratic game remain secure. . . . These are facts which the Government cannot belittle . . . as though they were bureaucratic indiscretions of a purely administrative sort . . . ." The crisis of confidence, the declaration continued, rose also from the widespread impression that the "Federal Government has played an unworthy and dishonest game of hide and seek with the Bundestag and the public, that members of the Federal Government do not take seriously the principles of constitutionalism and that the attempt has been made to absolve the Government of its responsibility through the never seriously meant releasal of state secretaries." They concluded: "In view of the late arrival of democracy in our country and the weakness of its tradition the crisis of confidence can only be lifted through an unmistakable act of political decency. In the well-established democracies a crisis of these dimensions would have caused the resignation of the Government. We therefore believe that a thorough-going internal reconstruction of the Government to be a prerequisite for restoring the credibility of our political system."[18]

On the following day sixty-three professors at Bonn University made public the contents of petitions which they had sent to the members of the Bundestag. In a sharply worded condemnation of Adenauer's remarks in the parliamentary debate, of the authorities' deliberate misrepresentation of the facts of the case, and of the "mishandling by the Government of the entire episode," the petitioners found these and other

[18] *Der Spiegel,* November 28, 1962, p. 39.

circumstances not merely "peripheral phenomena." The academicians warned "they are signs of a deterioration of our political life. The authority of the state has been damaged and confidence in our democratic order is at stake." More serious than the impact of the affair on Germany's image abroad is "the political devastation at home" in the wake of the controversy. And they further pointed out: "Bad domestic political style is like an insidious disease. It lays hold of the good powers which are most certainly not lacking in our parliament, our parties, and our bureaucracy. It interferes with the development of a civic consciousness. As college teachers we have an obligation to introduce the youth to the state. Events such as these of recent weeks work against this task. We cannot therefore remain silent."[19]

On November 2 an open letter from 29 political science and public law professors, reading like a *Who's Who* of professional political scientists in West Germany, was addressed to Bundesrat President Kurt Georg Kiesinger, who was acting as federal president in the absence of Heinrich Lübke, touring India on a state visit. Alluding again to the crisis of confidence now confronting the government and bitterly charging that "not once have the people been accurately informed of the circumstances" surrounding the affair, they concluded that the restoration of public confidence "seems to be possible now only if the responsible ministers' conform to the principle of accountability by assuming the consequences for their conduct.[20] Similar declarations, signed by an additional 394 university professors, instructors, and teaching assistants, appeared publicly between November 22 and December 7, 1962.[21]

[19] *Ibid.,* 38–39.
[20] *Ibid.,* 38.
[21] Twenty-seven professors of Stuttgart *Technische Hochschule* (November 22, 1962); 285 professors, instructors, and teaching assistants of Heidelberg University (December 1, 1962); 47 professors of Karlsruhe

Restoring the Coalition

Somewhat belatedly, and against the backdrop of an escalating public concern, the Chancellor turned his full attention to the *Spiegel* Affair. At a cabinet meeting on November 20, he discussed with his CDU/CSU colleagues the possibility of reconstructing the FDP-CDU/CSU cabinet, excluding Strauss and Stammberger, with a minimal number of changes in the other ministries. The CDU executive secretary, Hermann Dufhues, argued for a drastic overhaul of the cabinet in order to restore "public confidence" in the coalition government and to remove personal "tensions" left in the wake of the controversy. To facilitate the plan Dufhues had already received an agreement from the CDU/CSU ministers to offer their resignations, permitting the Chancellor a free hand. Adenauer accepted Dufhues's suggestion. On November 22 he met with the executive committee of the CDU, in a special meeting in Berlin, to map the strategy for coalition negotiations.

On November 25 the Bavarians went to the polls to elect a new *Landtag.* Strauss's supporters had been calling for a massive vote of confidence for the battle-scarred but still popular (in Bavaria) Defense Minister. But, with the decision already made to remove Strauss, the Bavarian election, whatever its results, could not save Strauss's position.[22] The CSU showed a slight increase in its popular vote (47.5 percent), as compared with its 1958 vote (45.6 percent). The SPD increase was larger, with its vote moving from 30.8 percent in 1958 to 35.3 percent. The FDP's share remained about

Technische Hochschule (December 3, 1962); and 35 instructors and teaching assistants of law and social science at Münster University (December 7, 1962).

[22] Moreover, Adenauer was encountering increasing opposition within the CDU Bundestag *Fraktion,* and particularly from his close adviser, Minister for Special Questions Heinrich Krone, to the retention of Strauss. Within these circles the position then being taken was that Strauss would first have to "rehabilitate" himself, outside the Bonn cabinet, before he could re-establish a claim to a ministerial post.

the same, 5.6 percent in 1958 and 5.9 percent in 1962.[23] On November 30 Strauss announced that he would "resign" his ministerial post.

Twice during the *Spiegel* Affair Adenauer had tactlessly aggravated the dispute between the FDP and the CDU/CSU. When, on October 31, the FDP confronted Adenauer with its terms for remaining in the cabinet, the Chancellor had unnecessarily antagonized his coalition partners by allowing his cabinet to discuss, in the absence of the FDP ministers, the *Sozialpaket* and the 1963 budget proposals. In both of these policy areas the FDP had staked a particular claim to influence. The FDP responded, as we have seen, on November 2 by warning the Chancellor that it would withdraw from the cabinet if its terms were not met. On that occasion Adenauer had succeeded, with the Hopf-Walter Strauss formula, of appeasing the FDP without significantly disrupting his government. On November 13 Adenauer had brazenly challenged the FDP's claim to importance by publicly revealing that Hopf would be returned to active service. In the negotiations with the FDP during the remaining days of November, the Chancellor and his advisors discovered that the party, reacting to these repeated rebuffs, had raised the price for returning to a coalition: Adenauer would have to resign, if not immediately at least at some specific time in the near future. The FDP had finally returned to its 1961 pre-coalition strategy of *ohne Adenauer.*

In an effort to soften the demands of the FDP, Adenauer resorted to a tactic he employed in the fall of 1961 when the FDP was insisting on Adenauer's retirement. After securing the approval of a bare majority of the CDU/CSU Bundestag *Fraktion,* he instructed his negotiators to explore the possi-

[23] *Die Landtagswahl in Bayern am 25. November 1962 (Endgültiges Ergebnis, Ausgegeben am 5. Dezember 1962),* published by the Bavarian Land Statistical Office.

bility of a "grand coalition" with the Social Democrats. On December 4 the SPD executive committee agreed by a vote of 26 to 13 to discuss with the Christian Democrats the basis for such an arrangement. Formal negotiations began that day, even while negotiations with the FDP were being continued. Adenauer wanted the SPD to agree to two major conditions in exchange for the privilege of entering the cabinet. No insistence would be made by the Social Democrats on a specific date for Adenauer's retirement from the chancellorship and they would support a move in the Bundestag to convert the Bundestag electoral law into an exclusively single-member constituency system. The FDP complained of these obvious pressure tactics of Adenauer, but did not call off its negotiations with the CDU/CSU.

On December 5 the SPD negotiating team reported to its Bundestag *Fraktion* the terms of the Adenauer proposal. Without specifically accepting either of them, the SPD deputies authorized a continuation of the talks with Adenauer's group. However, the report carried by the German news agency, *Deutsche Presse-Agentur* (DPA), of the SPD meeting announced that the *Fraktion* had decided it could accept Adenauer as chancellor only upon the condition that he fix a time for retirement in the near future. Six months was rumored to be the maximum time the group was willing to serve in a coalition under Adenauer's leadership.

Upon learning of the decision of the SPD *Fraktion,* as reported by the DPA, that the chancellorship would have to be included within the items of a coalition bargain between the SPD and the CDU/CSU, Adenauer's office issued the statement that "the continuation of the negotiations between the delegations of the CDU/CSU and the SPD, which were scheduled again at 10:30 A.M. tomorrow, have been cancelled . . . ." The DPA withdrew from the news service wires almost simultaneously with the appearance of Adenauer's statement its original version and substituted the following account of the announcement by Franz Barsig, spokesman for the Executive Committee of the SPD: "Barsig mentioned that the SPD negotiating delegation retained flexibility. Their hands had not been tied by the *Fraktion*. They would take up all policy and personnel questions in the negotiations." When informed of Adenauer's cancellation of the meeting scheduled for the next day, SPD Bundestag *Fraktion* chairman Ollenhauer sent a wire to Adenauer: "My dear Herr Chancellor, the news release upon which you apparently based the cancellation of the meeting planned for tomorrow morning, 10:30, has just been laid before me. The account in this release is not a correct interpretation of the present position of the SPD Bundestag *Fraktion*. I am attaching the wording of our decisions and repeat that it was and is my view to take up these decisions with you."

In response to Ollenhauer's conciliatory message, Adenauer agreed to meet privately on December 6 with the Social Democratic leader. When, however, Ollenhauer had to insist during the discussion that the SPD wished to examine "all" personnel questions before entering a coalition with the CDU/CSU, Adenauer countered that he could only interpret this position as including the question of determining when the Chancellor, himself, would resign. To take up the question of who should be chancellor, he added, exceeded the boundaries originally established for negotiating with the SPD.[24]

It had now become clear to Adenauer that there was no longer any advantage to continuing the coalition discussion. He confidentially informed his advisors that he was prepared to fix a specific date for his retirement, to be effective prior to the opening of the fall session (October, 1963) of the Bunde-

[24] Various accounts of the events leading up to the abortive meeting between Adenauer and Ollenhauer have been summarized in the *Archiv der Gegenwart, Jahrgang 1962*, XXXII, 10286-B ff.

stag. The way was open for the return of the Free Democrats to the cabinet. On December 7 the government crisis was ended. By compelling Adenauer to agree to a final date for his resignation, the FDP was now achieving what it had tried, but failed, to achieve in 1961: the end of the Adenauer era.

Seven ministerial changes were announced on December 11 in the new CDU/CSU-FDP cabinet, including the changes in the ministries of justice and defense. Kai-Uwe von Hassel, minister-president of Schleswig-Holstein and one of four deputy national chairmen of the CDU, was appointed as Strauss's replacement, to be effective January 15, 1963. Stammberger was replaced by his FDP colleague, Ewald Bucher. The "working paper" upon which the new coalition was premised stipulated that the Christian Democrats would not pursue during the life of the coalition any plan to modify the electoral system; that "cooperation" between the coalition parties must be "bettered"; that no new policies were anticipated in the fields of finance, agriculture, and social walfare; and that all financial, social, and economic questions should be "discussed between the coalition partners for the purposes of finding mutually acceptable answers." Mende, later in a press conference, paid tribute to the SPD for its "honorable" conduct in refusing to accept the CDU/CSU offer to form a "grand coalition" and "destroy," through a new electoral law, the third force in West German politics.[25]

Public Reaction

During the formative and bargaining stages of the *Spiegel* Affair, did the press reactions correlate with the reactions of the broader public? Did the responses of the parties correlate with the responses of their supporters? Upon whom did the public fix responsibility for the *Spiegel* Affair? What in the public mind was the most objectionable feature of the *Spiegel*

[25] *Archiv der Gegenwart, Jahrgang 1962,* XXXII, 10302-A.

case? Was the forced resignation of Strauss consistent with the desires of the public? Public opinion surveys conducted in November and December, 1962, by the *Institut für Demoskopie* suggest partial answers.

The *Spiegel* Affair was probably the most publicized political controversy in the history of the West German Republic. By November 22, 1962, 91 percent of the representative population sample (sixteen years of age and over) "knew" of the *Spiegel* Affair.[26] A second survey, conducted between November 28 and December 6, shows that a remarkable 96 percent of the sample had "heard" of the Affair.[27] This degree of awareness was uniformly high among all sex, age, and political-orientation categories. How well the public was informed about the complex controversy is not revealed in the survey, but the communications system had undoubtedly secured a large "attentive" audience during the *Spiegel* Affair.

As noted in Chapter Three, a sampling of press reaction immediately after the *Spiegel* raids revealed two primary causes of criticism against the authorities: (1) the methods used in the action, with particular implications for freedom of the press; and (2) the motives for the investigation, especially in light of *Der Spiegel's* earlier encounters with Strauss. The criticisms of the broader public also seemed to have clustered around these two specific objections. A public opinion survey conducted between November 10 and 22 (Table IV) reveals 31 percent objecting to the actions because of the methods used (the second response) and 16 percent objecting because of questionable motives (the first response). Combining these two responses a majority (57 percent) of the men and a plurality of the entire sample (47 percent) were critical of the *Spiegel* action. Earlier we had noted that 62

[26] Neumann, as cited on p. 4, footnote 2.
[27] *Ibid.*, p. 8.

percent of the press sample was critical, either for motivational or procedural objections.

Table IV

Public Reactions to the *Spiegel* Investigation,
Public Opinion Survey,
November 10–22, 1962*

QUESTION:

"Here are three men discussing the events concerning *Der Spiegel*. Would you look it over. Which of the three has expressed what you also think about the matter?"

*The first
one says:*

"Basically I don't think that the suspicion of treason has anything to do with it. The whole thing has been set in motion to silence *Der Spiegel*. Basically this is what it's all about."

*The second
one says:*

"Basically one can't object to an investigation of treason, for through it can be determined whether the suspicion is well founded. But the way in which it was carried out against *Der Spiegel* cannot be approved on any grounds. Things happened there that cannot be tolerated in a constitutional state."

*The third
one says:*

"I find the suspicion of treason a very serious matter. In such cases the police must certainly proceed very quickly and decisively. It concerns in no way *Der Spiegel* alone, but also the persons who give such secret information about our national defense to the press."

	Entire Sample	Men	Women
	(Percent)	(Percent)	(Percent)
The first one is correct:			
They simply wanted to silence *Der Spiegel*	16	21	12
The second one is correct:			
Nothing basically against the investigation, but the manner and means are disapproved	31	36	26
The third one is correct:			
Treason is a serious matter	27	30	25
Undecided	17	9	24
Have not heard of it	9	4	13
	100	100	100

* Source: Neumann, p. 15.

In a separate survey (Table V) the SPD followers were most (56 percent) inclined to question the motives behind the *Spiegel* raids, although a significantly high proportion (47 percent) of the FDP followers had the same concern. Only in the case of the Christian Democratic followers was the sample predominantly sympathetic with the authorities' undertaking the action. Thus the roles the three parties played in the formative phase seem to correlate reasonably high with the attitudes of their respective followers. These surveys neither confirm nor deny, of course, a causal relationship between party roles and followers' attitudes.

Table V
Attitudes Concerning the *Spiegel* Investigation,
by Party Orientation,
November 10–22, 1962*

	They wanted to silence *Der Spiegel*	It was the duty of the authorities to step in	Not Questioned
Of every 100 followers of the CDU/CSU it was said	19	54	27 (100)
Of every 100 followers of the SPD it was said	56	15	29 (100)
Of every 100 followers of the FDP it was said	47	30	23 (100)

*Source: Neumann, p. 14.

How did the public view Strauss's role in the *Spiegel* Affair? And should he have resigned? To the second question a clear majority said yes. (Table VI)

Table VI
Should Strauss Resign? Public Opinion Survey,
November 28 – December 6, 1962*

QUESTION:

"If it were up to you: Should Strauss resign, or should he remain Defense Minister?"

	(Percent)
Resign	54
Remain	31
Undecided	12
Have not heard of the matter	3
	100

* Source: Neumann, p. 28.

Table VII suggests that *Der Spiegel's* exposés, prior to the *Spiegel* Affair, had already harmed Strauss's public image. Thus 64 percent of those who responded that he should resign mentioned the Fibag Affair and "other unclarified matters" as the reason for their attitude.

Table VII

Why Should Strauss Resign? Public Opinion Survey,
November 28 – December 6, 1962*

QUESTION:

"And why (should Strauss resign)? Could you tell me this on the basis of this list? (List presented.)

	Entire Sample	Persons who wanted Strauss to resign (54 percent = 100)
	(Percent)	(Percent)
I believe Strauss should resign—		
because he acted improperly in the *"Spiegel"* Affair	40	73
because of the Fibag Affair and other unclarified matters	35	64
because he wants atomic weapons	17	32
because he lied as Defense Minister	14	26
because one hears that he is sometimes drunk and not in control of himself	12	22
Not questioned	46	—
	164	217

* Source: Neumann, p. 28.

Table VIII reflects the strong suspicion, in spite of his repeated denials, of more than a third of the sample that Strauss ordered the arrest of the *Spiegel* publisher and editors.

Table VIII

Who Ordered the *Spiegel* Arrests? Public Opinion Survey,
November 28 – December 6, 1962*

QUESTION:

"Who really ordered the arrest of the *Spiegel* reporters and publishers?"

	December, 1962 (Percent)
Strauss	36
Federal Prosecutor's Office, Federal High Court	12
Other judicial authorities	3
Defense Ministry	2
Adenauer	4
In general: The government	2
Freiherr von der Heydte	2
Other responses	4
It is not yet determined	7
Don't know	30
Have still not heard of the criminal investigation against *Der Spiegel*	4

* Source: Neumann, p. 30.

The above findings are confirmed in more detail by another set of surveys conducted in December, 1962, and January, 1963, by EMNID Institute.[28] Based on population samples drawn from West Berlin, Rhineland-Palatinate, and Lower Saxony and employing a reputational approach ("Who, in your opinion, has had his reputation most damaged by the

[28] These surveys, carried out under private contract, are contained in files M 30252/2-RP, 12903; M 21252/12-NS, 04722; and M 21162/12-BL, 04712 (EMNID Institute, Bielefeld).

consequences of [the *Spiegel* Affair]?"), the EMNID surveys indicate that in all categories (sex, party orientation, *Land,* size of area of domicile, religion, and level of education) Strauss is most frequently cited.[29] The range of the percentages selecting Strauss varied, depending on the category of the respondents, from some 54 percent to 82 percent. Generally, a higher percentage believed Strauss's reputation was most damaged if the respondents (1) lived in cities and larger communities than in smaller towns and rural areas, (2) belonged to or sympathized with the SPD and the FDP than with the CDU/CSU, and (3) had completed a course of higher education resulting in or equivalent to the *Abitur* (baccalaureate).

Denouement

Under constant prodding from the SPD in the ensuing weeks and apparently in an almost painful effort to reconcile the conflicting versions of the ministries about the controversial aspects of the investigation, the official *Spiegel* Report, begun at Adenauer's request on November 13, 1962, was finally made public on February 4, 1963.[30] It confirmed the

[29] The respondents were asked to select the most incriminated personality or agency from the following list:

SPD	Strauss
CDU	Stammberger
FDP	The German judiciary
Hamburg senate	*Der Spiegel* and its staff
The federal government—domestically	Mende
The federal government—abroad	Brandt
Adenauer	

The item that ranked second for most respondents, but failing to get a majority of respondents, was "The Federal government—abroad."

[30] Der "Spiegel"-Bericht, Darstellung der Vorgänge beim Ermittlungsverfahren gegen Verleger, Redakteure und Informanten des Nachrichtenmagazins "Der Spiegel"—Bericht der Bundesministerien des Auswärtigen, Des Innern, Der Verteidigung und der Justiz, reprinted in the *Bulletin des Presse—und Informationsamtes der Bundesregierung* No. 23 (February 5, 1963), 195–204. The report alludes to an earlier version and adds that

conclusion that Franz Josef Strauss was substantially guilty of the two major accusations made against him during the *Spiegel* Affair. On his own initiative, and possibly upon the suggestion of State Secretary Hopf, Strauss personally phoned German Military Attaché Oster in Madrid on the night of October 26, 1962, and ordered him to request the Spanish authorities to have Ahlers taken into immediate custody.[31] Strauss resorted to this procedure after learning from Hopf that evening that neither the Federal Criminal Office nor the Federal Prosecutor's Office had been successful in its efforts to execute in West Germany the arrest warrant against Ahlers, for the simple reason that Ahlers was in Spain and possibly en route to Tangiers. In the *Spiegel* Report both the Federal Prosecutor's Office and the Justice Ministry insist that Hopf was told that, because the charge against Ahlers was a politi-

---

this report represents the second draft of the original version. The report was transmitted to Adenauer on January 31, 1963, before being released to the public (February 4, 1963) by the Minister of Justice. For a point by point analysis by the SPD Bundestag *Fraktion* of the contradictions committed by various spokesmen for the Adenauer Government during the Affair, as compared with the versions contained in the *Spiegel* Report, see the study published following the release of the *Spiegel* Report: *Bericht der Sozialdemokratischen Bundestagsfraktion über die "Spiegel"-Affäre durch die Bundesregierung* (Bonn, 1963).

[31] Two officials of the German Embassy in Madrid, in whom Oster confided on the night of October 26, 1962, are quoted in the *Spiegel* Report to the effect that Oster that night told them that the Defense Minister, in his phone conversation with Oster, indicated that he was acting with the approval of both the Chancellor and the Foreign Minister (Gerhard Schröder). The Ministry of Foreign Affairs then adds, in the report, the comment that neither the Foreign Minister nor the State Secretary of the Foreign Ministry even knew at that time of the arrest warrant against Ahlers. *Der "Spiegel"-Bericht,* 199–200. If the statements of the above cited German Embassy officials are correct, Strauss must have given Oster a highly exaggerated version of what was happening in West Germany on the night of October 26. Strauss reportedly mentioned that some twelve military officers had already been arrested (none had yet been arrested), that Augstein had fled to Cuba (he was in Hamburg), and that the investigation had a direct bearing on the Cuban missile crisis, the security of Germany and NATO. *Der "Spiegel"-Bericht,* 199.

cal crime, they could not legally resort to the regular channels of either Interpol or rendition procedures in securing in Spain the arrest of Ahlers.[32] Whether Hopf in turn revealed to Franz Josef Strauss the legal impediments to the seizure in Spain of Ahlers is still in dispute.[33] Assuming for the moment that the Defense Minister was not told by his state secretary of the legal difficulties, Strauss is still liable to the charge that he misrepresented both to the public and to the Bundestag his role in the Ahlers incident by insisting he had been *asked* by the investigating authorities to assist in the arrest of Ahlers. This request was never made of Strauss. His invoking the argument of *Amtshilfe* (official assistance), therefore, during the affair in justifying his part in the arrest of Ahlers is incompatible with the evidence in the *Spiegel* Report.

Strauss also misrepresented both to the public and to the Bundestag his role in the Stammberger episode. During the affair he denied knowledge of any deliberate attempt to keep the impending raids and arrests secret from the Justice Minister. The *Spiegel* Report specifically confirms that two days prior to the raids and initial arrests, in a conference with Hopf and State Secretary Walter Strauss of the Justice Ministry, Defense Minister Strauss orderd that Stammberger not be

---

[32] *Der "Spiegel"-Bericht*, 197–98.

[33] In June, 1963, the public prosecutor in Bonn initiated a process against Strauss, Hopf, and Oster for illegally and in violation of their authority causing the seizure in Spain of a German citizen. At least thirty-one additional suits were filed against Strauss by private citizens for his allegedly violating the rights of a German citizen. The suit filed by the Bonn public prosecutor rested on Paragraph 132 of the German Penal Code, which renders an official liable for knowingly violating the jurisdiction (in this case that of the Federal Prosecutor's Office and the Foreign Office) of other agencies in implementing a criminal investigation. Although the immunity of Bundestag deputies was lifted from Strauss to permit the charges to be filed, the Bonn prosecutor abandoned the case in view of his inability to prove whether Strauss knowingly violated his jurisdiction by ordering the arrest of Ahlers. State Secretary Hopf refused to submit sworn affidavits either confirming or denying that he had told the Defense Minister of the legal impediments to the arrest of Ahlers.

informed in advance of the action planned against *Der Spiegel.* In giving this order, Strauss cited the authority of the Chancellor.[34] Ignoring for the moment whether Adenauer explicitly authorized the circumvention of Stammberger, the conclusion must nevertheless be drawn that Strauss abused the truth during the *Spiegel* Affair. Strauss ordered the circumvention of Stammberger; this fact Strauss refused to admit during the affair.

A third major accusation made against Strauss during the affair, that he personally instigated the investigation against *Der Spiegel,* appears unwarranted. The initiative was first asserted by the Federal Prosecutor's Office, although the possibility remains that the idea for the investigation originated outside the offices of the federal attorneys.[35] It was after the instigation of the investigation, all accounts in the *Spiegel* Report agree, that Strauss asserted his authority in the investigation.

The evidence in the *Spiegel* Report also sheds new light on Adenauer's role in the *Spiegel* Affair. In the Bundestag debates the Chancellor left the impression that he learned of the *Spiegel* investigation "at the last possible moment."[36] He actually learned of the investigation at least eight days prior to the actions of October 26, 1962.[37] Adenauer also implied in the debates that he first learned of the investigation from the federal attorneys.[38] According to the *Spiegel* Report, Strauss, not the legal officers, first informed Adenauer of the investigation under way against *Der Spiegel.*[39] The evidence is inconclusive concerning Strauss's later contention that his

---

[34] *Der "Spiegel"-Bericht,* 196.

[35] See above, pp. 77–78.

[36] *Deutscher Bundestag, Stenographischer Bericht, 4. Wahlperiode, 45. Sitzung* (November 7, 1962), 1955.

[37] *Der "Spiegel"-Bericht,* 195.

[38] *Deutscher Bundestag, Stenographischer Bericht, 4. Wahlperiode, 45. Sitzung* (November 7, 1962), 1955.

[39] *Der "Spiegel"-Bericht,* 195.

role in the investigation had been authorized by the Chancellor. Apparently this was Strauss's interpretation of the blanket endorsement given him by Adenauer to cooperate fully with the Federal Prosecutor's Office for the purpose of bringing to justice "all persons regardless of rank or position" who had trafficked in state secrets.[40] In any event, Adenauer's reluctance during the bargaining stage of the affair to take a stronger position against Strauss may, in retrospect, have been due not only to the tactical consideration of not wishing to alienate the CSU Bundestag deputies but also to the Chancellor's insecurity in his own mind as to whether Strauss had acted with proper authority.

The *Spiegel* Report supports the conclusion that the federal attorneys, enjoying considerable immunity from criticism during the formative stage of the affair, were extraordinarily casual in discharging their administrative obligations to the Justice Minister. The statutory relationship between the Federal Prosecutor's Office and the Justice Ministry imposed, it can be reasonably argued, three specific reporting obligations upon the federal attorneys in charge of the *Spiegel* investigation: (1) to inform the Justice Ministry as soon as the investigation assumed the characteristics of one that required court orders and police action; (2) to include in their report, or in a subsequent report, specific mention of the planned police actions against *Der Spiegel* and its staff; and (3) to report personally to the head of the ministry, the Justice Minister, in passing on the above information to the ministry. The first obligation was technically met through the letter of October 18, 1962, arriving in the Justice Ministry on October 22, but inexplicably not reaching Stammberger's desk until October 24. Neither of the other two obligations was satisfied and there appears to have been no attempt by the federal attorneys to fulfill them.

[40] *Ibid.*

In 1963 the federal attorneys completed the preparation of their case against Augstein, Ahlers, and Colonel Martin. In the midst of speculation that the court might delay its decision until after the 1965 Bundestag election, a decision was announced on May 13, 1965.[41] The Third Senate of the Federal High Court, in a preliminary hearing, dismissed the charges of treasonable publication against Augstein and Ahlers and held open without prejudice the charge against Martin of passing confidential information from the Defense Ministry to *Der Spiegel*.[42] Although considering the possibility that "state secrets" may have been contained in both the Foertsch article and an earlier 1962 article[43]—the court alluded to seven categories of data which may not have been fully revealed previously to the public and which may have been of such a nature as to be susceptible to the state secret classification—it concluded that the evidence was insufficient to the major holding that state secrets, hitherto unpublished,

[41] *6 StE 4/64 (Bundesgerichtshof,* Third Senate). Charges against all others who had initially been arrested or questioned were either formally dropped or appeared unlikely to reach the stage of preliminary hearing. Colonel Wicht was eventually transferred from the Defense Ministry and assigned to the staff of an army corps of the Bundeswehr. Immediately after the *Spiegel* raids of October 26, 1962, *Der Spiegel* filed a constitutional complaint with the Federal Constitutional Court *(Bundesverfassungsgericht)* against the search and seizure methods still being employed against its offices and archives. In its decision of November 8, 1962, the Constitutional Court ruled that the complaint was without basis, since, the court reasoned, the next issue of *Der Spiegel* had already appeared without unconstitutional interference and there appeared to be no future endangering of the freedom of *Der Spiegel* to continue its publication schedule. *1 BvR 586/62.*

[42] In 1966 the last major court decisions arising out of the *Spiegel* affair were rendered. In a 4–4 decision the Federal Constitutional Court dismissed the constitutionality complaint of *Der Spiegel* against various aspects of the search and seizure action; the Federal High Court ordered proceedings dropped against Martin; and in December, 1966, the Court dismissed charges against Schmelz. See Schoenbaum, *The Spiegel Affair,* 209–17.

[43] The other 1962 article ("Stärker als 1939?") appeared in the June 13 issue, pp. 16–20. The Foertsch article was the sequel to and more lengthy continuation of the analysis begun in the June 13 article.

may have been treasonably published, i.e., "so as to endanger the security and well being of the Federal Republic." The court took into account not only the difficulty of factually determining whether the disputed data had been publicly revealed somewhere in the world prior to the appearance of the *Spiegel* articles, but it also noted such circumstances as the apparently untreasonable intent of the publisher and author, the effort by Ahlers prior to the publication of the articles to check out the state secrets problem with Colonel Wicht of the Federal Intelligence Agency, and the improbability that the material endangered the Republic because of the inability of any hostile power to establish the credibility of the information. The cautious and delimiting wording of the opinion, and the political controversy surrounding the case, warned against easy generalizations about the impact of the opinion on the future status in West Germany of the law of treasonable publication. The West German press generally welcomed the decision but renewed its plea for a uniform federal press law clarifying the boundaries between press freedom and treasonable publication.[44]

[44] Cf., for example, Ernst Müller-Meiningen, Jr., "Die Lehren aus dem Spiegel-Fall," *Süddeutsche Zeitung,* May 22, 1965; and Günter Kohlmann, "Dem Verratsparagraphen fehlen die klaren Begriffe," and "Der Verratsparagraph muss neu gefasst werden," in the *Handelsblatt* (Düsseldorf), May 25, 26, 1965.

Chapter VII

EPILOGUE

Adenauer's pledge to resign in the fall of 1963 cleared the way for the selection by the Christian Democrats of Ludwig Erhard as his successor. Until the final vote in the CDU/CSU caucus (April, 1963), Adenauer persisted in his opposition to Erhard, maintaining that the personable architect of the "economic miracle" lacked both the diversity of political experience and qualities of leadership essential for an effective chancellorship. Adenauer retained the national chairmanship of the CDU until 1966, periodically taking time off from the writing of his memoirs to criticize the endangering by the Erhard government of the Franco-German rapprochement to which Adenauer, while chancellor, had given so much emphasis.

Erhard succeeded Adenauer as party chief and seemed determined after the 1965 Bundestag election to try to assert his leadership over both the party and his coalition with the FDP. In this he failed. His inability to resolve the differences within his own party, the pressures exerted against his leadership by the CSU under Strauss's leadership and the Adenauer "loyalists" within the CDU, and the FDP's abandonment of Erhard during the budget dispute in the fall of 1966 finally led to the ousting of Erhard and his replacement by Kurt Georg Kiesinger as the chancellor of the newly formed Grand Coalition between the SPD and the CDU/CSU. Thus Ludwig Erhard, who ineffectually but clearly called during the *Spiegel* Affair for greater sensitivity on the part of the government to the nature of the public protest, was himself to experience but a brief sojourn at the pinnacle of power.

Erhard's ally in foreign policy and defense questions,

Gerhard Schroeder, obviously miffed by Strauss's conduct during the *Spiegel* Affair and lending his support, discreetly but surely, to the front against Strauss that forced his resignation in December, 1962, was relieved in 1966 of the Ministry of Foreign Affairs to make way for the SPD's Willy Brandt. Although Schroeder was then reassigned to the Defense Ministry portfolio, he had suffered a net loss in influence in the new coalition government and by 1967 appeared to be no nearer to the chancellorship than his erstwhile rival Strauss.

After resigning his cabinet position, Franz Josef Strauss assumed in 1963 the leadership in the Bundestag of the CSU *Fraktion*, upon whom the larger CDU continued to depend for support that enabled it to remain the largest party of representation in the Bundestag. The *Spiegel* Affair exposed what had been increasingly evident for years: not only structurally but in more significant ways the CDU and the CSU are separate political parties. Particularly under Strauss's leadership, the CSU had become an independent variable in the West German party system, rendering somewhat premature the speculation about the emergence in the Bonn Republic of a cohesive two-party system. Exploiting his bargaining power as leader of the CSU *Fraktion*, Strauss returned to power in 1966, this time as finance minister. His "rehabilitation" had been made possible through the SPD's willingness to coalesce with the CDU/CSU in forming the Grand Coalition.

Wolfgang Stammberger, the forgotten man of the *Spiegel* Affair who had entered a wedge of dissent that served as an important, if unforeseen, impetus to an escalation of the controversy, lost his ministerial post in the reshuffling of the cabinet by Adenauer in December, 1962. In 1964 Stammberger announced his departure from the ranks of the FDP in favor of the SPD. In justifying the transferral of party membership Stammberger reasoned that only the Social Democrats could prevent Strauss's return to a ministerial post.[1] The *Spiegel* Affair ended Stammberger's career as justice minister; the formation of the Grand Coalition in 1966 ended his career as a prophet.

The FDP, taking credit for the forced resignation of Strauss in 1962, campaigned in the 1965 Bundestag election with the promise to continue Strauss's isolation from ministerial power.[2] Not only did the Free Democrats fail to secure an electoral reward for their asserted accomplishment, but by withdrawing their support from Erhard in 1966 they also set in motion the events leading to Strauss's acceptance as finance minister. Following the formation of the Grand Coalition, the FDP therefore became in the Bundestag the party of the opposition, a role hardly consistent with its third force concept of pre-*Spiegel* Affair days. The Siegfried of the *Spiegel* Affair, the FDP later resembled a Don Quixote.

In short, for the dissidents who framed their reactions in terms of personalities, who perceived the *Spiegel* Affair as a morality tale in which the "good" people would, hopefully, prevail over the "bad", the outcome cannot be altogether satisfying.[3] Even for the more dispassionate observer, the end of the affair was marked by several touches of irony. But

[1] *Deutscher Bundestag, Stenographischer Bericht, 129. Sitzung* (June 5, 1964), p. 6255; *Archiv der Gegenwart, Jahrgang 1964,* XXXIV, 11253.

[2] Bundesparteileitung der Freien Demokratischen Partei, *FDP-Politiker stehen Rede und Antwort, Eine Dokumentation zur Bundestagwahl 1965* (Bonn, 1965), 29, 45, and 149; "Die Situation der Parteien vor der Bundestagswahl," (position paper prepared by the FDP national office for private circulation, mimeographed, n. d.), 14–15. The 1965 Bundestag election results, in percentages of popular votes cast on the second or *Land* list ballot (comparative 1961 figures in parentheses): CDU/CSU: 47.6% (45.3%); SPD: 39.3% (36.2%); FDP: 9.5% (12.8%).

[3] Walter Strauss was appointed, soon after the Affair, to a seat on the European High Court. The appointment had generally been anticipated prior to the *Spiegel* Affair. Hopf later became president of the *Bundesrechnungshof.* There were some personnel gains, of course, for the pro-*Spiegel* side in the controversy. Augstein remained free and as vigorous as before in directing *Der Spiegel;* Conrad Ahlers became assistant director of the Federal Press and Information Office.

whatever one's judgment of the personalities involved or of the justice of their fate, the *Spiegel* Affair represents a significant episode in the development of the Bonn system. Without attempting to overload the case with a theoretical thrust that cannot be sustained, it remains to suggest why this is so.

If a sizable number of participants in a political system are suddenly antagonized by, and wish therefore to protest, a specific act of the authorities, how do they translate their attitudes into demands upon the political processes? The *Spiegel* Affair points to the key role which the press can play in articulating the attitudes and circulating them broadly in the political community. At least one variable, however, in the *Spiegel* case interferes with the extension of this conclusion to the level of a generalization about the Bonn system. If the procedures employed in the investigation had been similar, but the object of the investigation had been a person or organization without a press function, would the response of the press community have been as vigorous and hostile? The question need not detract from the contributions which the press made to the intensification of the issues. It does suggest that *Der Spiegel* had the good fortune to have for its ally an institution that is peculiarly equipped in a pluralistic, participatory system to mobilize quickly criticism of public authority.

If the articulation mechanism during the *Spiegel* Affair performed impressively, the same can not be said for the "conveyor" apparatus. By this we mean that the dissidents, when confronted with the sluggishness of the Adenauer government in responding to the criticism, seemed temporarily stymied in extracting acceptable explanations and concessions. It was at this point that the FDP played its primary role in the *Spiegel* controversy. Only when the Adenauer government seemed threatened with the loss of its controlling majority in the Bundestag did it begin to respond in earnest to the flow of dissent. Does this then validate the FDP's claim to the third force function within the Bonn system? Perhaps so, but not as much as the FDP later claimed. The apparent ease with which the CDU/CSU diverted the FDP from the major areas of the controversy by offering the Hopf-Walter Strauss formula weakens the Free Democrats' claim to an exclusive and calculated role in exposing the government's, and Strauss's, position. A tactical error by Adenauer, evidencing a basic insensitivity to the nature of the controversy, returned the FDP to a more relevant course, from the dissenters' perspective, when he announced that Hopf would be returned to duty in the Defense Ministry.

Operating from its position as the party of opposition that simplified the type of response it would make, the SPD from the outset focused more consistently than the FDP on the major areas of the controversy. Although in the initial stage of the Affair it could not dislodge Strauss or exact tangible concessions from the Adenauer government, it did force the Bundestag debates during which Strauss's position, if not fully exposed, was weakened to the point of encouraging the dissenters to intensify their original demands. Both the SPD and the FDP served to translate the criticisms into demands upon the political processes. Neither alone achieved the final result, and the contributions of both the SPD and the FDP have institutional implications for the Bonn system. The use by the SPD of the Question Hour device to initiate the *Spiegel* debates in the Bundestag dramatically exposed the government's weakness in explaining and defending the methods employed in the *Spiegel* investigation. Whatever its deficiencies in other situations, the Question Hour cannot be discounted as an occasionally relevant and effective tool of opposition and confrontation. Moreover, while a balanced assessment of the FDP in West German politics must be approached from a perspective that transcends the limited scope of a single case, the party's role in the *Spiegel* Affair suggests that the third force rationale is not entirely irrelevant to the Bonn system.

State Secretary Walter Strauss's role in the *Spiegel* Affair also has institutional implications. Within the West German ministries the state secretaries occupy politico-bureaucratic positions, rooted in tradition and characterized neither by the well-established principle of political neutrality of the British permanent secretary nor, in contrast, by the complete political partisanship of an individual minister's *cabinet* in the French system. The state secretaries enjoy certain prerogatives of civil servants; at the same time they are partisan officials, subject to transferral for political reasons, entitled to and expected many times to have active party affiliations, and authorized to represent their ministerial superiors in relatively high policy matters. But the potential role conflict of their position does not excuse the conduct of Walter Strauss. Surely he violated the presumed relationship of confidence that is minimally to exist between a West German minister and his state secretary when he accepted the instruction from Defense Minister Strauss to keep Stammberger uninformed of the impending police action. The Walter Strauss incident gives credence to the suspicion in Bonn that the major party in a coalition government will wish, if possible, to "encircle" the ministers of the minor coalition parties with politically reliable state secretaries. The personnel problem over which coalition parties haggle in Bonn includes, for good reason, not only the ministerial posts but also the state secretary positions.

Important for an understanding of the controversy surrounding the *Spiegel* investigation was the apparent inability of the authorities to perceive that their assertion of the Legality Principle was not a credible defense against the mounting criticisms. And it was the gap between the critics' questions and the government's responses that gave the decisive impetus to the *Spiegel* Affair. The Legality Principle asserted that investigations and determinations of suspected violations of law are purely juridical functions, removed from interference or discretionary participation by the "political" agents of the state. Most advocates of constitutionalism would find it difficult to quarrel with this principle; it seems to embody the general notion highly congenial and intertwined with the constitutionalists' assumption that the judiciary is to be relatively shielded from the partisan pressures of discretionary exercises of authority, and that the adjudication of legal disputes is not appropriately amenable to the political processes. But the assertion by the government of the Legality Principle encountered two difficulties, one factual and the other conceptual.

The credibility of the Legality Principle could not be sustained unless, in fact, the *Spiegel* investigation appeared to be free of inappropriate influence from the "political" agencies and officials. The role which *Der Spiegel* had played in postwar Germany and the skirmishes in the past between *Der Spiegel* and prominent West German political personalities, particularly Franz Josef Strauss, placed a heavy responsibility upon those who decided to undertake and implement the investigation to insure at the outset that improper tampering with the Legality Principle be avoided. Under the most careful and discreet of circumstances, a police action against *Der Spiegel* would arouse considerable public interest. When the police action immediately received this publicity and did not appear to have been conducted in a manner fully consistent with the Legality Principle, the *Spiegel* action was transformed into a political controversy. Then, as the controversy moved to its second stage, that of a fully developed political affair, the question of the Legality Principle was enlarged to include a separate, but related, question, that of the credibility of the Adenauer government. When it became increasingly apparent that the government could not refute the critics' charge that the principle had been violated and, instead, seemed inclined either to ignore or belittle the validity of the protests, the controversy prompted a debate about a "crisis of confidence," with thematic overtones of the German past and the frailty in Germany of the presumed norms of a responsible parliamentary and democratic political system.

A second, and more basic, obstacle to the credibility of the Legality Principle as a defense against the public protest is that law and politics will not remain separate, in theory or in practice.[4] The political implications of "legal" processes, and the legal implications of "political" processes, are not of course distinctively German phenomena, but the problem took on added significance in West Germany in light of the German past, symbolized, for example, by the relatively easy transition made by a number of jurists from the Weimar to the Nazi systems. From the moment the investigators in the Federal Prosecutor's Office decided to move forward with a search and seizure action against *Der Spiegel* and its editors, it became increasingly difficult to sustain the distinction between law and policy. Not only did Franz Josef Strauss's conduct disprove the *Spiegel* investigation to be a purely legal matter, but also, and rather curiously, his responses suggest that he recognized from the beginning that the investigation was at least as much a policy matter as a legal matter. His error was not that he failed to see the policy aspects of the *Spiegel* investigation, but that he drew the wrong conclusions, on the basis of this perception, as to his proper role in the investigation.

Adenauer, not Strauss, epitomized the problem. If the Chancellor had been able to sense the policy nature of the investigation, that it could not fail to arouse public criticism, that it would in fact have political repercussions, he may or

[4] Particularly relevant for the point we are suggesting here is Otto Kirchheimer, *Political Justice: The Use of Legal Procedure for Political Ends* (Princeton, 1961).

may not have tried to dissuade the Federal Prosecutor's Office from proceeding. But surely he would at least have made certain that the government prepare itself for the expected criticism and make every effort to minimize, in advance, the validity of the public protest. And the most obvious way to shore up its position in advance of the criticism would have been an unequivocal instruction from Adenauer to Strauss that the latter stay entirely out of the investigation, including the implementation of it. At least eight days prior to October 26, 1962, Adenauer had the opportunity to give the instruction when conferring with Strauss about the investigation. Whether Strauss would have followed the advice is uncertain; that the Chancellor never gave the advice is significant. This is not to suggest that Adenauer simplistically be made the scapegoat of the affair. But in assessing the style of the Bonn political system, the Chancellor's insensitivity to the policy aspects of the *Spiegel* investigation is at least equal in importance to the poor judgment of one of his ministers.

APPENDIX I

THE FOERTSCH ARTICLE

Translator's Note: Except for the pictures (mainly photographs of the personalities prominently mentioned), a biographical sketch of Inspector-General Friedrich Foertsch that stands separate from the text of the article, and two charts depicting respectively the organization of a typical Bundeswehr mechanized infantry division and the relative military strengths of NATO and the Eastern bloc, the Foertsch article (as found in *Der Spiegel,* October 10, 1962) is reproduced here in its entirety. Although responsibility for the translation is mine, I wish to record my appreciation to Mrs. Heinz Velmeden of the Department of Foreign Languages, University of Houston, for her assistance with the initial version.

BUNDESWEHR

Strategy
Conditionally Prepared to Defend

> *One can only, then, influence American policy when one engages in politics with the Americans and when one does not engage in politics against the Americans.*
>
> Federal Defense Minister Franz Josef Strauss on March 20, 1958, in the German Bundestag.

The Chancellor left his capital of Bonn. Just as the Fuehrer had done in the early hours of May 10, 1940, at the beginning of the campaign in the west, he went now to his command bunker in the Eifels.

Accompanying the Chancellor were members of the Federal Defense Council and the command echelon of the Bundeswehr.

Extreme danger of war existed. "Fallex 62" (Fall Exercise 1962), a NATO staff manuever, passed from the "alert stage" to a "defend stage."* U.S. General Norstad, NATO commander in the European theater, had given the "general alarm" after the West's most forward positions had been attacked.

On this 21st day of September, in Cadenabbia, Konrad Adenauer played boccia. Special Affairs Minister Heinrich Krone, Konrad Adenauer's closest political confidant, had assumed the role of chancellor in the manuever. Franz Josef Strauss in his Riviera retreat nursed his nerves which had been assaulted by the Fibag Affair and the fight over the succession to the premiership of Bavaria. To the amazement of his colleagues he passed up this important exercise, while U.S. Defense Secretary McNamara came to West Germany to observe for 48 hours the conduct of "Fallex 62." The Federal Defense Minister's role in the manuever fell to the Bundeswehr Personnel Chief, Ministerial-Director Karl Gumbel.

Meanwhile, Major General Count Kielmansegg, otherwise commander of the 10th Mechanized-Infantry Division in Sigmaringen, directed the Bundeswehr. But the Bundeswehr Inspector-General, four-star General Friedrich Foertsch, was not taking a vacation as were his chancellor and his minister; he observed, step by step, the execution of the military exercise, giving the highest ranking German soldier valuable information about the war preparedness of the Federal Republic and the combat readiness of its military forces.

"Fallex 62" was the first NATO maneuver premised on the assumption that the third world war would begin with a large-scale attack in Europe.

---

* In a wargame, two sides, blue and red, oppose each other on the map. The person in charge, who plans the game, fixes the initial positions of both sides, with the leaders then directing on their own initiative; the blue leader with his forces, the red leader with those of the assumed enemy. In a Plan-Exercise, such as "Fallex 62," only one side plays, while the operations of the opponent are determined by the planners. War-games and Plan-Exercises are teaching and instructional devices of the military command staffs. They serve both to train and to test the operational, personnel, and supply needs in war planning.

The third world war began on that Friday, almost three weeks ago, in the early evening hours. The directors of the exercise allowed an atom bomb of medium force to explode over a Bundeswehr airbase. Additional atomic strikes followed against NATO airbases and missile sites in the Federal Republic, and in England, Italy, and Turkey.

The Russians failed, however, with this first atomic strike to destroy the retaliatory power of the Atlantic Pact.

About two-thirds of the West's atomic missiles remained intact. The 14-day "alert stage," preceding the Russian paper attack, had been utilized by NATO to camouflage its missiles and to put a large number of its planes in the air or on prearranged sidings.

However, even the immediate counterattack by these NATO units was not able to nip in the bud the Red aggression. The East retained sufficient forces and atomic bombs to push its attack forward.

Within a few days large areas of England and the Federal Republic were totally destroyed. In both countries the fatalities numbered ten to fifteen million. The losses were even greater in the United States, which had been hit in the meantime by several Soviet hydrogen bombs.

The chaos was inconceivable—even discounting the fact that in both the execution of the maneuver and the testing of emergency procedures more atomic devices were assumed to have been exploded than the Russians in a crisis presumably could and would employ.

This chaos hindered the advance of the similarly depleted and hard-hit Communist divisions. Nevertheless they could—because of the scarcity of NATO troops—occupy vast areas in the northwest of the Federal Republic, including Schleswig-Holstein. Hamburg was not defended, a price which the Hamburg Interior Minister Helmut Schmidt had already reconciled himself to before this exercise—just as formerly, under similar circumstances, the Hamburg Reich Governor, Karl Kaufmann, had done. The military was also not interested in suicidal street-fighting.

The purpose of "Fallex 62" was to test the combat readiness of NATO and the functional capability of the staff, and above all to test the emergency procedures for the civilian population. Several civilian agencies and officials therefore participated in the exercise—the interior ministers of the federal and *Land* governments, *Land* premiers and parliamentarians, in addition to the federal postal and transportation ministries.

It demonstrated that the federal government's defense preparations are entirely inadequate, the lack of a state of emergency law being only one of many deficiencies.

First to collapse was the public health service. It was short of field hospitals, medicine, and physicians. In the case of food supply and the maintenance of vital industrial and transportation facilities the situation was no better. Air-raid precautions failed completely. Controlling the flood of refugees was impossible. In a very short time the telecommunications system was out of order.

Officials and observers taking part in the maneuver—among them the Bonn history professor, Walther Hubatsch, and representatives of the Federation of [German] Industry—were shocked by the results of the maneuver. Federal Interior Minister Hermann Höcherl had to admit that in such a catastrophe only those things which had been done in advance would be of any help. He summarized the inadequacy of the preparations: "Under the present circumstances virtually no one has a chance."

Already obvious during the "alert stage," that is even before the attack began, were the defects of the Bundeswehr.

The American ground units in western Europe were ready within two hours for combat with 85 percent of their full strength. In contrast the nine mobilized divisions of the Bundeswehr, already under NATO's command system, were neither fully manned nor adequately supplied with weapons or equipment. Only one-fourth of the positions established for military doctors were staffed. For the hundreds of thousands of Bundeswehr reservists who had their active duty behind them and who—as the war players assumed—reported to the army administrative offices, there were no officers, no noncommissioned officers, and, even worse, no weapons.

The Territorial Defense (TV) units, with their few awkward engineering groups, were hardly capable of carrying out their assignments. Not a single TV unit was available for opposing the tanks which had broken through the lines.

NATO's command headquarters rated the allied forces according to one of four categories: fully prepared to attack; conditionally prepared to attack; fully prepared to defend; conditionally prepared to defend.

Today—after almost seven years of Germany's rearming and after six years under the official guidance of her Commander-in-Chief Strauss—the Bundeswehr still gets the lowest NATO rating: conditionally prepared to defend.

Confronting such inadequate forces on the central front in Europe, even in normal times, is a solid first-class Eastern force: ten armored and ten mechanized Soviet divisions with 6,000 mobile cannons and tanks, the bulk of them of medium type T 54, plus 1,000 heavy tanks of the type "Josef Stalin," all in the territory of the DDR [German Democratic Republic]; two Soviet divisions in Poland and four in Hungary.

Supporting the Soviet nucleus are six divisions of the National Peoples' Army [of the DDR], not to mention the six border divisions and three border brigades of the Peoples' Police [of the DDR], plus 13 Polish and 14 Czech divisions.

The Czechs have modern equipment, but are not particularly well prepared to use it. The Poles' equipment is not comparable, and they are also lacking a certain quality of fighting spirit. The National Peoples' Army with 2,500 tanks of mostly older types (T 34/85) took part in the Warsaw Pact maneuver last year, in the forward lines of operation, but their fighting skill is not highly regarded. The Russian divisions at the German central front are considered to be the elite of the Soviet army.

The Red army complex would presumably be able to smash a rescue operation by the NATO forces, with the Bundeswehr as the spearhead, in case of a West Berlin blockade—an operation which U.S. President Kennedy, in a conversation once with Bonn Ambassador Grewe, held to be unlikely in any event. Yet in the opinion of the general staff at NATO headquarters in Paris, their [the Soviet] counterthrusts would not be sufficient to push the Atlantic forces' line "out of position," even if they tried to blast their way forward with tactical atomic weapons.

A ground offensive from the East against the West requires the systematic deployment of the advancing units and strong reserves which can move up to support and replace those in the assault waves that are forced to retreat. Thus during the preparations for the building on August 13 last year of the Berlin Wall the Soviet army established in the DDR, as a precaution, several staff headquarters for those units that in case of a crisis were forced to fall back.

Deploying such troops by rail and highway the Soviets could, within ten days, bring to the combined striking force in the zone about 50 divisions from the Soviet Union's western provinces.

Red airforce transports for two airborne divisions, one of them a paratroopers' division, complete the Soviet deployment apparatus. All of the East's front-line units remain, even in peacetime, fully mobilized and equipped. Their forward progress in the "alert stage" is simply a matter of transportation.

NATO, on the other hand, to be able to deploy with an acceptable defense force, must first bring its active divisions to full strength and mobilize the reserves.

Of course, the front-line strength of the Soviet division, with 10,000 men plus the separate artillery and missile units, is less than the average 20,000-man strength of a NATO combat division, not including its own heavy artillery. Against this an aggressor needs, in terms of the entire front, a superiority of three to one for the assault. To deter or to be able to withstand such an operation, NATO must have between the Alps and the Baltic Sea at least 40 defending divisions against about 120 Red attacking divisions.

Contrary to this, the prevailing NATO forces available for the line of defense amount to exactly 33 divisions. The actual front-line strength today consist of 23 divisions:

five U.S. divisions, plus three regimental combat groups equipped with Davy Crockett atomic mortars;

three British divisions (including one Canadian brigade); two Belgian, two Dutch, and one Danish division;

nine Bundeswehr divisions (five mechanized infantry and two armored divisions, one airborne and one mountain division—the formation of a tenth division is nearing completion —with altogether about 2,000 tanks, 4,000 tank-cannons, and 700 self-propelled guns).

In addition, supplies and equipment for two U.S. divisions are stored in the Federal Republic; the troops can be transported by air within a week's time, demonstrated by the air transport exercise "Long Thrust," which took place the past year.

The American divisions are constantly kept at combat-readiness. The English divisions are at 60 percent of full strength; during "Fallex 62," therefore, British reserves had to be flown to Germany. The Dutch and Belgian units are also undermanned, and the Bundeswehr divisions, of which the mountain and airborne divisions are still short three full brigades, fluctuate between 80 and 90 percent of their effective strength following the introduction of the 18 months' compulsory military service.

To add to all this, NATO is short of fighter pilots to support the ground troops and conventional rocket mortars of the Russian type Stalin-Orgel.

In view of this inferiority of the West, NATO High Command asumes that the East, in case of war, would launch a large-scale attack with three massive prongs:

north of the Elbe toward Schleswig-Holstein, combined with airborne operations toward the Danish islands and Jutland, in order to gain the Baltic Sea gateway and to keep it open for their own naval forces, especially the submarine squadrons;

on both sides of the Autobahn Helmstedt-Cologne past the Ruhr Valley and across the Rhine;

from the Thuringian region to Frankfurt am Main and, for flank protection, toward the south to Nuremberg and Munich.

A secondary thrust from the Bohemian Forest through the Fichtel and Harz Mountains would contain the outflanked NATO forces.

The East can carry out this broad offensive—aim of attack: the North Sea and the Atlantic—with exclusively conventional firepower because of the weakly manned Western forces. For this purpose alone seven artillery and six to eight rocket mortar brigades are assigned to the 20 Soviet divisions in the DDR. To these is added a strong fighter aircraft group to support the tank thrusts with conventional bombs and aircraft fire.

The Soviet army divisions are at present deficient in tactical atomic weapons. Their caliber exceeds the size with which a division can effectively function in combat; because of the range they also lack the necessary reconnaissance and guidance systems.

It is at the army level that the Soviet forces first attain a tactical nuclear capability. These weapons are assigned to special units, thus insuring a purely conventional fighting capability at the combat division level.

The still all-too-weak, numerically, NATO divisions have thus, at present, no choice other than to counter the aggressor's superiority with the aid of tactical atomic weapons. This means of fighting, which in an operational air war favors the aggressor by permitting him to attack first the enemy's missile, air, and radar bases, gives the advantage to the defender in the opening stage of a ground war.

Both sides, aggressor and defender, are forced by the very existence of tactical atomic weapons to disperse their troops; the deployment areas will be thinned out. NATO's High Command staff figures that the East would extend its area of concentrated attack beyond the southern border of the DDR into Czechoslovakia and violate Austria's neutrality in order to gain the Danubian basis.

However, in order to break through the aggressor must focus his efforts at the central point of the attack, thus offering some rewarding targets to the defender's tactical atomic weapons.

With his tactical atomic weapons the defender may also be able to disrupt effectively the logistical lines through which the aggressor supplies his spearhead and brings up fresh troops—a consideration enhanced by the fact that the problem of reinforcement and supply is already complicated by the extensive mechanization and the use of weapons with substantially higher fire sequence than was true during the Second World War.

U.S. General Lemnitzer, until now the Chairman of the American Joint Chiefs of Staff and the next NATO Supreme Commander in Europe: "The Soviets' supply lines are fatally exposed."

But if the aggressor should succeed in a breakthrough and the front becomes fluid, then, of course, the use of atomic explosives by the defender will be difficult. Its own troops and its own civilian population will then be badly exposed and finding targets will be impeded.

The West did not have to be concerned with these problems when, after Stalin's Berlin blockade and the putsch in Czechoslovakia, it agreed in 1949 to the North Atlantic Defense Treaty. At that time the Americans had an atomic monopoly. Nor did their atomic mastery appreciably suffer from the production of the Soviet A-bombs in the early 1950's, since the USA continued to hold its superiority in the field of ballistic missiles.

But the war picture which the NATO strategists envisaged even then was not altogether satisfactory, in spite of the atomic superiority: against an invasion of western Europe by the massive Soviet forces, the bombs could not be effectively used in the initial phase of the fighting, and sufficient defense units did not exist in the West, which had demobilized in 1945. In Lisbon, therefore, in 1952 the NATO Council discussed a Contingency Plan—which has long since become legendary—calling for 85 divisions by June, 1954, for the front extending from the North Cape to Turkey.

With this kind of military force, which did not include the

already projected twelve German divisions, the NATO leaders felt they could proceed to think in terms of the operational dream concept "forward strategy": the 85 NATO divisions foil a Soviet attack against western Europe and free, through "operation roll-back," the people of eastern Europe and the Soviet Union.

The Lisbon Contingency Plan together with the "forward strategy" concept remain paper projects. The European NATO members shied away from the expenses of large ground armies; instead, they placed their faith in "massive retaliation," in the blunt atomic clubs with which the Americans threatened to retaliate for a Soviet attack.

The lead which the Americans held over the Russians in the technology of producing atomic and hydrogen weapons, and also delivery systems, seemed at first to justify this defense doctrine, even after the initial Russian nuclear successes. NATO's armies languished.

NATO's planners had to admit, however, that a substantial period of time would elapse before their "retaliation," their magic fire, that would engulf the Soviet Union, could stop the momentum of the Soviet combat divisions by destroying their sources of supply. From this recognition there emerged, following the abandonment of the Lisbon plan, the scheme to position at the Rhine the forward line against a Soviet attack.

The advocacy of this "fall back" planned-surrender of the Federal Republic placed a stumbling block in the way of West Germany's rearming. Bonn's first defense minister, Theodor Blank, had already insisted in 1952, during the initial discussions of the Federal Republic's defense contribution, that the West's defense strategy be converted from "fall back" to "forward defense"—at the very latest at that point where the bulk of the Bundeswehr forces were prepared to make a stand: to the most advanced line near the border [between East and West Germany].

General Collins, at that time Chief of Staff of the American Army, assured the Bonn rearmer that a revision would be made in the defense plan, according to Blank's suggestion, as soon as the Bundeswehr had reached the level of capability implied by such a change. That was in July, 1953, by chance Blank's first trip to America where he discussed the situation in the operations room of the U.S. Joint Chiefs of Staff.

From that moment on, Blank—today Federal Labor Minister— worried over the fine points of a rearmament schedule that called for 500,000 soldiers to be recruited within four years.

Within this hasty recruiting scheme, which would presumably satisfy NATO's requirements for the "forward defense," three developmental targets for the Bundeswehr were ultimately fixed: 1956—96,000 men; 1957—270,000 men; 1959—500,000 men.

However, both Blank and his chief advisers, Generals Heusinger and Speidel, miscalculated. After Germany's rearmament got under way on November 10, 1955, their projected targets could not be attained; everything was lacking—officers, noncoms, weapons, camps, training sites.

Bonn's NATO partners became skeptical. Franz Josef Strauss, since 1953 in Adenauer's second cabinet, first as Minister for Special Affairs, then Minister for Atomic Affairs, saw his chance. He wanted Blank's position.

In the Hamburg weekly, *Die Zeit,* he admonished his cabinet colleague Blank: "One should not, merely to fulfill a quota, set up voluntary military forces unsuitable to (modern) conditions." In opposition to Blank's remedy of resorting to compulsory military service, Strauss devised the meaningless prescription of a "quality army."

Six years later, following the Athens NATO Council meeting in late May, at which the Americans advocated the idea of stronger conventional military forces for NATO and Blank's concept had therefore been justified in retrospect, Strauss tried to obliterate the traces of that illusory dialectic devised during his ruthless competitive struggle with Blank. In a "Position Paper of the Federal Defense Minister," concerning the Athens Conference and directed to the Bundeswehr, the statement is found: "We have in the past—it was at the time when the SPD branded the formation of 500,000 conventional troops as 'nonsense ripe for the museum'

—always supported the position that we in Europe need a strong measure of conventional fighting power."

In May, 1956, of course, Strauss had attacked his predecessor Blank with the slogan, the Bundeswehr needs atomic weapons; in contrast Blank persisted in supporting the thesis of his program that conventional weapons are more important. Eventually, however, Blank got tired: "Leadership in defense policy means more to me than martyrdom."

On October 16, 1956, Strauss took over the leadership of military policy. He immediately went about establishing his "quality army," and indeed he did it through a ruse. Arbitrarily he differentiated, which the NATO plans had not considered, between wartime forces and peacetime forces of the Bundeswehr. A wartime strength of 500,000 men he equated with a peacetime force of 350,000 men and the organizational period for the individual units was extended.

In doing this Strauss was smart enough not to abandon entirely the orginally planned final goal of 500,000 men. Rather: "If we once have reserves, then we can certainly fill in" from peacetime strength back again to wartime strength.

Strauss was lucky. His manipulations were obscured by the Pentagon's theoretical tendency, at that time known as the "Radford Plan," which defined the military policy of the Eisenhower administration:* the U.S. Army, reduced in size, would serve primarily as a "trip-wire," which when crossed by an aggressor anywhere in the world would unleash a global atomic war.

The Soviets, in contemplating the western military forces, oriented themselves vis-à-vis the latter according to the maxim of their Tank-Marshall Rotmistrow: "It is quite clear that atomic and hydrogen weapons alone, that is, without the decisive operations of modern land armies, cannot determine the outcome of a war." Soviet General Krassilnikow elaborated this thesis: The conduct of an atomic war demands not "the reduction of troop strength but, to the contrary, its increase, for the danger grows

* Admiral Radford served from 1953 to 1957 as the American Joint Chiefs of Staff Chairman.

that whole divisions will be wiped out and, in order to replace them, large reserves will be needed."

At the same time, however, the Soviets steadily increased their stocks of atomic and hydrogen weapons. And their Sputnik rockets proved to be carriers of a transcontinental range.

NATO countered with Plan MC 70, an armaments and operations directive of the North Atlantic Military Committee in Washington. It recommended for the period beginning in 1958 and ending in 1963 the following goals: 30 divisions alone in the NATO sectors of Middle Europe; and tactical atomic weapons for all of these divisions as well as the NATO air forces.

Experience shows that both goals, during the period MC 70 is in effect, that is, through the end of next year, will not be reached. The goal stipulated for middle Europe is still short seven divisions.

Equipping the divisions and airforces with tactical atomic weapons has also not been fully accomplished.*

According to MC 70, each Bundeswehr division gets one Honest John battalion, each corps one to two Sergeant battalions. The Honest John battalions are not yet complete; the Sergeant battalions are just now in the formative stage.

The German Air Force has had available up to now only two combat-ready Nike battalions. And only a small part of the five fighter-bomber squadrons of the Luftwaffe is equipped for atomic sorties.** Their twenty-four Matador missiles, which in the meantime became obsolete, were replaced by three to five Pershing missile battalions (range of the Pershing: 600 kilometers). The

---

* The tactical atomic weapons of the NATO troop units consist of the following short range missiles: Lacrosse (Range: 32 kilometers); Honest John (40 kilometers); Sergeant (150 kilometers); Corporal (140 kilometers); Redstone (400 kilometers); the multi-purpose artillery 17.5 centimeters (up to 50 kilometers) and howitzers 20.3 centimeters (up to 23 kilometers); the missiles Matador (750 kilometers) and Mace (1200 kilometers); the ground-to-air rocket Nike Hercules (altitude of 50 kilometers); and the atomic trench mortar Davy Crockett (up to 10 kilometers).

** In addition to the five fighter squadrons, each with 50 planes, the Luftwaffe has available two additional fighter squadrons, one reconnaissance, and one transport squadron. Altogether it has 600 sortie aircraft.

training of the German Pershing teams has already begun in America.

The detonators for the assembled and assigned American atomic warheads, as provided by MC 70, remain, until used, under lock in the SAS sites (special ammunition sites). These sites, guarded by troops in rotation from all NATO countries, are hidden in the troop concentration areas, so that they are immediately available. American officers, standing by at all times, hold the keys.

Before the first atomic shot can be fired from these sites, the NATO Supreme Commander in Europe must have received permission from the U.S. President. Only then may the Supreme Commander release to the commanding generals of the corps the detonators for the atomic warheads of the lower KT range*, and indeed only according to the plan of fire of the different sites with various detonation values. The corps can themselves direct the fire or can give the divisions a free hand. Commanding generals or division commanders issue the fire command to the artillery commander. The command order determines the target, the firing sequence, and the desired effect; these details are communicated to the higher commanding authorities and to the airforces. The artillery commander gives the order to fire directly to the forces.

Following a similar scheme of command, NATO airforces deliver atomic bombs. About two-thirds of the atomic capacity available in Europe is stored at airforce bases. These explosives belong to the medium KT range.

Along with the American medium range missiles which are both stored in England, Italy, and Turkey and mounted on submarines, the atomic firepower of the air forces is still considered the strongest sword of NATO. Additionally, units of the strategic air command of the U.S. Air Force are assigned to the defense of Europe. Still, the danger of being shot down faces the bombing units: the U-2 losses over the Soviet Union and Red China have shown that ground-to-air rockets function accurately in high operational altitudes.

* The Hiroshima bombs of the Americans in the summer of 1945 had an explosive force of 20,000 tons (20 kilotons = KT) of customary explosives. This force belongs today to the lower range.

The confidence of the NATO staff is still based on the American advantage over the Soviet Union in the production of atomic weapons. The United States has—according to U.S. Defense Secretary McNamara at the Athens NATO conference in May—manufactured, so far, four times more nuclear material for warheads than the Soviets.

America alone holds 97 percent of the total atomic war materials in the West, a force which mathematically is sufficient to take care of up to 90 percent of the militarily relevant targets in the East two to three times over. The remaining 10 percent of the targets in the East are not reconnoiterable or are so mobile that they could not with certainty be covered even with greater Western atomic capability. A NATO war game disclosed two years ago the West's capability in atomic saturation: on the same Baltic seaport three atomic bombs fell at the same time. Reason: the NATO strategists are sure that the Soviet army, because of the vulnerability of its supply routes, will withdraw with parts of its reserves to the sea outlets; in the navy it is described as the "Baltic Sea Runway."

Three war players from three separate command positions therefore each directed an atom bomb to this particular Baltic seaport.

To bring order into the management of the atomic weaponry system and to insure coordinated firing, the Pentagon has established a "General Command" of the American armed forces, which coordinates the plan of fire. A liaison staff of the general command is attached to the European NATO Supreme Commander in Paris.

This target coordinating office admittedly cannot answer the basic questions, whether use will be made at all of atomic weapons, or in which situations they will be used, or what types of atomic weapons will be used. The answers to these questions are made difficult by the following considerations:

> the reciprocal stalemate position between the strategic nuclear weaponry systems of both sides, in which the aggressor

can also be destroyed by the subsequent response of the attacked;

the equipping of Soviet front-line troops with tactical atomic weapons;

and consequently, in the opinion of America, the growing danger of local—conventional or limited atomic—conflicts in Europe, caused, for example, by the Berlin Crisis.

In the stalemate situation America could be tempted to accept the localized successes of the Soviet Army in a struggle in Europe with NATO units, which are still numerically inferior, in order to avoid a strategic nuclear exchange that would be disastrous to both sides. And the Soviets conversely could be misled by the strategic nuclear balance of terror to attempt just such limited thrusts and to occupy the territorial "hostages."

The then Chief of Staff of the U.S. Army, General Taylor, at the beginning of 1959 had, therefore, already sought an increase in the conventional forces prescribed by MC 70. But the Republican Eisenhower administration was not inclined to dole out more money for conventional weapons or armaments. For the same reason the Europeans also shied away from higher military expenditures.

The Eisenhower administration conceived a remedy by which, after tactical atomic weapons without much ado had been brought forward to the European front, strategic nuclear weapons would also be brought under the command of NATO. This the Americans assumed would compensate for their lack of intercontinental missiles.

So at the end of 1960, while Eisenhower was still in office, in the initial drafts of the directive MC 96—MC 70 was to expire at the end of 1963—they offered to their European allies more than 100 medium-range missiles of the Polaris type with a range at that time of 2,000 (today 3,000) kilometers. The Polaris missiles could not only be launched from submarines, but could also cover targets on the Western European mainland. Even the Bundeswehr was to receive an allotment of these missiles.

Bonn's Defense Minister Strauss enthusiastically received the missile offer, while all other NATO partners to this day remain skeptical and cautious. Strauss fancied himself to be realizing his goal—sharing American atomic power and thus getting a piece of the atomic sovereignty. In any event he believed the Polaris project would take out of the hands of the French their instrument of hegemony in Europe, the atomic *force de frappe* (deterrent power).

But the moderate and responsible staff members of the European NATO Supreme Command in Paris were not deluded by the Polaris offer into failing to note that now, as before, a discrepancy existed between the hopes of deterrence and the means of deterrence at the lower levels of the defense system.

War games in NATO's headquarters in Paris showed: NATO's lines of defense are insufficiently manned and reserves are not available, so that the defense units themselves, in the event of limited thrusts from the East, must bounce about here and there from one sector to another, as long as they do not counter with atomic firepower. Lateral movements such as these, however, dangerously exposed broad sectors of the front.

NATO's countering with atomic strikes against an aggressor also equipped with tactical atomic weapons threatened, however, to set in motion the so-called atomic escalation: Whoever is inferior at one stage of an atomic conflict turns to the next higher caliber.

As a result of the war games, NATO headquarters concluded that the army units must be brought up to full strength and that through a system of "graduated deterrence" the "atomic threshold" must be raised; the point in time at which atomic weapons would be needed to withstand a Soviet attack must be deferred.

Among the ranking officers who plotted, directed, and evaluated such war games in 1959, and belonging to the highest echelon of the Atlantic military hierarchy, was Bundeswehr Lieutenant-General Friedrich Foertsch, since the first of January of that year the "Deputy Chief of Staff, Plans and Policy," in NATO Supreme Command Europe.

Foertsch later drafted a resumé of his work in the Atlantic headquarters: "I conveyed to my colleagues there the idea of not always shooting first with atomic weapons."

Revisionist efforts in the European NATO Supreme Command, formed since the beginning of 1960 [sic, 1961?] by the new Democratic Kennedy administration, had ripened by last fall into plan-recommendations to the NATO governments: the European army units should not only be brought to full strength but also expanded and then deployed closer to the line of demarcation so that local border violations can be countered without using atomic weapons. The deterrence to conventional encroachments by the East's forces is strengthened through the power of credibility.

Tactical atomic weapons nevertheless remain with the European NATO divisions, because the Soviets also have these tactical weapons, though not in the divisions but at the army level. U.S. General Lemnitzer said of the American theory, according to which tactical atomic weapons should be removed from the front units and relocated toward the rear: "That would be foolish; the weapons, if needed, could not in all probability be returned to the front." It is still an open question whether tactical atomic weapons would not be better placed under a special command, as in the Soviet Army.

The Polaris offer as outlined in the first draft of MC 96 was set aside in favor of more conventional reinforcements. U.S. President Kennedy discreetly concealed his lack of interest in such a NATO atomic force by advising the Europeans to agree first and foremost on a general control system for these weapons.

Kennedy had American NATO Ambassador Finletter explain in the Atlantic Council that the ground forces should have priority and that a Polaris system, if one day it were created, would in any event have to be paid for in cash dollars by America's allies.

America's Defense Secretary McNamara expressed it more clearly: "In four to six years we want to be so far along that Europe can be conventionally defended against a massive, conventional attack."

In January of this year the Bonn government directed its NATO

Ambassador, von Walther, to accept the new plan proposals of NATO's staff—"as a basis for further planning," as Ambassador von Walther conditionally put it: "We shall," he carefully noted, "have to work out the details later."

Actually, from the beginning Bonn's Defense Minister Strauss rejected the new proposals. He did not trust the Americans; they would, in the event of war breaking out and in order to protect their country from the Soviet's strategic nuclear weapons, hesitate too long to introduce atomic strikes.

Strauss: "Today one cannot accept a war with conventional means as the lesser of evils merely because he believes he can thus avoid the penalties of an atomic war. . . . Atomic weapons will not be abolished by this kind of acrobatic act of self-deception." The Minister maintained that atomic deterrence would lose its credibility if NATO prepared for a conventional war.

The crisis that has been accelerating since 1958 over Berlin argued, of course, against Strauss's theories; the danger of localized encounters became apparent to everyone. It forced the West to plan military operations which at the beginning are only possible with conventional forces and which assume that the West does not want to initiate an atomic war.

Thus NATO strategists considered, for example, the immediate closing of the Baltic Sea exits should the Soviets blockade West Berlin. A sanction of this sort, however, requires conventional defense preparations in case the Soviets try to break out of the Baltic Sea closure.

On the other hand, Franz Josef Strauss, both admired and denounced for his rhetorical boasting of strength, did not want to reinforce the West Berlin position with force. In the critical days following August 13, 1961, he opted, after an inner struggle, against every energetic course of action and accused Mayor Brandt of playing with fire.

When the new plan proposals of NATO were submitted to Bonn, Strauss directed Inspector-General Foertsch's staff, under the supervision of Major General Schnez, to draw up a strategic evaluation.

With Moltkesian thoroughness, the young war gods of the Bonn Ermekeil barracks sketched several war situation studies. In them was the initial premise of the staff exercise "Fallex 62": the Soviets start a large-scale attack against Europe with atomic strikes on both the missile sites, runways, and communications centers of NATO and ground units in the defense perimeter near the border.

The West German general staff officers, however, could not agree on the conclusions to be drawn for Atlantic strategy. Strauss's press officer, Gerd Schmuekle, called attention to their differences of opinion in a newspaper article: "There are some generals who stubbornly insist that a war in Europe would not last beyond 48 hours. Others speak of 48 months. The difference between the two estimates reflects the distance in conception that generally separates the airforce and army experts from one another as soon as the talk turns these days to the mode of warfare."

One group of general staff officers, supported by German officers assigned to NATO staffs, argued: Only a strong German land force can enhance the deterrent factor and prevent the Soviets from making an attack of this sort. Also, an increase of German troops alone guarantees the "forward defense" in the border zones. In a memorandum to Inspector-General Friedrich Foertsch, the Germans assigned to NATO Supreme Command pointed out that more [West German] troops would increase the political weight of the Federal Republic in the Atlantic Alliance; in contrast, Bonn's push for medium range missiles only arouses distrust.

Other general staff officers of the Bundeswehr, however, thought that NATO could best counter a first atomic strike from the East if the idea, debated years ago in the U.S., is accepted of a "preemptive strike" which would come prior to a Soviet atomic strike, and at that moment when the Soviet's intention to attack is clearly apparent.

Their recommendation: NATO needs its own atomic force, independent of the U.S.A., at the expense, if necessary, of conventional weapons.

Airforce General Kammhuber, up to the end of last month Inspector of the *Bundesluftwaffe,* had already entertained several ideas in 1955 at the NATO air manuevers, "Carte blanc," at which a similar initial war phase was tested. At that time Kammhuber argued "that the Bundeswehr must have a weapon that is effective up to the Urals. Otherwise we are only satellites."

With the Starfighter program, Strauss and Kammhuber laid the foundation for this wonder weapon: fighter-bombers that could carry atomic warheads and could later be replaced by missiles.

The fighter-bombers are doomed for the preemptive strike, because, designed as they are for the kilometer-long concrete runways, they would be seriously endangered by missile attacks or bombs dropped during the enemy's initial attack. The question remains whether they would be able to find undamaged landing strips upon their return from their first flight to the front.

For all detachments, of course, widely dispersed secondary landing fields are established, including concrete bunkers for storing the planes, and provisional landing facilities on the *Autobahnen* are to be built, but an atomic warhead exploding near the runway would destroy the radar equipment, without the assistance of which a Starfighter can be landed only with difficulty.

The Strauss people completed their war situation studies, although the American government long ago rejected the "preemptive strike" idea. It contradicts the defensive nature of the Atlantic Alliance. That the West would never be the first to launch an attack, and that the Soviet Union knows it is regarded in the Western capitals as having a "stabilizing effect" on the political situation throughout the world.

Combat instructions of the NATO airforces are therefore based on the idea of an immediate counterattack after the initial attack. They pinpoint missile sites, air fields, and above all the most vulnerable spots of the Russian aggressor: the long supply lines. Battlefield Europe is to be contained at the Vistula.

At the same time NATO ground units have the assignment of stopping the advancing enemy in the deployment area between the Vistula and the border.

Until 1958 the Rhine was considered the main line of defense. The weak NATO divisions would only have been able to detain a massive attack between the border and the Rhine. Several lines of resistance, supported by natural barriers, would also have to be held for certain periods of time in order to secure the communications stations of the fighter-bombers and missiles which are located west of those lines.

Planners at NATO figured that it would be days later before an atomic counterattack on the East's communications and supply lines would have an effect on the attacking army. According to NATO estimates, however, the Soviet units would be forced to re-group, no later than at the Rhine.

General Friedrich Foertsch in the European Supreme Command of NATO, his predecessor as the Bundeswehr Inspector-General, General Adolf Heusinger, and General Hans Speidel, Army Commander in the NATO Middle European Command, finally succeeded in having the NATO main line of defense moved from the Rhine farther to the east.

After August 13 of last year the American NATO Supreme Commander Norstad, considering the possibility of an eventual skirmish at the border, also ordered the border region to be defended. Peoples' Army or Soviet units that penetrated would be pushed back over the border.

On Norstad's order a Dutch brigade advanced at that time to Bergen-Hohne in the Lüneburg marshes for the defense of the border areas.

That which the first German Defense Minister, Theodor Blank, had wanted to achieve by the end of the fifties was now finally accomplished on the drawing board: "the forward defense."

But obviously, even today, as "Fallex 62" has demonstrated, the NATO Supreme Command lacks the forces to implement effectively this operational concept.

Although the Algerian war is over, France's General-President de Gaulle refuses to assign the French divisions released in Algeria to the Atlantic High Command. To the contrary, three-fourths of the French Army is retained by de Gaulle under national command. The army paratrooper corps of General Massu, garrisoned in Alsace and Lorraine, is among these divisions.

De Gaulle commands this corps west of the Rhine as his personal operational reserve force, as "intervening troops," under leash. With it he would like to be able to operate according to his own taste in case of a Soviet breakthrough toward the Atlantic. Meanwhile, NATO Command Middle Europe urgently needs Massu's corps for a task closer to the front. For the front sector, including the Bavarian capital Munich, which the French have to hold in southern Germany, is only weakly occupied, to such an extent that Munich could not be defended any more effectively than Hamburg or Hanover.

The commanding officer in the middle European NATO sector, General Speidel, reassures himself about the notorious French attitude of hostility toward NATO: "When it begins, Massu will be there."

But even if Massu should come, and if Speidel adds the French corps in Alsace-Lorraine to his middle European striking force, and if at the end of next year all twelve projected German divisions should be placed at his disposal, the NATO General will still not have sufficient forces under his command. Speidel needs, both in his own judgment and that of the NATO Supreme Command in Paris, at least 35 divisions for his sector of middle Europe —in as much as he is to defend the Federal Republic initially near the border and not between the Weser and the Rhine.

The new war plan of the Bundeswehr, TF (troop command) 62, assigns, in the event of atomic war, to each division a defense sector 25 kilometers wide and for a defensive effort without atomic weapons each division has a sector 12 kilometers wide. General Speidel, on the other hand, must assign (with the forces currently available for the divisions in the middle European defense area) a defense sector of more than 30 kilometers wide.

Under these conditions a single breakthrough by the aggressor can turn the entire front in middle Europe upside down. The Soviet General Staff plans accordingly to be on the Rhine in seven days, as revealed in its own war games.

The new NATO concept "forward defense" is intended to frustrate this plan: in addition to bringing to full strength the projected divisions, mobile "defense brigades" are to protect the border sectors, especially in the critical north German lowlands. Their tactical mission includes the blunting of small thrusts and obtaining sufficient time for the deployment of operative units during concentrated attacks.

Gaining time is undoubtedly essential, since the mobile NATO divisions in the Federal Republic are frequently so situated, due to the shortage of training sites and the geographical narrowness of the West German territory, that their deployment must be effected by risky criss-crossing movements toward the front.

Also, mine fields are to block those border sectors, such as the Bavarian Forest, which are supported by natural barriers so that active units like the U.S. regimental combat groups will be free.

Joining these advanced units and border patrols, NATO divisions are to make a stand without atomic fire against a massive attack launched by the Soviets in a purely conventional manner, and are to force the enemy to a "pause." The "pause," during which diplomats negotiate, forces in the most extreme case a single and carefully determined atomic strike commensurate with the pressure of the attack.

Only when this "selective strike" fails to have the desired effect will the "hour of retaliation" arrive.

The new NATO requirements for this atomically guaranteed "forward defense" are contained in the fourth draft of Plan Directive MC 96. It is to be in effect from 1964 to 1970; the Atlantic Council wants to consider in December who will be responsible for implementing its various aspects during the first three years of this period.

The new directive, requiring more money and troops from all NATO governments for strengthening the conventional forces, places the following obligations on the organizational structure and strength of German ground forces:

in addition to the twelve projected divisions, four mechanized defense brigades with stronger reconnaisance and engineering battalions;

completion of the air-borne division (up to now only two weak brigades), so that it is serviceable as a motorized infantry division;

a combat strength of all mobile units of about 100 percent, so that they are combat ready in a few hours, excluding commanding officers and men on leave and sick call.

Only after Defense Minister Strauss had approved, albeit with reluctance, this program *en gros* did he allow the details to be worked out. The command staffs of the Bundeswehr and of the ground forces went to work with slide rules and huge statistical charts.

Result: the present strength of the Bundeswehr—today, 375,000 men—would have to climb from the originally planned but far from being reached figure of 500,000 to 750,000 men, if *all* NATO requirements and *all* national requirements, including the one reserve of personnel for the medium range missiles, are to be met. This represents more troops than before the 1939 mobilization.

Defense Minister Strauss later cited this enormous figure when he publicly attacked the Americans because of their plan, although requirements of this size for the Bundeswehr were suggested neither by Washington nor by NATO.

Also, NATO knows that the Federal Republic cannot bring about this kind of armed strength within a reasonable period of time. They don't have the troops. They don't have the money.

At any rate, the personnel situation, which was critical from the beginning, is the most troublesome one for the Bundeswehr organizers. Replacements cannot be found at the officer and noncommissioned officer levels. Established positions in many companies are only half filled, and every now and then officers and noncoms, to satisfy the need for instructors, have to complete themselves one course of training after another.

A rough estimate by the financial experts of the Defense and

Finance Ministries showed that a 750,000 man-Bundeswehr, together with Strauss's special missile contingents, would take about 30 billion marks annually, three to four billion of which would be spent just for the German share of a European atomic force.

However, Federal Finance Minister Starke allocated to the Defense Minister a maximum of 20 billion marks (1962, 15 billion; 1963, 18 billion) annually in the future for the entire Bundeswehr.

The administrative staff of the armed services thereafter submitted two additional and more realistic estimates:

> a Bundeswehr of 580,000 men—the expense including the cost of missiles, 23 billion marks; without missiles, 20 billion marks;
>
> a Bundeswehr of 500,000 men—the expense including the cost of missiles, 20 billion marks.

The administrative staff of the army indicated its preference for the first of these two proposals. With 580,000 men the Federal Republic could also finance the NATO requirements, even allowing for an eventual reserve of 20,000 troops for the missile units, if the superfluous equipment such as expensive Starfighters and destroyers is reduced.

Strauss rejected this suggestion: "An atomic bomb is worth as much as a brigade and, besides, is much cheaper. We cannot permit any reduction in our standard of living and our exports. Neither do we want to abandon our missile claims."

In his "Position Paper" on the Athens NATO conference in May of this year Strauss had written: "In Athens I have not warned in vain of overestimating the German capacity in this (conventional) area. Conventionally, we have done our part. . . . If a strengthening of conventional forces is desired, it can not be done by us."

The Bonn Defense Minister prefers to spend his share of the federal burget for atomic firepower than for conventional weapons, even though it may mean that with 500,000 men the urgent request of NATO's leaders for more M (mobilization) day units cannot be met.

M-Day-Units are those which are already sufficiently staffed and equipped so that they are combat ready in minutes (airforce, missile units, radar units) or hours (ground and naval striking forces). "Fallex 62" proved that there must be a large number of these M-Day-Units, since reserve units can no longer be quickly mobilized.

The German Defense Minister thought he could meet NATO halfway with a skillful sleight of hand. He wanted to offset the lack of troops with a small-scale weapon, the Davy Crockett atomic mortar.

Strauss refused to get disturbed by reports from his officers in Washington. In the American army general staff, the question whether Davy Crockett could replace conventional artillery was laconically answered: "By no means!"

Strauss nevertheless instructed his staff aides to consider a new troop structure. If each mechanized infantry battalion were equipped with an atomic mortar, the artillery divisions could be eliminated and the number of battalions could be further reduced. It would thus be possible to meet the demands of the Atlantic High Command for a higher degree of combat readiness.

Strauss himself described the advantages of arming with Davy Crocketts: "There is an American field atomic weapon of very short range and of limited effect. A single shot from this weapon has the same effect as, say, a round of 40 or 50 shots by an entire artillery division."

Washington promptly rejected the Bonn armament idea, since it would mean that tthe German divisions would lose completely their conventional fighting capability.

The reorganizational plan of the Minister also encountered opposition in the Bundeswehr. Only on the staff of Inspector-General Foertsch and among his personal staff did Strauss find support.

Military affairs journalist Adelbert Weinstein, consistently well-informed on official policy, disclosed in the FAZ [*Frankfurter Allgemeine Zeitung*]: "In the Bundeswehr itself followers (of Minister Strauss) are by no means to be found only among the modern officers. Except for General Heusinger and Inspector-

General Foertsch, however, only a few adhere . . . without reservations to the military policy views of Strauss."

In Bonn the demarcation line, described by Strauss-confidant Weinstein, runs roughly between the staff chiefs in the Bundeswehr on the one side and those of the ground forces on the other. The dispute is analogous to the historic division in Hitler's time between the Wehrmacht High Command (OKW) and the Army High Command (OKH).

At that time the OKW, supported and favored by Hitler, increasingly gained influence at the expense of the OKH. Today the Bundeswehr staff admits without reservation, in the wake of similarly fluctuating and roulette type intelligence data supplied by the Defense Minister, to its military views and defends them with Straussian verve.

The Ministry's robust press chief, Schmueckle, took to the field in the Stuttgart weekly, *Christ und Welt,* against the American theorists of the new NATO strategy: "With their subconscious enthusiasm for war, these planners are prey to the strangest imaginations. . . . They discount the new war situation in Europe and superimpose upon it the fallacious patina of conventional armed conflict."

Schmuekle lectured his comrades in the [West German] army: These (American) ideologues are supported by a military establishment which, with all its ability, cannot grasp the mission of the army in the atomic age, and whose tenacious memory is still preoccupied with tank thrusts and encircling movements in the style of the Second World War. . . . Ah, how vividly men dream of past achievements!"

For nights on end the matter was discussed in the officers' mess of the military academies and field battalions. Lieutenant Colonel Count Bernstorff, tactics instructor at the army officers' school in Hamburg, tried to get Army-Inspector Zerbel to reply to Schmuekle. But Strauss's press chief is untouchable. And Count Bernstorff retired.

Colonel Karst, expert in "education" at the Ermekeil barracks in Bonn, sent to *Christ und Welt* a reply to Schmuekle's essay;

main point of criticism: Schmuekle's tone is impertinent. The newspaper's editors refused to publish the reply.

Karst sent his article to the inspectors of the army, airforce, and navy, and also to Inspector-General Foertsch, who during his service with NATO had been against the emphasis on atomic weapons.

However, Bundeswehr Inspector-General Foertsch had changed his mind. While with NATO's Supreme Command Foertsch had recognized, in the course of precision general staff work, that the conventionally premised "forward defense" promised more security than the uncredible atomic deterrence, and not the least so for the Federal Republic.

Inspector-General of the Bundeswehr since April 1st of last year, Freidrich Foertsch was no longer able to withstand the vehement garrulity of his commander-in-chief.

Franz Josef Strauss tried unceasingly since the beginning of June of this year to persuade the American Defense Secretary McNamara in Washington to be satisfied with 500,000 German troops. But the American had long ago discovered that the Germans would not be able to provide at full combat strength the divisions and brigades needed by NATO. The American was annoyed.

As compensation Strauss offered "some other elements," namely border patrol units, consisting of an active nucleus that is expanded in any emergency through reservists. McNamara held such units to be merely makeshift arrrangements.

Six weeks later U.S. President Kennedy appointed his military advisor, General Taylor, to be chairman of the Joint Chiefs of Staff and announced the departure of General Norstad. General Taylor had resigned as chief of staff of the U.S. Army in 1959— an event as inconceivable in the Bundeswehr as in Hitler's armed forces—because he could not get accepted his strategy of "flexible reaction" as opposed to the official doctrine of "massive (atomic) retaliation" in the Republican Eisenhower era. Even at that time the American Supreme Commander of NATO, Norstad, had shown sympathy for the European desire for an autonomous

NATO atomic power. The new Democratic U.S. President Kennedy admonished Norstad: "Remember, you are an American."

When Kennedy appointed Taylor as General Staff Chief at the same time he released Norstad from the NATO Supreme Command, Bonn's Defense Minister Strauss sounded the alarm. The change in personnel was to him a welcome occasion to demonstrate before the world against the new NATO proposals that had been drawn up nine months earlier and to have his objections confirmed by the German public.

Ignoring the warnings of the Federal Foreign Affairs Minister Schroeder, the Foreign Office State Secretary Carstens, and even of the Bundeswehr Chief of Staff Schnez, a friend of the Minister, not to jeopardize relations with Washington, the Minister mobilized a campaign against the defense policies of the Kennedy administration.

Strauss declared in an interview with Weinstein: The West's divisions could only be "raised in value" by tactical atomic weapons (of the Davy Crockett type). With modern weapons deterrence begins at the most forward positions. In contrast, America's Defense Secretary McNamara: "We have to be able to meet situations in which an atomic response is either inappropriate or quite simply inconceivable."

Strauss further contradicted the American view that even the smallest atomic weapons on the Western defense line at the Iron Curtain could trigger a massive world war. He hinted that he regretted not being able to act as de Gaulle, who "in practice simply ignores American remonstrances."

McNamara had said that in certain situations only conventional divisions could prevent war. Strauss found this opinion "debatable"—particularly since not 30 but 60 to 100 divisions which could not be afforded would be necessary in Western Europe.

According to McNamara, the big atomic weapons in a large-scale war serve primarily military goals. According to Strauss, "this contradicts the essential nature of the atom bomb, which is a political weapon by which one can add to the civilian population's fear of bombardment."

Strauss's demagogy enraged the Americans; it terrified the German army generals. The contention of the Bonn Defense Minister that 60 to 100 divisions are necessary in Western Europe for deterrence found no support among the military.

Generals Heusinger and Speidel, as well as Foertsch's successor at NATO, Major General Mueller-Hillebrandt, all agree that 40 divisions are adequate if the units are constantly maintained at combat readiness. The money for them is there as long as Europe, including the Federal Republic, renounces the costly ostentation of missiles.

To make plausible such a renunciation and to remove the European fear of Russian missiles, McNamara declared: "The United States is just as concerned with that part of the Soviet atomic striking force which can reach Western Europe as it is with that which can reach the United States. We have placed the atomic defense of NATO on a global basis." The American Defense Secretary argued in favor of a division of labor in the Western Alliance, thereby reducing expenditures.

Nevertheless, Strauss persisted in his missiles and decided against NATO's proposals: 500,000 troops are enough.

On the 17th of July, Franz Josef Strauss, accompanied by Inspector-General Friedrich Foertsch, presented himself to Chancellor Konrad Adenauer in the Palais Schaumburg. Strauss received Adenauer's approval for his new plan estimates.

The Defense Minister's numbers game and, above all, his offer to spare the federal budget, won the Chancellor over. General Foertsch seconded the Minister with an artistic display of strategic technicalities. Adenauer responded with the advice, very simply, to replace the missing brigades with "little flags on the map;" whether these brigades would be ready in 1966 or 1967 was not very important. But one must at least keep up appearances before NATO.

Commander-in-chief Strauss and his Inspector-General marched off satisfied. The lesson of "Fallex 62" was not yet available. It says: With missiles in place of brigades and atomic mortars in place of troops, a forward defense by the Bundeswehr is not possible; an effective deterrence remains doubtful.

APPENDIX II

THE THIRTY-FOUR NEWSPAPERS CONSTITUTING THE SAMPLE UPON WHICH
TABLES 1, 2, AND 3 ARE CONSTRUCTED[a]

Newspaper	Place of Publication	Political Orientation	Circulation	Primary Region of Circulation
1 *Aachener Volkszeitung*	Aachen	CDU	79,327	Aachen and environs
2 *Der Abend*	Berlin	Independent	91,118	West Berlin
3 *Abendzeitung*	Munich	Independent	104,684	Bavarian, especially Munich
4 *Allgemeine Zeitung*	Mainz	Nonpartisan	106,369	Mainz and the "Rheinhessen" region
5 *Badische Neueste Nachrichten*	Karlsruhe	Independent	130,245	Karlsruhe and environs
6 *Deutsche Tagespost*	Würzburg	Independent-Catholic	14,200	German Federal Republic, West Berlin, abroad
7 *Frankfurter Allgemeine Zeitung*	Frankfurt	Independent-liberal civic foundations	258,554	German Federal Republic, West Berlin, abroad
8 *Frankfurter Neue Presse*	Frankfurt	Independent (pro-CDU)[b]	110,301	German Federal Republic

APPENDIX (CONTINUED)

Newspaper	Place of Publication	Political Orientation	Circulation	Primary Region of Circulation
9 *Frankfurter Rundschau*	Frankfurt	Nonpartisan, liberal (pro-SPD)	114,300[c]	Frankfurt and Rhine-Main area
10 *Handelsblatt*	Düsseldorf	Independent-business	33,500	German Federal Republic, West Berlin, abroad
11 *Hannoversche Presse*	Hanover	Independent (pro-SPD)	146,300[c]	Lower Saxony
12 *Industrie Kurier*[a]	Düsseldorf	Entrepreneurial-antisocialist	26,346	German Federal Republic, West Berlin
13 *Kasseler Post*	Kassel	Middle-class, nationalistic, independent	20,910	Kassel and environs
14 *Kölner Stadt-Anzeiger*	Cologne	Nonpartisan, independent	169,650[c]	Cologne and environs
15 *Kölnische Rundschau*	Cologne	Independent-Christian Democratic	161,067[c]	Cologne and environs
16 *Der Kurier*	Berlin	Independent	23,628	West Berlin

APPENDIX (CONTINUED)

Newspaper	Place of Publication	Political Orientation	Circulation	Primary Region of Circulation
17 *Mannheimer Morgen*	Mannheim	Independent	132,164	Baden-Württemberg and Rhineland-Palatinate
18 *Der Mittag*	Düsseldorf	Independent-nonpartisan	59,300	German Federal Republic and neighboring countries
19 *Münchner Merkur*	Munich	Independent (pro-CDU)	174,844	Munich and Bavaria
20 *Neue Rhein Zeitung (Neue Ruhr Zeitung)*[e]	Cologne	Independent	231,944	Cologne, Düsseldorf, and Aachen
21 *Rhein Zeitung*	Koblenz	Independent (pro-CDU)	177,898	North Rhineland-Palatinate
22 *Rheinische Post*	Düsseldorf	Christian Democratic	265,064	Düsseldorf and Rhine-Ruhr areas
23 *Ruhr-Nachrichten*	Dortmund	Independent-Christian	187,885	Rhineland, North Rhineland-Westphalia

APPENDIX (CONTINUED)

Newspaper	Place of Publication	Political Orientation	Circulation	Primary Region of Circulation
24 *Saarbrücker Allgemeine*	Saarbrücken	Independent	36,950	Saarland
25 *Süddeutsche Zeitung*	Munich	Nonpartisan-independent	224,188	**Munich, South Bavaria, and German Federal Republic**
26 *Stuttgarter Zeitung*	Stuttgart	Independent	143,577	Baden-Württemburg
27 *Der Tag*	Berlin	Independent-Christian Democratic	24,083	West Berlin
28 *Die Welt*	Hamburg, Essen, Berlin	Independent	267,183	German Federal Republic Berlin, abroad
29 *Weser Kurier*	Bremen	Independent-nonpartisan	119,321	Bremen and environs
30 *Westdeutsche Allgemeine*	Essen	Independent-	418,482	Ruhr area
31 *Westdeutsche Rundschau*	Wuppertal	Nonpartisan (pro-SPD)	13,180	Wuppertal and environs

APPENDIX (CONTINUED)

Newspaper	Place of Publication	Political Orientation	Circulation	Primary Region of Circulation
32 *Westdeutsches Tagesblatt*	Dortmund	Independent	24,299	Dortmund, Hagen and Münster
33 *Westfälische Rundschau*	Dortmund	Neutral	228,551	Münster, Dortmund and Arnsberg
34 *Wiesbadener Kurier*	Wiesbaden	Nonpartisan	63,378	Wiesbaden and environs

a Unless otherwise indicated, the source for the political orientation, circulation figures, and regions of primary circulation distribution is *Die deutsche Presse 1961.* The 1961 edition was the most recently published edition prior to the *Spiegel* Affair.

b The indication in parentheses of a proparty orientation suggests a general editorial sympathy with the views of that political party, even though the newspaper does not formally claim a party orientation. Wherever these references appear in this table, they are based on the author's judgment and material contained in *1963 Editor and Publisher Yearbook,* and Walter H. Mallory (ed.). *Political Handbook of the World* (New York: Harper, 1961), 78–80 (published for the American Council on Foreign Relations).

c Figures based on Mallory, *Political Handbook of the World.*

d Appears four times weekly.

e Appears under both titles cited here.

INDEX

Abendländische Akademie, 77
Abendpost (Frankfurt): interview with Franz Josef Strauss, 121
Abendzeitung (Munich), 69
Academicians. *See* Faculty
Acht-Uhr-Blatt (Nürnberg): statement of Franz Josef Strauss in, 122–23
Adenauer era, 103, 162; and *Kanzlerdemokratie,* xiii–xiv
Adenauer, Konrad, 93, 95, 108, 109, 114n29, 116, 117, 142, 176, 180; on Ahlers episode, 147; and *Bundestag* bribery case, 11; and 1961 *Bundestag* election, 20–21; coalition strategy of, 150–51, 152–53, 158–62; and Fränkel case, 73n 13; and FDP, 107-109; on Wolfgang Hopf's leave of absence, 147; perception of *Spiegel* controversy, 183–84; retirement as Chancellor, xix; and Schmeisser case, 12–13; and SPD, 160–61; in *Spiegel* Bundestag debates, 129–32, 133; in *Spiegel* controversy, 151
Adenauer, Ludwig, 38, 39, 99, 128
Ahlers, Conrad, 36, 43, 51, 57, 57n 28, 63n8, 64, 65, 66, 70, 73, 90, 98, 135, 136, 138, 153, 178n3; arrest of, xvii, xiv, 55–56, 76–77, 124–25; charges against, 57, 63; preliminary trial of, 174–75
Allgemeine Studentenausschüsse, 60
Allgemeine Zeitung (Mainz), 74
Almond, Gabriel: and political culture, 8–9
Amtshilfe, 171
Andersch, Alfred, 61
Association of German Periodical Publishers *(Verband deutscher*

Zeitschriftenverlager): on *Spiegel* action, 80
Augstein, Josef, 46, 57n28; arrest of, 56
Augstein, Rudolf, 36, 37, 43–53 *passim,* 57, 59, 61, 75, 122, 123, 127, 130, 133–35, 153, 178n3; arrest of, xvii–xviii, 52–53; charges against, xviii, 63–64; editorial policy of, 4–6; and founding of *Der Spiegel,* 3; preliminary court trial of, 174–75; and Schmeisser case, 13
Baden-Württemberg, 103
Baldwin, Hansen W.: on Foertsch article, 33–34
Barsig, Franz, 161
Basic Law (Bonn), 74, 130; Article 5 (censorship), 88; Article 35 (Amtshilfe), 136; constructive vote of confidence, 126n
Bavaria: Landtag elections, 95, 125, 148–50, 152, 153, 158–59; and Franz Josef Strauss, 19
Bavarian Journalists' Association, 80
Bavarian Party: and Bundestag bribery case, 12
Becker, Erhard, 72
Becker, Hans Detlev, 56, 64
Berlin (West): public response to *Spiegel* controversy in, 168–69
Berlin Wall, 109; and Bundestag election, 21
Bild-Zeitung, 47, 82
Blank, Theodor, 54
Blank Office, 54, 136
Blankenhorn, Herbert: and Schmeisser case, 12–13; and Franz Josef Strauss, 16
Blücher, Franz, 102

Böhm, Anton: on postwar Germany, 7
Bohrer, Harry: and the founding of *Der Spiegel,* 3
Bonn Correspondents' Association: reaction to the *Spiegel* action, 79–80
Bonn system, xv, 155, 179–80, 184; characteristics of, xiii; criticisms of, xiii–xiv; public attitudes toward, xiv, xxii, 8–10; view of *Der Spiegel* toward, 6
Bonner Rundschau, 75
Bracher, Karl Dietrich, 155
Brandt, Willy, 177
Braun, Karl Willy: and Fibag Affair, 21
Brawand, Leo, 46
Brentano, Heinrich von, 146
Bribery, 57, 63
British Press Control Authority: and founding of *Der Spiegel,* 3
Buback, Siegfried, 43, 49, 50
Bucher, Ewald, 162: and Fibag Affair, 26
Bulletin des Presse-und Informationsamtes, 153
Bundesgerichtshof. See Federal High Court
Bundesnachrichtensdienst. See Federal Intelligence Agency
Bundestag, 66, 90; and 1950 bribery case, 11–12; Council of Elders, 27; committee of inquiry in Fibag Affair, 25–29; question hour in, 180; rules of procedure, 98, 98n7; *Spiegel* debate in, xviii, 127–41
Bundestag Library, 83
Bundesverfassungsgericht. See Federal Constitutional Court
Bundeswehr, 63, 67, 130; and Fallex 62, 31; and Foertsch article, 31–36 *passim,* 186–216 *passim*
Busse, Herman, 144

Chaloner, John: and founding of *Der Spiegel,* 3
Christian Democratic Union (CDU), 69, 71; and 1962 Hesse Landtag election, 146. *See also* CDU/CSU
Christian Democratic Union/Christian Social Union (CDU/CSU), 79, 93–95, 100, 102, 110n22, 142, 145; and Bundestag bribery case, 11–12; and Bundestag elections, 20–21, 104; and Fränkel case, 73n13; and FDP, 106–109, 121, 123–27, 158-59, 162; and Fibag Affair, 26–29; and SPD, 160–61
Christian Social Union (CSU): and CDU, 177; and Franz Josef Strauss, xviii, 15, 19, 149, 177. *See also* CDU/CSU
Coalition: of CDU/CSU and FDP, 121, 123–27, 158–62; CDU/CSU and SPD negotiations of, 159–61; between CDU/CSU and SPD, 178–79 and personnel question, 181
Codetermination *(Mitbestimmung),* 102
Conrad, Paul, 56
Conservatism, 102, 103
Constitutionalism, 156
Courts. *See* Federal Constitutional Court; Federal High Court
Credibility; of Adenauer government, 156–57, 181–84
Cuban missile crisis, xxii, 69, 110, 123, 142, 170n31

Dagens Nyheter (Stockholm), 65
Dahlgrün, Rolf, 28
Daily Mail (London), 33
De Champs, Bruno, 72, 73
Defense, Federal Ministry of, 52, 54, 56, 62, 75. *See also* Strauss, Franz Josef
Dehler, Thomas, 102
Demonstrations. *See* Students
Denazification, 138
Deutsche Presse-Agentur, 160
Deutsche Tagespost (Würzburg), 75, 76
Döring, Wolfgang, 108, 116, 147, 151; in Bundestag *Spiegel* debates, 133–34

Dolata, Werner, 47
Dortmunder Ruhr-Nachrichten, 148
Dreyfus Affair, xx
Düsseldorf Revolt: in FDP, 107–108
Dufhues, Josef Hermann, 69, 72, 74, 98, 158

Elections: Bundestag (1961), 19–20, 108–109; Bundestag (1965), 178, 178n2. See also Bavaria, Hesse
Electoral systems, 104–107, 160, 162
Emergency power: under Basic Law, xxi, xxin6, 71, 71n
EMNID Institute: public opinion polls of, 168–69
Engel, Johannes K., 44, 47, 53, 56
Enzensberger, Hans Magnus, 61
Erhard, Ludwig, 20, 120, 176, 178; on Spiegel controversy, 150
Erler, Fritz, 101, 144n; in the Bundestag Spiegel debates, 130–31, 139
Extradition, 153–54; agreement between Spain and Germany, 77, 90

Faculty: attitudes on Spiegel controversy, xix, 60–61, 155–57. See also Protests
Fallex article. See Foertsch article
Fallex 62 (Fall Exercise '62), 30–31, 55, 62, 186–216 passim, esp. 186–90
Federal Constitutional Court (Bundesverfassungsgericht), 16; and Der Spiegel complaints, 174n41, 174n42
Federal Criminal Office, 99, 130, 132. See also Security Group
Federal High Court (Bundesgerichtshof), 35–36, 49, 50, 66, 119, 130, 132; and Conrad Ahlers, 174–75; and Rudolf Augstein, 174–75; examining judge of, 40, 63; and Alfred Martin, 174–75, 174n42; and Hans Schmelz, 174n42
Federal Intelligence Agency (Bundesnachrichtendienst), 56, 175; and Adolf Wicht, 52n

Federal Press Conference (Bundespresskonferenz): on Spiegel Action, 79
Federal Press Office, 16, 178n
Federal Prosecutor (Generalbundesanwalt). See Federal Prosecutor's Office
Federal Prosecutor's Office (Generalbundesanwaltschaft), xvii, 35, 68, 69, 72, 73n13, 75, 75n, 96n, 97, 115, 119, 122, 130, 132, 137, 149; and Ahlers episode, 76–77, 90; and the Bonn police action, 41; charges against Der Spiegel, 57, 63, 64; and Hamburg police action, 42–43, 49, 50, 52; and Friedrich August von Heydte, 78n; jurisdiction of, 37–39; and Justice Ministry, 111–12, 112n, 173
Fibag Affair, 17–29, 66, 69, 90, 100, 114, 167
Finanzbau-Aktiengesellschaft (Fibag). See Fibag Affair
Fischer, Erich, 37, 46
Foertsch, Friedrich, 30, 186–216 passim
Foertsch article, 29–36, 49, 57, 64, 68, 69, 75, 90, 101, 136; and Conrad Ahlers, 54–55; and Federal High Court, 174–75. See also Appendix I
Foreign Affairs, Federal Ministry of, 63n, 170n31; and Ahlers episode, 76–77, 90. See also Gerhard Schröder
France: and Schmeisser case, 12–13
Fränkel, Wolfgang, 73n13
Frankenfeld, Alfred, 110n22
Frankfurter Allgemeine Zeitung, 66, 72, 85, 86, 134, 154
Frankfurter Rundschau, 54, 69, 135
Free Democratic Party (FDP) 20, 59, 92, 93, 95, 100–103, 142; and Bundestag elections (1961), 19–21; coalition with CDU/CSU, xviii, xix, 107–109, 118–21, 119–27, 151–52, 158–59, 162; and

Fibag Affair, 24, 26–29; and Landtag elections (Bavaria), 149; (Hesse), 146; and proportional representation, 107*n*; response to *Spiegel* action, 101–17; and Third Force idea, 104–109
Freiheit, Die (Mainz), 68

Gates, Thomas: and Fibag Affair, 17
Gehrmann, Kurt, 74, 75
Generalanzeiger newspapers, 82–83
Gerlach, Hans, 69
German Journalists' Association (*Deutscher Journalistenverband*): on *Spiegel* action, 80
German Party (DP), 93, 108
Germany (East): government of, 73*n*13
Germany (West): political culture of, 8–10
Gerstenmaier, Eugen, 128, 150*n*14; in the Bundestag *Spiegel* debates, 129–30, 131
Gollancz, Victor: and founding of *Der Spiegel*, 3
Grass, Günter, 61
Great Britain. *See* United Kingdom
Gruppe 47, 62*n*6, 7
Güde, Max, 112*n*

Hamburg, 31, 103; Assembly, 110*n* 22; criminal police, 39, 44–45, 63, 63*n*8; *Land* government, 98–100, 109, 114, 114*n*29
Hamburger Echo, 42, 67
Hannoversche Presse, 67
Hase, Karl-Günther von, 154
Hassel, Kai-Uwe von, 162
Heimatzeitungen, 82–83
Heinemann, Gustav, 26
Henrich, Hans, 67
Hermsdorf, Hans, 131
Hess, Ernst, 48
Hesse, 103, 110*n*22; *Landtag* election (1962), 94, 146
Heuss, Theodor, 102
Heydte, Friedrich August von der, 75*n*, 77, 78*n*

Hitler, Adolf, xvii, 155; and Hitlerism, 8
Höcherl, Hermann, 110*n*22, 128; in the Bundestag *Spiegel* debates, 137
Hölzl, Josef, 38
Hoogen, Mathias: and Fibag Affair, 25, 26
Hopf, Wolfgang, 115, 132, 178*n*3; and Ahlers episode, 138–40, 170–71; leave of absence of, 123–24; and *Spiegel* investigation, 122–23, 128–29
Hopf-Walter Strauss formula, 124–25, 142, 147, 159

Institut für Demoskopie: opinion polls of, 163–68
Intellectuals: reactions to *Spiegel* action, 58–62
Interior, Federal Ministry of, 79, 99, 110*n*22, 128–29. *See also* Höcherl, Hermann
International Police (Interpol), 73, 73*n*14, 77, 128, 171
International Press Institute, 81
Italy, 8

Jacobi, Anneliese, 53, 54
Jacobi, Claus, 7, 43–56 *passim*
Jaene, Hans Dieter, 39, 52
Jahn, Gerhard, 100*n*12; and Fibag Affair, 28–29
Jahr, John, 52, 80
Jahrbuch der Öffentlichen Meinung, 9
Jaspers, Karl, 7
Johnson, Uwe, 61
Jurgens, Cürd, 62*n*
Justice, Federal Ministry of, 60, 96*n*, 111, 116, 119, 123, 131; and Federal Prosecutor's Office, 111–12, 112*n*, 173. *See also* Wolfgang Stammberger

Kallai, Gyula, 41
Kapfinger, Hans E.: and Fibag Affair, 17–21 *passim*
Kasseler Post, 71

Kennedy, John F., 33, 125, 142
Kiesinger, Kurt Georg, 157, 176
Kilb, Hans, 14*n*
Kirchliche Hochschule (Bielefeld), 60
Kölner Stadt-Anzeiger, 69, 151
Kohut, Oswald, A., 110*n*, 140; in the Bundestag *Spiegel* debates, 137–138
Krone, Heinrich, 148, 158*n*

Land, Erhard, 45
Landesverrat. *See* Treason
Legality Principle *(Legalitätsprinzip)*, 96–97, 93*n*, 121, 181–84
Leonhardt, Rudolf Walter, 62*n*6
Levacher, René. *See* Schmeisser, Hans Konrad
Liberaler Studentenbund, 59
Liberalism: and FDP, 101–106
Lieser, Kurt: and Zind Affair, 14*n*
Lohmar, Ulrich, 97, 98
Lojewski, Werner von, 75
Lower Saxony, 104; public opinion in, 168–69
Lübke, Heinrich, 60, 123*n*, 148, 157

Malaga (Spain), xviii
Mannheimer Morgen, 72
Martin, Alfred, xviii, 56, 57, 57*n* 28; preliminary court trial of, 174–75
Martin, Berthold, 98
Matthiesen, Johannes, 48, 49, 50
Mayer, Hellmuth, 153–54
Meier, Reinhold, 102
Mende, Erich, 102, 108, 111, 116, 117, 123*n*, 144, 147, 151–52; in the Bundestag *Spiegel* debates, 132; on coalition crisis, 121, 125–26, 162; comments on Franz Josef Strauss, 144, 149–50
Metzger, Ludwig: in the Bundestag *Spiegel* debates, 136–37
Mexico, 8
Military policy: of Franz Josef Strauss, 31–36, 186–216 *passim*
Military secrets, 35, 61, 62, 90, 149

Miramar-Haus (Hamburg), 42, 43, 45
Der Mittag (Düsseldorf), 68
Mittelstand, 94
Mommer, Karl, 101, 127, 128*n*6
Monde, Le, 65, 66, 77
Morocco, 136
Müller-Meiningen, Jr., Ernst, 80
Münchner Merkur, 68, 149
Muller, Josef, 16

National Democratic Party (NPD), 106*n*17
National Socialism, 6, 154
National-Zeitung (Basel), 65
Nationalism: and FDP, 103
Nazi Germany xvii, xxi, 8–9, 154
Neue Gesellschaft, Die, 98
Neue Rhein Zeitung (Cologne), 74, 135
Neue Zürcher Zeitung, 65
Neuermann, Paul, 114*n*29
Neues Deutschland, 64
News Chronicle (London): and founding of *Der Spiegel*, 3
News Review (London): and founding of *Der Spiegel*, 3
Newspapers (West German): circulation figures of, 82–83, 83*n*, 218–22; classification of 82–83; content analysis of, 83–91; politicalorientation of, 87, 218–22; reactions to *Spiegel* action of, 62–79; selected sample of, 218–22
North Atlantic Treaty Organization (NATO), 30–33, 170*n*31
North Rhine-Westphalia, 103, 107; Interior Ministry of, 39, 99, 110*n* 22, 128; Land government of, 98–100, 109

Ollenhauer, Erich, 93, 161
Ossietsky Affair, xiv
Ossietzky, Carl von, 59
Oster, Achim, 128, 135, 136, 139, 170, 170*n*31

Passauer Neue Presse, 17
Police action; against *Der Spiegel's*

Bonn office, 39–42; against *Der Spiegel's* Hamburg office, 42–51
Political affair: conceptualization of, xv–xviii
Political asylum, 42
Political crime, 77, 90
Political culture: of West Germany, 8–10, 104
Pragmatism: and West German politics, 8–10
Precensorship, 67, 68, 74, 75, 80, 88, 114n29, 127, 149
Press: associations of, 79–81; criticisms of *Spiegel* action, xiv, 62–79, 81–91, 163; freedom of, xiv, xxiii, 66, 67, 69, 80, 88, 97; reactions to Bundestag *Spiegel* debates of, 134–35. *See also* Newspapers (West German)
Press Evolution Section (Bundestag Library), 83
Pressehaus (Hamburg), 42–53 *passim*
Presseverband Berlin, 80
Professional Association of Hamburg Journalists, 79
Proportional representation, 104–105, 105n16
Protests: faculty, 60–61; intellectuals, 61–62; student, 58–60, 96
Public opinion, 96, 121; on the Bundestag *Spiegel* debates, 140–41; on the *Spiegel* police raids and arrests, 58–62, 80–89, 163–66; on Franz Josef Strauss's resignation, 167. *See also* Newspapers; Protests

Rapp, Alfred, 66, 67
Rhein Zeitung (Koblentz), 68
Rhineland-Palatinate: public opinion in, 168–69
Richter, Hans Werner, 61
Ring Christlich–Demokratischer, 59
Ritter, Gerhard, 154, 155
Ritzel, Heinrich, 129, 131
Röhm putsch, 42
Ruhr-Nachrichten (Dortmund), 71

Saar, 107
Saarbrücker Allgemeine Zeitung, 68
Sänger, Fritz, 97
Schäfer, Friedrich, 145n6
Schäffer, Fritz: and Bundestag bribery case, 11, 12
Schleswig-Holstein, 31, 162
Schloss, Lothar: and Fibag Affair, 18, 19, 21
Schmeisser, Hans Konrad (alias René Levacher), 12–13
Schmelz, Hans, 41, 52; dismissal of charges against, 174n42
Schmidt, Helmut, 39, 99
Schmidt, Otto: in the Bundestag *Spiegel* debates, 129
Schneider, Hans-Roderich, 39
Schröder, Gerhard, 146, 177
Schütz, Karl, 44, 45, 48
Schumacher, Kurt, 93
Security Group (Federal Criminal Office), xvii, 39, 69, 110n22, 129; and Ahlers episode, 55, 76–77, 124–25, 136, 139; and the Bonn police action, 40–41; and Hamburg police action, 42–53 *passim*; jurisdiction of, 37–39
Seuffert, Walter; in the Bundestag *Spiegel* debates, 130, 131, 132
Simoneit, Ferdinand, 41
Social Democratic Party (SPD), xiv, xix, 54, 59, 68, 75, 76, 118, 126, 142, 145; and Konrad Adenauer, 160–61; and coalition negotiations of 1962, 159–61; and elections (Bundestag) 19–21, 104, 178n2; (Landtag) 146, 158; and Fibag Affair, 18, 21, 23–25; and the FDP, 106, 126–27; Godesberg program of, 93, 93n; Presidium of, 100–101; reactions to *Spiegel* actions, 95–101; and Schmeisser case, 13; and Franz Josef Strauss, 20
Socialist Unity Party (SED), 64
Soviet Union, 103
Sozialdemokratischer Hochschulbund, 59

Sozialistischer Deutscher Studentenbund, 59
Spain, 63n8, 65, 66, 70, 73, 90, 98, 138; and Ahlers episode, xvii, xix, 76–77, 124
Speidel, Hans, 12
Spiegel, Der: and Bundestag bribery case, 11–12; and Kilb Affair, 14n; and Taubert Affair, 13n8; and Zind Affair, 14n; passim, esp. 3–36
Spiegel Committee: and the Bundestag bribery case, 11–12
Spiegel Debates. See Bundestag
Spiegel Report, 153, 169–74, 169n30
SS (Schulzstaffel), 137, 140
Stammberger, Wolfgang, xviii, 60, 79, 121, 127, 132, 144, 151; and Federal Prosecutor's Office, 173; and Fränkel case, 73n13; joins the SPD, 177–78; reaction to Spiegel action of, 111–17; replaced as Justice Minister, 162; resignation offer of, 116–17
Starke, Heinz, 129, 151
State secretary: role of, 181
State secrets, 63, 67, 68, 75
Stern, Der, 42
Strauss, Franz Josef, xiv, 54–73, passim, 76–79, 88–96 passim, 115, 116, 120–23, 143–49 passim, 152–53, 158–59, 176–80 passim; and Konrad Adenauer, 20; and Ahlers episode, xviii–xix, 77, 121, 124–25, 135–37, 146, 170–71; in the Bundestag Spiegel debates, 135–40; and CSU, 19–20; and Fibag Affair, 17–29 passim; public attitudes toward, 167–68; and Der Spiegel, 14–17. See also Defense, Federal Ministry of
Strauss, Walter, 115, 116, 132, 138, 139, 178n3, 181; and Stammberger incident, 127–29, 123–24, 171–72, 181
Students: reaction to Spiegel actions, xiv, 58–62, 96, 115, 155. See also Protests

Süddeutsche Zeitung (Munich), 68, 71, 85, 134

Tangiers (Morocco), 55, 110
Taubert, Eberhard, 13n18
Technische Hochschule: of Karlsruhe, 157n21; of Stuttgart, 157n 21
Third force, concept of: and the FDP, 104–109, 126, 180–81
Third Reich, xvii, 72. See also Nazi Germany
Time (U.S.): compared with Der Spiegel, 3–6
Times (London), 65
Torremolinos (Spain), xvii, 55
Toyka, Rudolf, 39
Treason, xxi, xxii, 57, 63, 74, 75, 90, 97, 111, 123, 129–33 passim, 135, 154; and treasonable publication, 34, 57, 96, 175
Tunisia, 56

United Kingdom, 3, 8, 31, 104–105
United States, 8
University: of Berlin (West), 115; of Bonn, 115, 156; of Cologne, 69; of Frankfurt, 115; of Freiburg, 115; of Göttingen, 60; of Hamburg, 59, 115; of Heidelberg, 157n21; of Münster, 157n21; of Munich, 115; of Tübingen, 155; of Würzburg, 77. See also Faculty; Protests; Student; Technische Hochschule

Verba, Sidney, 8–9
Vine, George, 33

Wehner, Herbert, 97, 132; in the Bundestag Spiegel debates, 129, 133, 137
Weimar Constitution: article 48 of, 71, 71n
Weimar Republic, xix, 8, 103
Welt, Die, 74, 76, 85
Weltbühne, Die, 59

Weser Kurier (Bremen), 67
Westdeutsche Allgemeine Zeitung (Essen), 68, 74
Westdeutsche Rundschau (Wuppertal), 135
Westfälische Rundschau (Dortmund), 77–78
Weyer, Willi, 99, 100, 100*n*11

Wicht, Adolf, xviii, 52*n*, 56, 57*n*28, 175
Willke, Jochen, 69
Woche, Diese, 3

Zeit, Die, 42, 84*n*29
Zind, Ludwig, 14*n*
Zoglman, Siegfried, 143